For our mothers, Penny and Jane

Vaccine Anxieties
Global Science, Child Health and Society
Melissa Leach and James Fairhead

A Web of Prevention
Biological Weapons, Life Sciences and the Governance of Research
Edited by Brian Rappert and Caitríona McLeish

Democratizing Technology
Risk, Responsibility and the Regulation of Chemicals
Anne Chapman

Genomics and Society
Legal, Ethical and Social Dimensions
Edited by George Gaskell and Martin W. Bauer

Nanotechnology
Risk, Ethics and Law
Edited by Geoffrey Hunt and Michael Mehta

Vaccine Anxieties

Global Science, Child Health and Society

Melissa Leach
and
James Fairhead

London • Sterling, VA

First published by Earthscan in the UK and USA in 2007

ISBN-13:   978-1-84407-370-2 paperback
ISBN-13:   978-1-84407-416-7 hardback
Typeset by JS Typesetting Ltd, Porthcawl, Mid Glamorgan
Printed and bound in the UK by Antony Rowe, Chippenham
Cover design by Susanne Harris

For a full list of publications please contact:

Earthscan
8–12 Camden High Street
London, NW1 0JH, UK
Tel: +44 (0)20 7387 8558
Fax: +44 (0)20 7387 8998
Email: earthinfo@earthscan.co.uk
Web: **www.earthscan.co.uk**

22883 Quicksilver Drive, Sterling, VA 20166-2012, USA

Earthscan publishes in association with the International Institute for Environment and
Development

A catalogue record for this book is available from the British Library

Library of Congress Cataloging-in-Publication Data

Leach, Melissa.
   Vaccine anxieties : global science, child health, and society / Melissa Leach and James Fairhead.
       p. cm.
   Includes bibliographical references.
   ISBN-13: 978-1-84407-416-7 (hardback)
   ISBN-10: 1-84407-416-1 (hardback)
   ISBN-13: 978-1-84407-370-2 (pbk.)
   ISBN-10: 1-84407-370-X (pbk.)
   1. Immunization of children–Complications–Great Britain. 2.
Immunization of children–Complications–Africa, West. 3. Vaccines–
Political aspects–Great Britain, 4. Vaccines–Political aspects–Africa,
West. 5. Vaccines–Social aspects–Great Britain, 6. Vaccines–Social
aspects–Africa, West. 7. Vaccines–Health aspects. I. Fairhead, James,
1962– II. Title.
   [DNLM: 1. Vaccines–Africa, Western. 2. Vaccines–Great Britain. 3.
Anxiety–Africa, Western. 4. Anxiety–Great Britain. 5. Vaccination–
Africa, Western. 6. Vaccination–Great Britain. 7. World Health–Africa,
Western. 8. World Health–Great Britain. QW 805 L434v 2007]
   RJ240.L43 2007
   614.4'7083–dc22
                                          2007025359

The paper used for this book is FSC-certified and totally
chlorine-free. FSC (the Forest Stewardship Council) is an
international network to promote responsible management
of the world's forests.

FSC
Mixed Sources
Product group from well-managed
forests and other controlled sources

Cert no. SGS-COC-2953
www.fsc.org
© 1996 Forest Stewardship Council

Contents

List of Figures

Acknowledgements

This book is the result of several forms of partnership and collaboration. As joint and equal co-authors, we embarked on this attempt to understand vaccine anxieties as a result of two convergent pathways: as anthropologists researching environmental issues over a 15-year period in West African worlds where health issues were often a greater priority and local understandings often linked both; and as parents bringing up young children in southern England at a time of anxiety around the measles, mumps and rubella (MMR) vaccine. Two focused, collaborative research projects enabled us to bring these two pathways together, and to engage with research partners, health authorities, scientists and parental support groups to conduct studies that spoke to their concerns.

The first of these was a project on 'Childhood Vaccination: Science and Public Engagement in International Perspective', kindly supported by the Science in Society Research Programme of the UK Economic and Social Research Council (ESRC grant L144250051). This combined research on parental thinking and practices around vaccination and MMR in Brighton, UK, and around both routine vaccination and vaccine trials in The Gambia. In the UK, anthropologist Michael Poltorak was a central member of the research team, helping to design the study and carrying out most of its interviews in Brighton. In acknowledgement of this core role and lead authorship of an article on which it draws (Poltorak et al, 2005), he appears as a co-author of Chapter 3. Jackie Cassell brought public health and survey expertise to the study, helping to design the survey component and analyse its findings, while Catherine Mercer helped with statistical analysis. Angela Iversen, Surrey and Sussex Local Health Protection Agency, helped us to identify and approach general practitioner (GP) practices, and to make the study relevant to the work of local health authorities. These team members appear as co-authors of papers reporting on specific aspects of the Brighton study's findings (Poltorak et al, 2005; Cassell et al, 2006b). We owe many thanks to the numerous parents, health professionals and local institutions in Brighton who participated in and helped facilitate the study. We are grateful to the UK study's advisory group, Graham Bickler, Health Protection Agency; Joanne Yarwood, Head of Immunization Information, Department of Health; Mark Jones, Director of the Community Practitioners' and Health Visitors' Association;

Isabella Thomas, Brighton parents' support group and Justice, Awareness and Basic Support (JABS); and Martina Pickin, Health Visitor, Brighton. We would also like to acknowledge practical support from Surrey and Sussex Health Protection Agency, South Downs National Health Service (NHS) Trust, and Brighton and Hove City Primary Care Trust, and to thank the East Sussex Local Research Ethics Committee for their permission. Support from the Citizenship Development Research Centre, funded by the Department for International Development (DFID) and the Rockefeller Foundation, enabled additional research on the MMR controversy which forms the basis of Chapter 4.

In The Gambia, social researcher and nurse Mary Small was a central member of the study team, helping to carry out interviews and ethnographic work and supervising the study's survey component. She appears as a co-author on earlier articles (Fairhead et al, 2004, 2006; Cassell et al, 2006a) from which material was drawn for Chapters 5 and 6. Jackie Cassell helped design and analyse the Gambian survey findings, and Catherine Mercer again carried out statistical analysis. Ousman Cham, Lamin Danso, Yankuba Manneh, Alagie Saidy and Mansata Sanneh formed an excellent team to carry out the survey interviews. We are grateful to the many parents, community leaders and health workers in the Gambia's Western Division and Upper River Division who participated in the study. Special thanks are due to the families in the village of Marikunda who hosted our family's stay there and to the staff of Sukuta Health Centre, especially Sally Savage. For their support and useful comments at various stages of the research we should like to thank the staff of the Expanded Programme on Immunization Unit of the Gambian government, Kebba Gibba, Yaimundow Jallow and Robert Ninson, and of the Medical Research Council Laboratories, especially Tumani Corrah, Felicity Cutts, Sam McConkey, Warren Stevens and Mariane van der Sande. Thanks are also due to the Gambia Committee on Traditional Practices (Gamcotrap) for logistical support and to the joint Gambian Government/Medical Research Council (MRC) Ethics Committee for granting ethical approval for this component of the research.

The second project, 'The Cultural and Political Dynamics of Technology Delivery: The Case of Infant Immunization in West Africa' was funded by the Committee on Social Science Research of DFID, whose support we also gratefully acknowledge. This project co-funded our research on routine immunization in The Gambia, and enabled a detailed anthropological study in Guinea and a set of comparative studies by country-based researchers in Sierra Leone and Nigeria. In Guinea, Dominique Millimouno of the Centre Universitaire de Recherche sur le Développement (CURA) and Dr Alpha Ahmadou Diallo of the Ministère de la Santé Publique were co-researchers in the study, conducting fieldwork and providing many important insights. They co-authored several articles which we draw on in Chapter 5 (Millimouno et al, 2006; Fairhead et al, forthcoming). Many thanks are also due to S. E. Professeur Mamadou Saliou Diallo, the then Minister of Public Health, Dr Mohamed Sylla, the national coordinator of the Health and AIDS Project, Dr Cornelius Oepen of this same project, Dr N'Nah Djenab Sylla, Head of Research and Documentation at the Ministry of Public Health, and other members of the Guinea study's advisory group and research ethics committee for their kind support and inputs. We are grateful to the Regional and Prefectoral health directorates of Faranah, Kissidougou and Dinguiraye. We are particularly indebted to the local health centre staff and the many parents in our study localities who gave generously of their time to discuss child health and vaccination issues with us.

Maryam Yahya, Clifford Kamara and Ayodele Jegede conducted related studies in their own countries under the auspices of the project (Yahya, 2005, 2007; Jegede, 2005; Kamara, 2005) and to which we refer in Chapter 5. We would also like to thank others who contributed insights at our regional West African workshop held at the MRC Laboratories, The Gambia on 21–22 June 2005, including Kebba Jobe, Mamanding Kuyate and Francis Sar.

Except where explicitly acknowledged, the views expressed in this book are those of ourselves as authors, and not of any of our research partners or funders, either in the UK or West Africa.

Back in Sussex, we are grateful to colleagues in the Anthropology Department of the university and in the Knowledge, Technology and Society (KNOTS) team of the Institute of Development Studies for their insights, encouragement and comments at various stages of these projects – especially Gerry Bloom, Henry Lucas, Ian Scoones, Hilary Standing and Linda Waldman. We gained valuable ideas and feedback when presenting parts of this material at seminars and workshops both in Africa and in the UK, and owe thanks to their numerous participants. At home and in West Africa, Cassie, Rory, Xanthe and Francesca were often with us during this research and gave it special meaning – many thanks to them, and to Elisa Eade and Penny Leach who helped make this family anthropology possible.

List of Acronyms and Abbreviations

AIDS	Acquired Immune Deficiency Syndrome
BMA	British Medical Association
BSE	Bovine Spongiform Encephalopathy
CEPT	Chief Executive Policy Team
CJD	Creutzfeldt-Jakob Disease
CSM	Committee on Safety of Medicines
CURA	Centre Universitaire de Recherche sur le Développement
DETR	Department of the Environment, Transport and the Regions
DFID	Department for International Development
DH	Department of Health
DTP	diptheria, tetanus and pertussis
EPI	Expanded Programme on Immunization
Gamcotrap	Gambia Committee on Traditional Practices
GAVI	Global Alliance on Vaccines and Immunization
GFATM	Global Fund to fight Aids, TB and Malaria
GP	general practitioner
HIV	Human Immunodeficiency Virus
HPA	Health Protection Agency
HPI	Health Partners International
IAVI	International AIDS Vaccine Initiative
IEC	Information, Education and Communication
IHSD	Institute for Health Sector Development
IPR	intellectual property rights
IWC	Infant Welfare Clinic
JABS	Justice, Awareness and Basic Support
KNOTS	Knowledge, Technology and Society (Institute of Development Studies)
MAFF	Ministry of Agriculture, Fisheries and Food
MMR	measles, mumps and rubella
MRC	Medical Research Council
NGO	non-governmental organization
NHS	National Health Service

NID	National Immunization Day
NPI	National Programme on Immunization
OPV	oral polio vaccine
PCT	Primary Care Trust
PVT	Pneumococcal Vaccine Trial
SCSN	Supreme Council for Sharia in Nigeria
TRIPS	(Agreement on) Trade-Related Aspects of Intellectual Property Rights
UN	United Nations
UNICEF	United Nations Children's Fund
WHO	World Health Organization
WTO	World Trade Organization

1

Introduction: Global Technologies, Personal Worlds

A school teacher in the town of Gueckedou, on Guinea's border with Liberia sees rebel forces with child soldiers destroy his town in 2001, and worries that children's vaccination has created a strengthened but more violent generation.

A mother in southern England is taken to the High Court by her ex-husband over her refusal to allow their child to have the controversial measles, mumps and rubella (MMR) vaccination.[1]

Former guerilla fighters in a village in Mozambique seek vaccinations and are angry that government clinics will vaccinate only children, marginalizing their adult political rivals.

Datti Ahmed, a doctor and president of Nigeria's Supreme Council for Sharia Law, tells journalists: 'We believe that modern-day Hitlers have deliberately adulterated the oral polio vaccine with anti-fertility drugs and contaminated it with certain viruses which are known to cause HIV and AIDS.'[2] Polio soon resurges from Nigeria across Africa and beyond, sweeping aside the global polio eradication campaign.

Marlon Brando as 'Kurtz' in the film 'Apocalypse Now' relates how Viet Cong cut the arms off all the children that the US Army had inoculated with polio vaccine in a Vietnamese village. Yet this fictional refusal of cultural and spiritual pollution by America's campaign 'to win hearts and minds' has a factual base.[3]

Such scenes, unfolding in places across the globe, reveal how much more there is to vaccination[4] than children's health. Vaccination – and especially mass childhood immunization – is acclaimed as the most successful and effective form of public health intervention that there has ever been. It has acquired a special character, symbolizing high hopes of lives saved, diseases eradicated, and the power of medical technology in an apparent triumph of science over nature. Such hopes justify mass actions that appear to rise above politics. From the smallpox vaccination campaigns of 19th-century Europe, to the international community's growing investments in mass childhood immunization across the world, this technology offers a universal promise of disease control that can appear to trump national and local interests. Wars have been suspended for vaccination. In 1990s Sierra Leone, the United Nations Children's Fund (UNICEF's) immunization programmes continued to cross rebel front lines when even food convoys did not. Vaccines lend themselves easily to representation as an incontestable public good.

Vaccines are also special in linking the most global with the most local and personal. Aiming to reach every child on the planet, vaccination technology has a uniquely global character. Vaccines are produced, distributed and monitored within systems that are equally globalized. Yet vaccination reaches from the global into the most intimate world of parenting and care. At the needle point, the most global meets the most personal of worlds. As a technology, it enters the intense social world in which parents[5] and carers seek to help their children flourish, spanning genders and generations, comrades and communities, and advice givers. These are everyday worlds that vary enormously across the globe, and over time. Within them, some jostle for vaccination. Others jostle against. Through thinking and talking about vaccination, people often express a great deal about what they value, who they are and whom they identify with.

Controversies over vaccines feed cornerstone debates of our time. For while vaccination is easily represented as a universal, neutral good, it is actually deeply bound up with politics: with struggles over status, authority and value, writ small and writ large. Thus as some British parents from the 1990s refused to take their children to receive the MMR vaccination, fearing that it would trigger autism, the debates that swirled through policy, professional, media and popular circles ranged widely. They variously evoked notions of trust in government; of media responsibility; of scientific impartiality; of parental choice; of citizenship rights, and of the appropriate limits of government action and enforcement in a liberal democracy. From 2003, some northern Nigerian parents refused to take their children to receive oral polio vaccination, fearing that it would reduce their future fertility or infect them with HIV as part of a genocidal plot against Islamic Africa. Again debates and commentary expanded into far wider questions of governance. They invoked the relations between local and national government; trust in federal government and its global sponsors; the motivations of US foreign policy; scientific impartiality (Whose science? Whose vaccines?); the value of different health priorities, and, as Nigerian news spread across the airwaves and polio cases reappeared across the region, the role and responsibility of media in a globalized world.

This book is therefore a book about global technologies, governance and their intersection with social worlds. We explore how experiences of vaccination are simultaneously experiences of the body and its health, of social relations, and of wider governance and politics. At the same time, a focus on vaccination draws us into much broader public debates (and professional writing) about science and technology, and about the nature of contemporary society. We explore how debates thrown up around vaccination have animated existing public debates such as to affirm and put into play a range of stereotypes – about modern society, about western society, and about African society. What, we ask, is the validity of these ideas? What are they doing? And what might they be hiding?

A notion of anxiety is a central anchor in current debates and in our exploration of them. Anxiety, though, is a double-edged word. Used in a negative sense, anxiety implies a state of unease, worry or concern. Yet it also has a positive meaning, implying an earnest, focused desire for something, or to do something. Recent policy discussions and social science writing have emphasized the first, negative meaning. 'Vaccine anxieties', in this sense, are seen as worries about vaccines. Anxiety easily becomes part of an explanation for instances of public refusal or dissent from vaccination, or for controversies. Thus in the British MMR controversy, a negative sense of anxiety is invoked by commentators attributing vaccine refusal to parents' overblown sense of risk and loss of trust, whether ascribing this to everyone or to the 'anxious middle classes'. Some see this vaccine anxiety as a manifestation of a broader age of anxiety afflicting contemporary western society (Fitzpatrick, 2004; see also Furedi, 2001). A negative sense of anxiety tends to be manifested differently in discussions of Africa and Asia. Here, commentary has emphasized the role of particular individuals and groups in propagating anxieties, and their easy spread among populations who lack a modern understanding of vaccination. Vaccine anxieties, in this sense, are linked either with anti-vaccination 'rumours', or with collective resistance (e.g. Streefland, 2001). In both settings, anxiety is imaged in its negative sense in terms of a departure from an unproblematized acceptance of public health routines, towards greater, if misguided, reflection.

Yet such discussions, and the images of society that they produce, overlook the positive meaning of anxiety, and its implications. Anxiety can imply a striving for something and recognizing this is crucial. First, it attunes us to circumstances in which people are anxious for vaccination. Having a child vaccinated may not, in this sense, be a question of passive acceptance of established, normal public-health routines, but a matter of more active demand (see Nichter, 1995; Streefland et al, 1999). This positive sense of anxiety invites exploration of the issues, values and forms of knowledge underlying such demand, and the extent to which they match (or fail to match) the expectations of public health professionals and policy makers. And it draws attention to the sense of let-down that people may feel when their own expectations of vaccination – its availability or effects – are unmet. Second, a positive meaning of anxiety allows us to recognize that people can be anxious for child health and wellbeing more broadly – and that the place of vaccination in this can be more problematic. Where people dissent from, question or fail to respond as expected to public health messages, a common tendency – using a negative sense of anxiety – is to interpret this in terms of 'failure to understand', a 'breakdown of trust', and so on. But as we shall argue, it is more productive to ask, in a more positive sense, what people expect and desire around child health and why – and why at times vaccination is failing to match those desires.

Appreciating the positive in the double-edge of anxiety has broader implications for understanding public engagements with science and technology. Many debates about and explanations for controversies over public issues involving science are framed in terms of public (mis)understanding or lack of understanding of science, technology or its risks. In an extension of this 'deficit model', the lack may be not just of knowledge, but of trust – in both science itself and in its governance. The emphasis is on the negative – deficits of knowledge, deficits of rationality, deficits of trust – on the part of the public. And in response, scientific institutions are called to respond by winning hearts and minds.

But this well-established set of perspectives, in focusing on what people do not think or understand, misses what they do think and understand. It obscures why what they do think might make sense, as part of their everyday lives and experiences, values and conceptualizations of the issues involved. It misses the opportunity to identify the 'framings' – forms of knowledge, value and social commitment – that people bring to an issue, and which shape their anxieties about it, whether positive or negative. And it misses opportunities to identify mismatches between people's framings, and those of the institutions involved with science or governance. A positive perspective that focuses on the ways in which members of the public frame issues involving science and technology, in turn, suggests that similar questions should be asked of those developing and promoting technologies, or exerting authoritative governance over issues involving science. How, one might ask, do scientific and policy institutions frame the issues, and what kinds of knowledge, social and political values and commitments do these framings embody? This will shed light on why it is that scientific and policy institutions represent the public in the ways that they do.

The relevant question, then, is not how the public understand or engage with science and technology as if it were neutral and universal, but how different framings of a problem – among scientific and policy institutions, and a variegated public – have emerged. Crucially, however, we need to go beyond this 'symmetrical' approach (e.g. Jasanoff and Wynne, 1997) to consider how policy and public framings have emerged in relation to each other; how they interact. This is a core emphasis of this book. It is not enough simply to draw a contrast between science/policy and public framings, or between globalized and personalized ones, as if they were part of distinct, separate lifeworlds. Rather, crucial questions concern how these contrasts arise, become manifested and consolidated, and how the social and political interactions they shape themselves play into this.   → Main question of book

The problems with vaccination

At heart, this book is concerned with some very practical problems. It takes as a starting point the great gulfs that often exist between people's senses of themselves – the people, in this case, being parents and carers of children in diverse settings in Africa and Europe – and the stereotypes applied to them by health professionals, policy makers and media commentators. These gulfs are unhelpful for everyone.

peoples sense of themselves vs stereotypes of men

They are unhelpful for public health officials trying to increase immunization coverage, who often find their education and communication efforts ineffective. They are unhelpful for the funders and international organizations promoting large-scale disease eradication campaigns, when they lead to these being derailed, and to diseases once again finding a foothold. They are unhelpful for parents frustrated in their engagements with health services. And they are unhelpful for those children who die as a result.

For many people, the problems of vaccination are not controversial. Rather, they are well-known and long established: getting good coverage through improving supply and infrastructure, and improving uptake through education. The challenges lie mainly in tackling the resource and system constraints that prevent vaccination technology and knowledge being extended to all. This book does not dispute the value of such efforts, but it does expose the limits of this comfort zone.

For others, the big challenges lie at a larger scale: in creating the right vaccines to tackle major and emergent disease problems, and developing cost-effective ways to deliver them. This book does not deny the crucial importance of such vaccine innovation, but it does show why grand challenges need to be matched with attention to how parents will engage with these efforts. It also shows that in a world of aggrandizing and globalizing vaccination programmes, parental understandings sometimes come to include dimensions of the larger political economy of vaccine development in ways that can prove problematic, feeding back to derail the programmes themselves. It is these gulfs which are the focus of this book. They recur in vaccination research, development and delivery; in routine mass childhood immunization and disease eradication campaigns.

Vaccination as technology and technocracy

Vaccination is high on both national and international policy agendas. Long-regarded as a highly effective, and cost-effective, public health intervention (WHO/UNICEF, 1996), mass childhood immunization is now receiving renewed international attention. While vaccines protect individuals, high levels of coverage can build up social or 'herd' immunity against certain infectious diseases, so personal and social immunity, and possibilities for disease eradication frame public health strategies. A variety of initiatives and investments are focusing on improving access to immunization services, expanding the use of existing vaccines and accelerating the development and introduction of new ones.

As technologies, vaccines are still in their infancy. New generations of 'DNA' vaccines are emerging. Needle-free delivery is being perfected. The promises of vaccines grown in plants or introduced into foods are materializing. Nano-science and technology offer as yet uncharted delivery techniques. New combinations of vaccines are constantly being created, offering greater efficiency and coverage as 'three-in-one' jabs become four-in-one, or five-in-one.

These technological developments contribute to a powerful vision of techno-logical progress. This vision encompasses vaccines against poverty and vaccines against excess. Thus unprecedented international investments target the 'killer diseases' associated with modern poverty. These portray vaccination as a key route to tackling pervasive ill-health in Africa and achieving the Millennium Development Goals to reduce childhood mortality, and as a moral imperative as part of global development efforts (Obaro and Palmer, 2003; Smith and Woodward, 2003). At the same time, solutions to the excesses of northern over-consumption through vaccination are envisaged, through inoculations against obesity, drug addiction and cancer.

In the context of these overall narratives of technological progress and promise, many lament how slow innovations have been for vaccines against malaria, HIV and other hard-to-tackle diseases that primarily affect the global south. They question the limited public funding that has been available for this, and the preference of pharmaceutical companies to focus on profit-generating markets – thus favouring curative drugs over vaccines, and northern over southern settings. To speed up vaccine innovation for development, a variety of new aid and philanthropic initiatives now link with pharmaceutical companies in innovative forms of partnership. These go beyond their common labelling as 'public–private' as they involve an array of coalitions between wealthy and poor governments, vaccine manufacturers, non-governmental organizations, research institutes, foundations and international health organizations, often involving protracted negotiations to launch and sustain. The largest of these is the Global Alliance on Vaccines and Immunization (GAVI) launched in 2000, together with its financing mechanism, the Vaccine Fund (Heaton and Keith, 2002; Muraskin, 2004, 2005). The International Aids Vaccine Initiative (IAVI) also brings together developing country organizations and northern research outfits, both public and private, to further HIV vaccine research and wider policy through operations in 22 countries. By 2004 IAVI had raised over $340 million (Chataway and Smith, 2006). The Global Fund to fight Aids, TB and Malaria (GFATM), launched in 2002 following a call by the UN Secretary General and a decision by G8 countries, is a large, international, independent public–private partnership designed to attract and manage significant new sums of money – from governments, foundations and the private sector – to address these three diseases, including through vaccine innovation and delivery.

While the aim is to extend vaccines to every person on the planet, their production has become increasingly concentrated, and is set to become more so as technological sophistication intersects with global regulation and patenting. Debates about intellectual property and generics will affect future production possibilities, including the viability of, for instance, small Asian companies that have been attempting to produce cheap vaccines for the poor.[6] Some argue that the restrictions on property rights are a real constraint to making them available, or to promoting public – as opposed to private, commercial – values.

In the regulation of vaccines and research into them, as for other pharmaceuticals, national issues encounter a world of global standardization. The trend of the past few decades has been to expand intellectual property regimes globally, and indeed an obligation is to comply with the TRIPS agreement under free-trade rules set by the World Trade Organization (WTO). In this context, the spectre of smaller companies becoming part of outsourcing arrangements in larger networked conglomerates controlled by big pharmaceutical companies seems likely. If such a scenario unfolds, and given the disincentives for large pharmaceutical companies alone to invest in vaccine development, the significance of international public–private–philanthropic partnerships in meeting vaccine development needs for the global south may increase further.

Aid funding in these partnerships is not entirely altruistic. First, the rich can catch the diseases of the poor. In a world of mobile people and microbes, eradicating infectious diseases is increasingly a global public good (Kaul and Faust, 2001) – an agenda of mutual north–south self-interest that has undoubtedly played a role in pushing immunization up international political agendas. In what Fidler (1998) calls microbialpolitik, infectious disease control has become central to international relations, as an international security issue. In this light, it is no surprise that a major funding source for the development of vaccines derives from the US military. Second, many of the component technologies that contribute to vaccine development can also contribute to the production of bio-weapons. This 'dual use' potential contributes to the stringency of the regulatory frameworks that surround vaccine development. It also contributes to a climate of fear that in turn supports geo-political and geo-commercial monopolization. In short, vaccines are produced within a very political economy. And while vaccines and vaccine technologies may be multiplying, their production is becoming increasingly concentrated.

The technology involved with vaccination extends beyond the vaccines themselves, to encompass a range of technologies of vaccine delivery – from needles, syringes and oral droppers, to refrigeration, transport and technologies of population registration and record-keeping. To make the technology work also demands interventions and strictures of timing, scheduling and coverage. Thus along with vaccination technologies have emerged vaccination technocracies, in the sense of institutional and governance regimes devoted to ensuring timely delivery and uptake.

While state governments and their health systems have assumed primary responsibility for vaccinating their citizens, there has long been an international dimension to vaccination technocracies and this too is increasing today. Thus a variety of global alliances and forms of international donor support have emerged to support health delivery systems. In many parts of Africa and beyond, donor funds have long been used to support immunization amid struggling state health systems. Impoverished governments have, with international support, sometimes attempted to maintain and expand vaccination delivery systems even as crises and trends towards privatization affect other aspects of their health delivery. That vaccination delivery has been sustained through protracted conflicts is an extreme example of this.

International investment in vaccination delivery has recently been spurred by arguments that it is a moral imperative as part of poverty reduction efforts. Whether underlain by such arguments or by global mutual self-interest in controlling disease, the result has been a proliferation of international initiatives to improve delivery and access to immunization services. International non-governmental organizations (NGOs) and global funds invest in the personnel, resources and infrastructure to spread coverage to the remotest rural regions.

Modes of vaccine delivery, their financing and international support to them vary. Sometimes immunization is embedded within wider strategies and systems to deliver primary health care and mother–child health services. This has been the focus of donor support mechanisms in recent years, with their emphasis on (health) 'sector-wide' approaches. Yet so-called vertical programmes, in which a dedicated set of institutions and financial arrangements are responsible for immunization, often persist. Recent global funding mechanisms focused on the control of particular diseases are tending to re-enliven a top-down, vertical approach, promoting globally orchestrated, highly focused campaigns such as the Global Polio Eradication Initiative – for which fleets of vaccinators move out across entire countries and regions at particular times of year, aiming to reach every child. How the campaigns intersect with the institutions and actions of government health systems often illustrates the power of global technocracies, and the limits these place on national sovereignty. White's (2005) argument that vaccination programmes in colonial and post-independence Africa were exercises in the practice of global or 'un-national' sovereignty may acquire renewed relevance in a world of global alliances against what are perceived as global disease threats. At the very least, it is evident that vaccination is not just a global health technology, but also part of a global health technocracy that is remoulding health services across the world.

Techniques for compliance

Vaccination delivery is not just about getting vaccines to those who 'need' them. It is also about getting those who need them to take them up. Put another way, what are conventionally described as 'supply side' concerns with vaccine availability, infrastructure and accessibility meet 'demand side' concerns with ensuring 'acceptance'. Vaccination technocracies deploy varied techniques which mobilize different modes of influence, and which are more or less legitimate and feasible according to the political setting in question.

First, some strategies have made use of force and compulsion. This was the case for the early smallpox eradication campaigns in 19th-century Britain, for instance, when vaccination was made mandatory. Colonial vaccination campaigns in many parts of Africa and Asia (e.g. Vaughan, 1991) similarly relied on compulsion and coercion, sometimes orchestrated and enforced by military troops. Similar strategies sometimes continued in the post-independence era, for instance in the smallpox vaccination campaigns that the World Health Organization (WHO) ran in Africa throughout the 1960s and 1970s (White, 2005) and in the approaches adopted by a number of national governments.

A second set of techniques to promote uptake has associated vaccination with (legal) rules linked to material benefits. For instance, proof of having had childhood vaccinations is a prerequisite to school entry in the US. In France, it is a requirement for access to certain welfare and tax benefits. In contemporary African settings, less formal rules and practices have linked vaccination to various material incentives. Having one's infant vaccinated can thus be a condition for access to other health or development benefits such as free anti-malaria bednets, or to avoid having to pay fines imposed by local clinics and their health workers.

Third, strategies aim at instilling vaccination as a habit, and inculcating a desire for it. The former emphasizes the incorporation of vaccination into parents' 'normal' routines and practices, so that it becomes an unproblematic matter of unthinking, passive acceptance or of community practices (social demand). Inculcating a desire, by contrast, emphasizes a more active form of demand (see Streefland et al, 1999). Techniques focused on education, persuasion and reminders to those who 'forget' address both. Thus in Britain, for example, a set of educational strategies through brochures and pamphlets, media and websites, and information and advice-giving by primary healthcare workers has in recent years been the main means to encourage compliance, aiming to persuade parents of the value and importance of vaccination. This is backed up by computerized child health surveillance systems and practices of sending call-letters and reminders. Through much of the 1990s, these techniques were also linked to material incentives offered to health workers through a system of giving extra financial benefits to doctors' practices that met immunization targets. Education-based strategies are also central across Africa. Thus the design and promotion of Information, Education and Communication (IEC) approaches have become central to the work of international agencies concerned with health. Government health ministries and their immunization departments frequently have dedicated information and education programmes. And in many settings, the 'health talks' that persuade and remind mothers why they should bring their infants for immunization have become a standard part of clinic routines.

These different strategies involve different relationships between public health institutions and parents. They also rely on particular assumptions about the nature of social and individual action; assumptions about what it is that brings people to have their children vaccinated, and to conform or not. But are these assumptions warranted? Are the institutions involved with vaccination and public health getting it right?

This book is an attempt to understand what does bring parents to have their children vaccinated, in different settings, and what leads them, sometimes, not to. To do this it considers parental vaccine anxieties in both their positive and negative sense. It is also an exploration of what institutions involved with vaccination and public health policy assume is going on, and the dynamic processes through which these worlds interact and shape each other.

Approach and strategy

As we have observed, there is hardly greater attention that someone can give to another than that which a parent gives to a child, and no greater field for anxiety. Childcare decisions involve both acute personal reflection, and intense social interest in societies everywhere.

In this meeting point between the global and the personal that is vaccination, it is unsurprising – perhaps inevitable – that clashes and concerns sometimes arise. Public concerns about vaccination, and controversies around it, date back as far as the technology itself (Allen, 2007). As we shall be exploring, these concerns are at once bodily, social and political. Analysis of them needs to address how the body and health are understood and experienced and the place of vaccination in this. It needs to address the nature of the social worlds that vaccination becomes part of; worlds that involve relations within families, communities and clinics. It also has to comprehend wider political experiences: people's encounters and imaginings about health and related institutions nationally and internationally, and the broader political and economic worlds in which they are embedded.

In this book, we make three key arguments. First, we argue that these three dimensions – the bodily, the social and the broader political – are more connected than might appear at first sight. We suggest that these dimensions co-emerge with each other in parental thinking and practice. A focus on vaccine anxieties – on instances where parents express anxious desire for or against vaccination – can reveal the particular ways in which these dimensions come to be coordinated. Second, we argue that, in a symmetrical way, one can recognize a parallel co-emergence in public health institutions and policy, where perspectives and practices also involve bodily, social and wider political dimensions. Third, we argue that these parental and policy worlds interact through encounters and in ways that shape both. The apparent distinctiveness of parental and policy worlds of knowledge and practice, and the gulfs that often appear between them, is thus not a matter of a priori distinction, but of making and re-making through actual practices of communicating and relating. Importantly, this means that these distinctions are open to change; to blurring and bridging in ways that could have positive outcomes for all concerned.

How parents understand and experience these bodily, social and wider political dimensions of vaccination occupies much of our attention in this book, not least because parents' own views and experiences have so often been submerged and obscured by dominant biomedical and policy framings of vaccination issues. Methodologically, a major aim is to rescue and bring to light parental framings, and to show how they make sense in their particular contexts. Secondary aims are to consider the perspectives of those involved with vaccination policy and delivery, and to examine how these framings interact: how the production of knowledge by institutions of policy and public health leads them to interpret and act in relation to parents in particular ways; and how parents embody and reflect on these interactions in ways that shape their understandings and action.

Research with such aims has to be grounded in particular places and cases. Not only have different countries taken starkly varied approaches to delivering and promoting uptake of vaccination, but the nature of emerging public debates around vaccines is also deeply inflected by local and national political history and culture, and by the legacy of particular interactions between populations and institutions of the state, of science, of civil society and of the media. For while vaccination is part of globalized technological and technocratic orders, the contrasting ways that different regions, countries and localities engage with these reveal different ways that bodily, social and political orders are co-experienced, and forged in relation to them.

Located, historical analyses of controversies around vaccination – whether of dissent to smallpox vaccination in Britain (Porter and Porter, 1988; Durbach, 2000, 2005) or to colonial vaccination campaigns in Africa (Vaughan, 1991; White, 2005) or Asia (Nichter, 1995) show the very varied forms that these have taken, linking with wider social and political issues of the place and the day. In a similar way, contemporary social science studies of vaccination often take pains to emphasize the specificity of their social contexts (e.g. Colgrove, 2006; Samuelsen, 2001). Such works call into question arguments that public controversies are part of a singular phenomenon that some have glossed as 'anti-vaccinationism' or an 'anti-vaccination movement' (Poland and Jacobson, 2001). They serve to qualify popular and policy views that today's vaccination controversies have developed and built from those of the past as part of a continuous, linear history (e.g. Wolfe and Sharpe, 2002; Baker, 2003). And they serve to qualify current arguments about the globalization of dissent, which hold that given the globalization of networks, pressure groups, media and internet communication, today's anti-vaccinationism threatens to become as global a force to be reckoned with as the pro-vaccinationism it opposes.

Yet located social studies of vaccination have also – often unwittingly – contributed to the emergence of stereotypes about place. Focused on particular places in either Europe and the US, or Africa and Asia, they have often framed their questions and interpreted their findings in line with wider policy and analytical debates dominant in, or about, those places. This has played into the emergence of contrasting analytical traditions concerned with Africa and so-called 'southern' settings on the one hand, and Europe and 'northern' settings on the other. The result has been the emergence of some powerful views that frame what is going on around vaccination in these places in very different ways. Thus, as we explore in more detail in the next chapter, dominant debates about Africa and 'southern' settings see instituting modern health services as the key problem, and link vaccine worries and controversies to collective concerns and 'resistance' grounded in religion or tradition, imaging them, in effect, as pre-modern. In contrast, dominant debates in and about Europe associate vaccine worries with individualized, misguided notions of risk and with a breakdown of trust, imaging these as phenomena of late or post-modernity. Both views image vaccination itself as quintessentially modern. Thus dominant debates cast African and European societies as engaging with modernity in sharply contrasting ways.

But neither analyses in terms of continuity – emphasizing the enduring nature and globalization of vaccine controversies – nor those that rely on and reproduce strong discontinuities between Africa and Europe are sufficient. What is needed is to address what is distinct about the ways vaccine anxieties have emerged in particular times and places, and to do so using an analytical framework that does not depend on any particular policy view or regional analytical tradition. This is what our approach aims to do. It is only in this way that the merits or otherwise of these broader arguments can be assessed.

To facilitate this approach, we deliberately focus on places and cases where vaccine anxieties would, at first sight, seem to conform closely with pre-modern or post-modern stereotypes. Thus we explore cases from the African Republic of Guinea and The Gambia, where modern health services are being extended, and increasingly integrating with 'traditional' practices. We look at the anxieties thrown up by the conduct of trials of new vaccines, in which reluctance to participate could be interpreted as grounded in 'tradition', religion or inadequate understanding of modern science. We also look at the controversy around polio vaccine in recent years in northern Nigeria, which could easily be interpreted as collective resistance orchestrated by religious and political leaders. In apparent contrast, we focus on the recent anxiety around the MMR vaccine, focusing particularly on how this has unfolded in southern England. This has become a case around which policy, popular and social scientific arguments articulate a loss of trust, emerging irrationality and misperception of risk, and increased individualism.

By focusing on unfolding processes in these locations, we can assess the validity of these dominant arguments, and reveal issues that they obscure. We can interrogate the validity of generic explanations that differentiate experiences across the globe, as well as those that attribute resistance to global connectedness. We can discern how the views and explanations circulating in policy circles and professional health communities are manifested and reproduced in particular places, and in engagements with parents. And we can consider conditions in which these interactions strengthen dominant views, and in which they might undermine them.

By considering, ethnographically, the nature of vaccine anxieties in particular settings, we attempt to avoid the pitfalls of studies that take policy dilemmas to frame their studies. Social science studies in which questions are framed by the terms of policy debate – or indeed by dominant regional analytical traditions – we will argue, can contribute dangerously to the reproduction of policy stereotypes, by providing supportive social science analyses that serve to uphold them. Instead, in our analyses of parental worlds, rather than start with a (policy-driven) question such as 'why do parents demand or refuse vaccination?, our ethnographic approach starts from considering parents' broader perspectives on raising a good healthy child in that setting, and how vaccination fits into this. In this respect, this book follows a strong tradition of ethnographies of technologies-in-use, and their users, attentive to the specificity of located knowledge and practice, and the specific transformations of meaning that technologies undergo in social settings (Richards, 1985; Latour, 1987; Fairhead and Leach, 1996; Mol, 2003). But it is also more than this. It is also an analysis of how dominant scientific and policy discourses are constructed, reproduced and put into practice (Keeley and Scoones, 2003; Fairhead and Leach, 2003; Agrawal, 2005). And to reiterate, by examining these together, the book is able to consider how each is implicated in the other.

Methods and structure

In exploring each focal case, we explore parental understandings and experiences of child health and vaccination, addressing bodily dimensions to vaccine anxieties. We explore the social relations of child care and vaccination, within families, communities and with 'frontline' health workers, addressing social dimensions to vaccine anxieties. And we explore parents' views and experiences of wider political and political–economic dimensions that have a bearing on vaccine anxieties. In parallel, we explore the views of those working in the vaccination policy and delivery worlds that these parents engage with, and the nature of these engagements.

A variety of research methods contributed to these inquiries. Central among these were informal conversations and participant observation in assorted social settings where parents take babies and small children. This enabled the research to pick up on ways that people talk about their children's health, and its responsiveness to social relationships. We also observed settings of vaccination delivery at a variety of clinics and health posts, to consider interactions between parents and with health workers. We complemented this more informal approach with interviews, both with some of these parents and with health workers, to consider their particular experiences and perspectives in greater depth. The majority of interviews took a narrative form, enabling people to speak widely around the issue and reflect what they regarded as most important (see Mattingly and Garro, 2002). For several of the cases, we developed and used a particular narrative method focused on the health biography of a particular child. In the British, Guinean and Gambian cases, we also built a questionnaire survey from the ethnography to consider the wider significance of the parental perspectives emerging. In all settings, we tracked how debates concerning particular vaccine anxieties were represented in broader popular and policy debate, drawing on sources from the media and policy documents. Later chapters detail how this set of methods was refined and conducted for each location.

Conducting ethnographic work in several sites involved a variety of forms of collaboration. Some of these were intense partnerships with social science researchers from the regions concerned. We also worked with parents' organizations and wider networks of colleagues who became part of the research in the different locations. Other forms of collaboration involved biomedical and public health research, policy and implementing agencies that face challenges to improve vaccine research and vaccination coverage. Our research was conceived in collaboration with several such agencies both in the countries concerned, and internationally, in the spirit of a shared interest in bridging gulfs between themselves and their publics. That we had different ideas about the nature of these gulfs was, in many cases, apparent at the start and only became more so as the research progressed.

The next chapter focuses on representations of vaccine anxieties that emerge from public health and policy institutions, drawing mainly on documentary and media sources. By critically exploring their framings and the stereotypes that emerge, we pave the way for a fuller justification of the analytical approach we take in the book. The following chapters apply this in case study settings. The first two case study chapters focus on south-east England, exploring different aspects of the vaccine anxieties that unfolded around the MMR vaccination. Thus Chapter 3 addresses how emerging uncertainties about MMR played into and altered parents' thinking and practices about immunization for their children. Chapter 4 explores the perspectives and practices of those more directly caught up in the controversy, concerned that the MMR vaccine had damaged their children's health – and how they interacted with the scientific and policy networks that soon emerged in opposition to them. The next two chapters address African settings. Chapter 5 explores bodily, social and wider political dimensions of 'routine' vaccination engagements in settings in The Gambia and the Republic of Guinea. This includes the case of oral polio vaccination in Nigeria as a dramatic instance of mass vaccination refusal. Chapter 6 extends these concerns in The Gambia to understand how anxieties around vaccine trials unfolded there.

In bringing these diverse British and West African cases together, our aim is less comparison than juxtaposition, to discern the particular ways that anxieties can play out in different locations. But rather than simply a juxtaposed set of ethnographies, the collection also adds up to what, in some respects, is a multi-sited ethnography (Marcus, 1995). This tracks a technology and technocracy through different geographical and social settings, to discern both the located meanings they acquire, and how their global characteristics are locally understood.

In tracking a global technology and technocracy in this way, and in exploring their unfolding mutual construction with social processes, we move beyond an anthropology of globalization that looks simply at how global phenomena are locally apprehended and interpreted. Considering a global technology across sites in both the global 'north' and 'south' enables, also, a critical engagement with distinct literatures that have emerged around each, including northern-focused science studies, and the anthropologies of modernity and postcolonial technoscience (e.g. Anderson, 2002) that address southern settings. Through this critical engagement, we aim to advance more productive and less bounded ways of understanding people's engagements with technology in a contemporary world. We aim, too, to recover modes of understanding and debate that better grasp the ways that people are actually thinking about, experiencing and imagining technologies. Vaccination provides both a potent lens through which to do this, and a set of practical challenges to which such an approach is essential. For, if the promises of vaccination are to be realized, even partially, then overcoming the gulfs between public and policy views of them will be vital. Understanding vaccine anxieties, in all their positive as well as negative senses, is an essential step towards this.

Notes

1   http://news.bbc.co.uk/1/hi/health/2093003.stm, accessed May 2007.
2   'Vaccine boycott spreads polio', News 24.com, South Africa, 11 February 2004.
3   See Norris (1998) and Mambro (2002).
4   While the term 'vaccination' refers to the act of vaccinating someone, the term immunization strictly refers to the process of 'making immune', and thus depends also on the body's (successful, immunological) response to a vaccine. In this book we use the terms interchangeably, as indeed does much professional and policy debate.
5   We generally use the term 'parent' in this book as shorthand for a child's main caregiver, while recognizing that this is, of course, not necessarily his or her biological mother or father.
6   See 'Indian pharmaceuticals: Good chemistry', The Economist, 4 February 2006.

2

Analysing Vaccine Anxieties

A great deal has been said and written about vaccination: about why people might want it, and especially why they sometimes appear not to. Much commentary and analysis has emerged from policy and public health institutions and in the media, and not surprisingly has blossomed in and around circumstances where vaccination acceptance seems to present a problem. This chapter begins by exploring these representations, and the images they describe of people and of society in Europe and Africa. The arguments that ensue in social science literature sometimes become part of this process.

Such dominant representations of vaccination rest on more generic concepts and arguments that are often deployed to characterize public engagements with science more generally. These include notions of ignorance and public misunderstanding of science; of risk; of trust and its breakdown; of rumour; and of resistance. Yet these are contested notions, and other strands of social science suggest problems in the ways the concepts are mobilized in dominant policy arguments. By reviewing these notions, we reveal a range of questions both about people's engagements with vaccination, and about public controversies involving science more generally, which invite exploration through an alternative analytical lens. The last part of the chapter lays out this analytical approach, which we use to address particular vaccine anxieties in the case study chapters that follow.

Dominant images of people's engagements with vaccination

The British context

In contemporary Britain the determinants of vaccination acceptance and uptake have attracted a great deal of commentary – in medical and public health journals, among social scientists, and in policy, popular and media discussion. Instances and periods when large sections of the public have appeared to reject vaccination – such as occurred in the 1970s and 1980s when fears were raised over the possible effects of pertussis (whooping cough) vaccination and in the 1990s when fears were raised over the MMR vaccine and its possible links with autism – have attracted most commentary of all. In this mass of unfolding debate, recurring themes have emerged.

A predominant theme is that apart from these moments, vaccination has become normalized for parents. From this perspective, although health services may still struggle to reach a minority 'underclass', for the vast majority bringing children for the expected vaccinations has become part of established parenting routines. Yet some individual parents, it is argued, depart from this norm by worrying about risks of vaccination. In this view, vaccine anxieties are primarily anxieties about risk.

Arguments about risk are evident in much policy debate and attempts at public education about vaccination. Risk comparisons have become a dominant communication tool, making quantitative comparisons of the risks and benefits from vaccination, or the risks from vaccination versus other kinds of risks. Risk was, for instance, the key theme of government communication to the public on the MMR issue, using quantitative comparisons of the relative risks of negative health effects from the MMR vaccination and from contracting measles naturally. A prime example is the government leaflet 'MMR. The facts' (Health Promotion England, 2001). As Hobson-West (2003) points out, this presumes that the 'facts' that parents want and need are quantitative comparisons of various 'serious effects' of the diseases, and 'vaccine reactions'. Such risk comparisons present the risks associated with the MMR vaccination as extremely low or negligible, and have thus been seen as a simple way to convince the public that MMR is safe, and to demonstrate the irrationality of refusal to vaccinate.

A related theme turns on the relationship between the individual and the social benefits of vaccination, suggesting that parents are acting selfishly in refusing to vaccinate. This argument acknowledges that if people are indeed (as is presumed) behaving as risk-minimizing individuals, then the rational route might be for them not to vaccinate, thus avoiding personal risk (however low) while gaining the collective benefits of herd immunity from the compliance of others (European Commission, 2001). Yet such 'free-riding', it is argued, if pursued by too many, will bring down vaccination coverage below the level required to ensure herd immunity, undermining the collective benefit of vaccination. This happened over MMR, where coverage in some parts of Britain fell well below the 95 per cent levels required to sustain population-level protection from measles. For certain diseases, it is the social, population-level benefits of vaccination that are paramount. For instance rubella is a mild disease in the individual but causes severe damage to unborn babies, and thus vaccination serves the social good of keeping disease levels low in the population so that the chances of a pregnant woman catching it are minimized. Given arguments such as these, vaccination-refusing parents can be imaged as selfish, prioritizing individual risks over the social good. Thus some have called for a re-framing of vaccination not as an individual choice but as a public duty (Science Media Centre, 2002, p5).

A range of arguments is forwarded to account for instances of parental refusal to vaccinate in the UK. First, some turn on the role of knowledge and information. Policy makers and public health professionals frequently link low vaccination uptake to public ignorance – of the value of vaccination, of evidence of vaccine safety, and of the 'real' nature of the risks (e.g. Elliman et al, 2001). It is also argued that the public underestimate the risks from childhood diseases such as measles as they no longer see widespread evidence of them, and of their complications (Bedford and Elliman, 1998, 1999). In this respect, it is suggested, vaccination uptake has become a victim of its own success.

Second, related arguments turn on the key role of local health professionals in providing education and information – and the consequences if they do not 'toe the line'. Thus Ramsay et al (2002), commenting on one of the Department of Health's regular immunization attitudes surveys, conclude that the advice of health professionals was key in maintaining uptake levels for MMR (see also Pareek and Pattinson, 2000). Yet other commentators suggest that nurses and health workers harbour their own private concerns either about the vaccine or the assurances of the health service, and in some cases, convey mixed messages about MMR, contributing to parental confusion (Whyte and Liversidge, 2001; Whyte, 2002; Smailbegovic et al, 2003).

Third, arguments relate parental refusal to vaccinate to misinformation and rumour. In some versions, pressure groups are seen as the prime culprits in spreading these to gullible parents. Thus André (2003), for example, suggests that 'a small group of so-called educated in developed countries', who constitute an 'anti vaccination movement', have been misclassifying health events after vaccination as vaccine reactions (see also Nasir, 2000; Poland and Jacobson, 2001). Fitzpatrick (2004) makes this argument in relation to MMR. Baker (2003) emphasizes the key role of pressure groups amid divided medical opinion during the British pertussis vaccine controversy in the 1970s–1980s.

Attention to pressure groups fades into attention to the 'irresponsible' media. Here, it is argued that mass-media coverage tends to miscommunicate and amplify risks to publics. Journalistic coverage of vaccine issues is held to have accelerated during the 1990s, with the majority of stories concerning vaccine 'scares' (Cookson, 2002). Some argue that public anxiety about MMR has been fuelled by (even created by) media bias and styles (Begg et al, 1998; Anderson, 1999), including the tendency to give undue coverage to personalized stories of alleged vaccine damage, and to 'David and Goliath' stories of struggles against the scientific establishment that make good copy. It is also because of a tendency for media stories to pit two sides of a controversy against each other as if the evidence for each side were 50:50, even when one side can muster only marginal data in support of its claims (e.g. Hargreaves et al, 2002; Ramsay et al, 2002; Science Media Centre, 2002).

Fourth, parental worries about or refusal to vaccinate are imaged as linked to emotion or irrational beliefs. These are seen to contrast with the reason and rationality driving evidence-based vaccination policy and governance. Thus, for instance, public health professionals and media commentary sometimes represent parents' refusal to have their children given the MMR vaccine as an emotional reaction, swayed by sympathy with other parents' stories of vaccine damage. Such arguments sometimes acquire a gender dimension: thus one television documentary tracking couples' views of MMR in the face of a variety of views of the vaccine's safety concluded that the mothers' opinions were largely driven by emotion, whereas the fathers paid more attention to the 'scientific evidence' presented. Some studies have linked 'un-reason', in scientific terms, with the beliefs of particular social and cultural groups. Thus Rogers and Pilgrim (1995) associate complete refusal to vaccinate with groups holding 'new age' beliefs and lifestyles. Others have argued that scientific irrationality is on the rise in British society more generally, as indicated, for instance, by the increasing popularity of alternative medicine (Fitzpatrick, 2004). Irrationality and un-reason about vaccination are, in this view, an exemplar of a wider trend.

Fifth, a breakdown of trust is invoked to explain people's reticence to vaccinate. Trust is talked about in various ways (see Hobson-West, 2007). General media commentary sometimes portrays people as distrusting a vaccine itself, as in media headlines such as 'Doctor blames ministers for loss of faith in MMR', and 'Parents trust in MMR jab halts measles epidemic'.[1] Other commentary has emphasized trust in doctors – in the General Practitioners who, assisted by nurses, usually deliver vaccines in the UK. It is argued that the kind of faith that people once placed in their doctors has declined (Hupcey et al, 2001; Ham and Alberti, 2002). This is seen as part of a move towards a less deferent society, where people do not automatically place faith in 'experts', including scientists and those in authority (House of Lords, 2000). In this context it is seen to be 'unlikely that the blind faith in the men in white coats will return' (Worcester, 2002, p36). Commentators have also linked what is seen as declining trust in doctors to people's fears that they no longer act in their patients' best interests. For example, some saw the economic incentives paid to doctors to meet immunization targets in the UK in the 1990s as reducing the priority of the patient's interest. The British Medical Association (BMA) eventually requested the abolition of 'target payments' because of the 'detrimental effect on the doctor/patient relationship resulting from the perceived link between medical advice and pecuniary interest' (BMA, 2002). A third set of arguments about trust has turned on people's trust (or otherwise) in government and the institutions that decide vaccination policy. Thus, for instance, media commentary has described people's distrust in committees that oversee vaccination policy because members have links with pharmaceutical companies. More generally, trust in government over vaccination is seen as part of generalized trust, or trust in 'abstract systems', that some analysts identify as a central feature of modern society (e.g. Luhmann, 1979). If such trust is breaking down, such analyses suggest, this signals a move into a different, late modern or post-modern societal order.

The African context

There has also been considerable commentary from policy makers, international and donor agencies, and medical and social scientists on people's engagements with vaccination in African settings. This dwells partly on the challenges of increasing vaccination coverage across the continent. Indeed recent, unprecedented international attention and investment in vaccination for Africa come at a time when routine immunization rates are stagnant or falling in many countries, as indeed they have been for much of the period since 1990. Redressing such declines in vaccination coverage, and ensuring that the proposed expansion of immunization programmes is effective and sustainable, have thus become key issues. Commentary also addresses instances where people and communities have refused vaccination.

Most policy and social science research is dominated by a focus on 'supply-side' issues: of the challenges of getting vaccines to those seen to need them. Thus Gauri and Khaleghian (2002) point to the significance of the quality of a country"s governance and healthcare institutions, and its relationships with international agencies, as key factors in explaining coverage, feeding through to shape specific problems in obtaining vaccines. In this vein, commentators point to the collapse of health systems in many African countries in the context of broader national economic, financial and governance difficulties (Simms et al, 2001). Problems in the infrastructure, financing, supplies, staffing and management of national immunization programmes are highlighted. Some see these as a mirror of more general health system collapse, although others argue that it has been hastened by donor and UN agency attempts at health sector reform which have generally moved away from a focus on vertical programmes such as immunization towards their integration into broad-based health sector approaches, to be implemented through decentralized approaches. There are concerns, and emerging evidence, that this might undermine the effectiveness and coverage of immunization interventions (Brown et al, 2001) especially where integrated, decentralized programmes emphasize cost control and end up underfunded, with insufficient management capacity (Simms et al, 2001).

Despite the focus on supply-side factors in explaining (low) coverage, more limited policy debate and social science writing have also drawn attention to social aspects of vaccination access. Many survey-based studies have associated failure to take up vaccination services, even when they are physically available, with social and demographic characteristics that are seen to limit access for certain individuals and groups. Often-cited characteristics include poverty, large family size, and discriminatory ethnic and migrant status (e.g. Hanlon et al, 1988; Heggenhougen and Clements, 1990; Eng et al, 1991; Gage et al, 1997). Discussions also highlight the ways that (poorly paid, poorly trained) frontline health workers sometimes contribute to access problems through lack of motivation and rudeness. They may, in this view, fail to make efforts to reach socially or geographically isolated parents, fail to mobilize and encourage future attendance, and put parents off by treating them with disrespect or embarrassing them.

At times, people do not take up vaccination even when it is accessible to them. In representing and explaining this, commentators commonly turn to a set of vocabularies that distinguishes 'acceptance' from 'default'; default being failure to comply with the regime on offer.

Several arguments are used to explain the reasons for such default. First, it can be linked to ignorance – especially ignorance of modern biomedicine. Those who default are thus imaged as those who have not yet come to understand the value of vaccination, in modern scientific terms. They have certainly not reached the state of what Nichter (1995) defines as 'active demand', or adherence to vaccination programmes by an informed public which perceives the benefits of and need for specific vaccinations. In a related set of arguments, default is linked to a lack of modern education in general. Thus in several studies, poor educational levels among mothers have been related to low vaccination uptake and seen as a cause of it (e.g. Cleland and Van Ginneken, 1988; Bicego and Boerma, 1993).

Second, in an extension of arguments about scientific ignorance, default has been linked to 'tradition' and religion. Non-uptake of vaccination may in this view reflect the persistence of 'traditional' beliefs and healing practices that either reject vaccination, or deter understanding of its biomedical benefits (e.g. Helman and Yogeswaran, 2004; Onuoha, 1981). A third set of arguments sees defaulters as those who do not bother to attend for vaccination because their priorities lie elsewhere. In some versions, this is linked to poverty and family size, and the need for hard-pressed mothers to spend their time in livelihood-seeking and everyday childcare tasks that leave little time or space to attend vaccination clinics. These are arguments that find support in certain studies of vaccination access. However, such failures are often imaged as due simply to degeneracy. Defaulters are then those with hopelessly misplaced priorities, incapable of making the correct judgements that would bring them to have their children vaccinated.

All these arguments, whether calling on ignorance, tradition or degeneracy, image defaulters as, in effect, pre-modern; not yet having acquired the knowledge, sentiments and habits that qualify them to be modern citizens.

Whereas these arguments focus on vaccination non-acceptance or refusal by individuals, other representations of African settings have emerged in commentary on apparent instances of mass-refusal of vaccination. Here, a dominant theme invokes the notion of rumour, and its capacity to spread rapidly among African populations that are, in turn, imaged as rather unreflective and gullible. Thus a consultant for UNICEF writes:

> *The vaccination programmes of recent decades have, to a certain extent, been the victims of their success. As morbidity and mortality have declined, so, too, has the African public's perception of the importance of some vaccine preventable diseases ... fears of side effects and rumours of long term repercussions of vaccination, never entirely absent, have surfaced as vaccination programmes have matured and approached their goals of polio eradication and tetanus elimination (UNICEF, 2003, p3).*

For many commentators, including international organizations such as WHO and UNICEF, anti-vaccination campaigns are involved in spreading and propagating anti-vaccination rumours that have negative influences on vaccine demand and uptake (UNICEF, 2003). Thus the director of UNICEF imaged the decision of the northern governors to boycott the polio vaccine in Nigeria as 'unforgivable' and grounded in 'baseless rumours'.[2] While usually taking root in one country, it is noted that with the ease of global internet communication such rumours are rapidly spread to 'an emergent anti-vaccine diaspora' (André, 2003, p594), in ways that threaten to derail the success of immunization globally (Obaro and Palmer, 2003). WHO, at the time of writing, had an entire website section devoted to 'combatting anti-vaccination rumours'.

A second theme attributes vaccine anxieties to collective resistance based on religion or traditional beliefs. Some policy and media commentary represented the mass-refusal of oral polio vaccination in northern Nigeria in this way, for instance, describing it as resistance by Islamic populations to what they saw as a genocidal conspiracy against them. In this vein, social science studies have highlighted the susceptibility of vaccination programmes in developing countries to such resistance (Streefland 2001, p166).

A third theme relates vaccine anxieties – and especially instances of mass refusal – to lack of trust. This is primarily seen as distrust of the state or global agencies that distribute and deliver vaccines. Such distrust has variously been linked, for instance, to past experiences of coercive colonial health campaigns (e.g. Feldman-Savelsberg et al, 2000), to problematic actions by international pharmaceutical companies (e.g. as in northern Nigeria),[3] and to economic reforms that have weakened the accountability of health services to local populations (Birungi, 1998). In some versions, African societies are imaged as experiencing a breakdown of trust precipitated by such experiences. More often, however, the image is of trust not yet having been established. In this respect, African societies are imaged as pre-modern, not yet having acquired the trust in institutions and abstract systems held to characterize modern societies.

Imaging contrasts

These analyses and explanations of people's engagements with vaccination largely emanate from institutions promoting public health and vaccination policy. Their arguments and terms of debate can easily be traced to the perspectives of doctors, scientists and health workers, and to their exasperation and incredulity with a non-compliant public. Usually social science studies adopt these framings to evaluate their significance. As we go on to consider, however, these arguments and the way they are framed can be problematic and embody assumptions that are open to contest.

The policy debates about vaccination coverage in European and African contexts have often proceeded in parallel, in terrain occupied by different institutions, agencies and analytical traditions. As the discussions above indicate, the result is to produce many contrasting images of 'Europe' and 'Africa', almost as if they were two worlds. Yet arguments about each do not just reflect separate strands of reasoning. Contrasting images of European and African society, and of the global 'north' and 'south' are in part produced as contrasts of each other within more global reasoning. It is useful to sum up these contrasts which often inform the tenor of policy debates.

A first contrast draws a strong distinction between views of risk in the global 'north' and 'south'. A concern with vaccine risks and side effects is, in this view, a luxury of those in the north no longer familiar with the childhood diseases ravaging the south, where the more important clamour is for vaccine access (Streefland, 2001; Obaro and Palmer, 2003). This evokes a broader contrast between late-industrialized 'risk society' (Beck, 1992) and a still-to-modernize 'underdeveloped society'.

Second, in a development of this argument, contrasts are drawn between the wealthy and the poor, and across class; distinctions that form a microcosm, within countries, of north–south differences. Thus poverty and 'underclass' status is associated with difficult access to health services, but also with compliance once reached. In contrast, worries about vaccine risks are associated with wealthier groups and the anxious middle classes.

A third contrast turns on rationality versus irrationality. Thus vaccine anxieties in the south are associated with incomplete (rising) scientific rationality in settings where 'traditional' beliefs still predominate. In the north, they are linked to a diminishing scientific rationality, or a rise of what is seen as irrationality in society.

Fourth, rumour and resistance are seen to play out in distinct ways in northern and southern settings. Thus images of the south emphasize collective resistance based on religion, and the spread of conspiracy-type theories. These spread easily among societies portrayed as mired in 'tradition', superstition or ignorance of science. In contrast, in the industrialized north resistance is imaged as individualized refusal grounded in parents' individual evaluation of risks to their own child, mediated through social networks and the media. Here, rumours based on 'wrong' science are seen to meet a receptive audience in people attuned to the values of the 'risk society'.

Finally, key contrasts turn on the nature of trust in north and south. Thus vaccine anxieties in the north are being cast as part of a generalized breakdown of trust in public institutions, and evidence of growing critical public engagement with scientific expertise. In contrast, southern debates tend to stress that trust is incomplete because it has not yet been achieved. They emphasize the unachieved or incomplete integration of expert science with 'indigenous knowledge' and beliefs. Thus while trust may be lacking everywhere, in the north it is seen to be diminishing, while in the south, it has not yet formed.

Across all these contrasts, an overriding image of a pre-modern south versus a late or post-modern north comes into view. If vaccination is a symbol of modernity, this would suggest that the south has yet to embrace it fully but that the north has moved beyond the tipping point and is already rejecting it. Projected over time, this contrast evokes the possibility that northern values may come to take root in the south, emerging as a logical progression through 'stages' of modernization and development. Projected over space, the danger is evoked that northern values will spread into and 'pollute' the south, through globalized media and movements of people and information. In either case, the emerging scenario might be a widespread loss of confidence in vaccination programmes worldwide.

Exploring key concepts

Each of the arguments and images that we have explored above are rooted in wider arguments about people and medicine, and people and science more generally, and in different European and Africanist traditions for theorizing and researching changing science–society relations. This helps to perpetuate the image of two contrasting worlds. Yet evaluating these wider arguments reveals further issues and questions which need to be explored.

Ignorance and misunderstanding of science

As we have seen, a common argument in both European and African settings explains vaccination refusal or default in terms of people's ignorance or mis-understanding – whether of the purposes and importance of vaccination, of vaccination and disease risks, or of biomedicine in general. Calling upon a lack of knowledge or understanding of scientific issues in this way represents a classic instance of what, in studies of science and technology in northern settings, has been termed the 'deficit model'. This originated as part of the wave of technological triumphalism and supportive studies of science that dominated during the 1950s and 1960s. Science was authoritative, objective and universal, and an unquestionable basis for expert-led decisions. Both failures of technology uptake and perceived crises of legitimacy in science among publics were deemed to be the result of public misunderstanding of science, a 'deficit' in public knowledge which should be filled through science education (see Collins and Evans, 2002 for a review).

The deficit model has been questioned from several angles emerging from 'northern' focused science studies, but finding echoes in literatures that have focused on 'southern' – including African – settings.

First, critics argue that where people do not accept or respond to scientific or technical interventions – including medical ones – as expected, this may reflect less a lack of knowledge or ignorance than distinct forms of experiential expertise grounded in everyday practice, knowledge and epistemology (Fischer, 2000).

Second, critics of the deficit model also argue that public understandings of science, grounded in people's own framings and experiential expertise, are often far more sophisticated and nuanced than is recognized. Such understandings focus not just on the content and methods of science, but also on its institutional embedding, patronage and control (Wynne, 1992; Irwin and Wynne, 1996). In other words, the public is often alert to the particular social and political commitments that underpin what may be presented as objective, neutral and authoritative science. This is illustrated in cases of 'citizen science' where people have explicitly engaged with and contested science and its advice by conducting their own research and experiments framed in different ways, whether for example in 'popular epidemiology' around issues of toxic waste pollution (Brown, 1992), or around HIV/AIDS diagnosis and treatment (Epstein, 1996). In such 'citizen science', publics engage critically with the scientific perspectives of expert institutions, either through funding or orchestrating their own scientific investigations, or through lobbying to transform research questions (e.g. Irwin, 1995; Fischer, 2000).

A third strand of critique thus turns the question round. Rather than presume that the perspectives of dominant scientific institutions are an objective, authoritative benchmark against which others' knowledge is lacking, questions are posed about the particularity and partiality of 'science'. In what some have termed a 'second wave' of science studies (Collins and Evans, 2002), the assumptions and practices of science have come under challenge. The framing of scientific questions, experimental methods, styles of investigation, modes of reaching closure, and treatments of risk and uncertainty are reconceptualized as social and political activities (e.g. Knorr-Cetina, 1981; Haraway, 1991; Barnes et al, 1996). They are shaped through particular sets of laboratory and other practices (eg. Latour and Woolgar, 1979; Latour, 1987), and through networks and relationships that enable them to acquire authority in particular settings (e.g. Pickering, 1992; Knorr-Cetina, 1999). Such arguments challenge the distinctions made between scientific 'experts' and other, non-experts. They would, for instance, force one to ask how the biomedical perspectives that drive and justify vaccination programmes arose, how they have become authoritative, and what broader social or political agendas might underlie and be supported by them.

These critiques thus recognize that what may be dismissed as ignorance is often, in reality, potentially valuable public knowledge and experience that can bring 'contributory expertise' to a decision or arena of technological application (Collins and Evans, 2002). However, much work in this vein sees the public's knowledge and expertise as valuable and legitimate only if it is continuous with western scientific rationality. Excluded, therefore, are 'fringe' sciences such as astrology, 'alternative' medical therapies, perspectives grounded in religion, and attention to 'folk knowledges' whose concepts and practices appear as discontinuous with those of western science. In a similar way, most work on citizen science has seen it as alternative *science*, conforming with the broad categories of science. Such emphases play down the ways in which people's knowledges develop in embedded relationship with local social processes and differences, concepts and moralities (see Leach and Fairhead, 2002). Different perspectives and forms of expertise may not easily combine, as they may represent fundamentally different ways of framing an issue, underlain by different social or political commitments (Stirling, 2005). The focus on knowledge and epistemology obscures more fundamental questions of ontology, or of the 'mutual embedding of natural knowledge and social order, their co-production' (Jasanoff, 2003, p392, also Jasanoff, 2004).

In contrast with northern-focused literatures, the co-production of knowledge about natural and technical phenomena with social processes has been a major focus of debates about rural people's knowledge in African settings. Rooted in social anthropology, this analytical tradition has long emphasized how knowledge and beliefs about 'technical' issues are often inseparable from questions of cosmology, morality, social relations and prevailing relations of authority. Concepts, ideas and metaphors that may lie at odds with western or biomedical rationalities may nevertheless make sense as part of their particular social and cultural settings. Thus, whether in agricultural, environmental or health arenas, local knowledge and western science, it is argued, are often rooted in incommensurable concepts and framings (Croll and Parkin, 1992; Fairhead, 1992; Scoones and Thompson, 1994).

It is broadly in this vein that some anthropologists have argued that whether or not people accept vaccination turns, in large measure, on how it engages with local knowledge, aetiologies and perceptions of disease (Streefland et al, 1999, p1707). In this view, vaccination refusal or resistance is seen to be grounded not in 'ignorance' but in alternative, socially and culturally embedded rationalities. However, these same works nevertheless suggest that demand for vaccination reflects a biomedical framing; either an informed public that perceives the benefits of and need for specific vaccinations (Nichter, 1995), or a population that generally appreciates biomedicine (Streefland et al, 1999). This overlooks the possibility that parents may value and actively seek vaccination for reasons grounded in socially and culturally embedded ideas that depart from, or even contradict, biomedical ideas. This possibility is underlined by works on Africa that emphasize the relative autonomy of 'indigenous' knowledges from scientific institutions, seeing the latter as relatively less embedded in society. They draw attention to ways of thinking – epistemologies – which are entirely at odds with those underlying, for instance, biomedicine, and yet are a way in which peoples' responses to technology are framed (White, 2005).

Such Africanist analytical traditions emphasizing the non-integration of local knowledge and expert science may, however, overplay the coherence of each (e.g. Last, 1980; Agrawal, 1995). This may obscure crucial ways in which knowledge and understanding are debated within societies, in ways interlocked with debates about social identity, difference and morality. It may also obscure important questions about how different forms of knowledge held by members of the public and by institutions involved with science, technology and policy interact, in ways that shape both (Long and Long, 1994). Such interactions are not just cultural – between different epistemologies, or belief systems. Fundamentally, as more 'northern' science studies reminds us, they are often social and political: encounters between framings that are themselves entwined with different social and political commitments (Stirling, 2005; Wynne, 2005), and whose interactions have economic and political dimensions (Farmer, 1999).

A set of questions thus arises about people's engagements with vaccination that are obscured by images of public ignorance. How do parents understand vaccination – how it works, what it does and does not do, and what benefits and dangers it may bring to their children's bodies? How do these conceptualizations of vaccination relate to people's broader ideas concerning child health, wellbeing and influences on it, in their particular, located 'worlds of babies' (Gottlieb and DeLoache, 2000)? How do these understandings relate to other fields of reflection and experience, for instance concerning the economy and social relations? Rather than be written off as irrational, superstitious or 'traditional', might views of vaccines that do not conform with western biomedicine be conceptually linked to ideas that do help people protect their children's health? Might vaccination refusal reflect judgements rooted in different calculus and starting points in understandings of child health and circumstance? Rather than ignorance of science, might parents' anxieties over vaccines reflect a different reading of science's uncertainties and politics?

Risk

Risk has become a dominant theme in popular, policy and media discussions of public engagement with science. It is a core concept in policy debates around vaccination. Much debate about the relationships between science and publics more generally has been cast in terms of risk, defined in narrow technical terms as a probability of a negative event, such as a vaccine-adverse event happening in a particular instance. A focus on risk presents it as amenable to prediction and management. In this framing of the issues and debate, publics are assumed to be aware of (or to misunderstand) risks in these same technical terms. It follows that a key challenge for policy is to educate the public towards a 'correct' understanding of 'real' risks.

This narrow, technical approach to risk and risk comparisons as a way of engaging the public in decisions over scientific and technological issues nevertheless makes a number of questionable assumptions. A first set of problems relates to the relationship between individual and social values and processes. First, this approach often assumes that an individual makes decisions through a comparison of risk – as when deciding whether to undertake a particular action, to accept a medical procedure, or adopt a technology. This presumes that there is in fact a moment of calculation by a single mind. Yet in reality, such questions are often dealt with in ongoing processes embedded in personal history, social relations and interactions, which may involve discussions among family members, peers or a wider community. In such processes, it may be very hard indeed to define a moment at which a 'risk calculation' would be made.

Second, this approach presumes that statistics about risks and benefits are convincing to individuals. Generalized risk calculations are grounded in a view of a general population, and an average person (in the case of vaccination, an average child). Yet this overlooks the possibility that people do not consider themselves and their particular child as average, and thus do not feel that these calculations could or should apply to them. As we shall see, in the case of vaccination, this puts questions of how parents themselves frame risks, in relation to their understandings of their own child's health, centre stage.

Third, this approach often presumes a conflict of interest between rather singular visions of the individual and public good; between being selfish and public-spirited. Yet people belong to many social worlds. Important as the ongoing debate about individual versus social risks and benefits is, it overlooks the variety of collectivities and forms of common good that people may already be part of, and that shape their thinking and practice around engaging with technologies. Indeed in the environmental context where similar 'tragedy of the commons' arguments have been rehearsed at length, a now very large body of work has contested the notion of the selfish risk-minimizing individual to show how people form community and group institutions of various kinds to manage the resources that are important to them (e.g. Berkes, 1989; Ostrom, 1990); communities that are often based on shared knowledges and values. This raises further questions about vaccination: what kinds of solidarities are emerging, among whom, and what serves to unite them?

A second set of problems relates to the nature of the uncertainties surrounding scientific and technological issues, and how far the notion of 'risk' is adequate to address these. As Beck et al (1994, p181) and others have pointed out, risk is only one response to what is an inherently uncertain world, that attempts to place order on it by 'making the incalculable calculable' (Hobson-West, 2003, p279). In some instances, such an attempt may be misplaced, or so badly at odds with the ways publics or particular groups in society frame the issue, as to perpetuate controversy rather than resolve it. Stirling (Stirling and Mayer, 1999; Stirling, 2003) has usefully distinguished between four types of incertitude. A genuine situation of risk prevails where there are calculable probabilities between known outcomes. Uncertainty prevails where the possible outcomes are known, but there is no credible basis for assigning probabilities to them. But also significant are situations of ambiguity, where there are major differences of subjective focus and framing, and ignorance, where we don't know what we don't know, and the possibility prevails that surprises or 'unknowable unknowns' might arise. In the vaccination arena, many issues and cases involve not just uncertainty, but ambiguity and ignorance. For instance the possibility that there exist hitherto unknown mechanisms is acknowledged by many vaccine scientists dealing with this rapidly advancing arena of science and technology. Thus new generations of DNA vaccines could have unforeseen effects in the body, or vaccines could interact in unpredicted ways with disease ecologies so that new resistances emerge. Publics, equally, have raised concerns about areas of ignorance, such as the long-term evolutionary consequences for human health of using vaccines derived from animal tissue (Hobson-West, 2003, p279). The potentialities for such unknown factors tends, however, to be little heeded by institutions charged with vaccination policy and programmes, for whom they are unwarranted distractions from the objective identification of risk within industry-standard parameters.

A third set of problems relates to questions of knowledge and its framing. Technical approaches to risk tend to presume that it has an objective and universal public meaning. Such views hold that risk is an objective, calculable reality, determined by 'sound science'. If public perceptions of risk depart from this, it is because they have become 'distorted' by social and emotional factors, and by misleading external influences such as media triggers. Whether knowledge of risk can be objective, or is always framed in ways that are inevitably 'positioned', has been discussed in a vast literature on risk communication applied to many issues, as well as to public health and vaccines (e.g. Bennett and Calman, 1999; Spier, 2002). Arguments are offered that public perception of risks from vaccines is amplified because they affect children and the vulnerable, because parents lack control over the outcome, and because damage is potentially long-term or fatal. Yet even this notion of 'risk perception' is problematic for the way it assumes a separation of actual and objectively calculated risk, distorting factors, and perceived risk. Public perceptions may neither be in line with these 'scientific' risk calculations, nor indeed framed in terms of risk at all. Rather than simply attempt to re-frame them as risk issues, as dominant approaches to vaccination policy and education have often done, might one instead address how people do understand and frame the issues concerned, as related to their own knowledge and perspectives and as a product of their history of interactions with policy institutions?

Thus a narrow, technical approach to risk can be extended to suggest a range of key questions around public engagements with vaccination. How do different people consider the various dimensions of incertitude involved with vaccination – to whom are they important and why? How do people's understandings of incertitude relate to their knowledge and understandings of their children's health? Are forms of social solidarity and community emerging around shared senses and experiences of risk and uncertainty? How do parents' framings of incertitude compare with the risk framings promoted by policy institutions, and how do they interact?

Trust

The concept of trust has been evoked in much policy and media debate as an explanation for public controversies about issues involving science and technology. There has been considerable talk, at least in the global north, of a 'crisis of public trust', whether in general or in relation to science (e.g. House of Lords, 2000; Cabinet Office Strategy Unit, 2002). Both academic and policy debate has focused on analysing this so-called 'breakdown of trust', and considering how trust can be rebuilt or restored. In this broader context it is not surprising that the question of trust has been raised in relation to vaccination controversies.

In relation to Britain, O'Neill (2002) suggests that 'loss of trust' is 'a cliché of our times'. The supposed deepening crisis of trust in contemporary British society has become commonplace in sociological and media arguments. These claim evidence of growing mistrust in key institutions and office-holders in public life, and in professionals of many sorts. In her lectures questioning this cliché, she portrays it well:

> *Citizens, it is said, no longer trust governments, or politicians, or ministers, or the police, or the courts, or the prison service. Consumers, it is said, no longer trust business, especially big business, or their products... Patients, it is said, no longer trust doctors (think of Dr Shipman!), and in particular no longer trust hospitals or hospital consultants (O'Neill, 2002, lecture 1, p2).*

Such a litany echoes many of the elements and contexts of mistrust that analysts have suggested are relevant to contemporary vaccination anxieties in the north. A deepening decline of trust more generally offers a seemingly powerful explanation for the rise of such vaccination controversies. In contrast, analysts of African settings who invoke the concept of trust more often suggest that trust has not yet been established.

However, the frequent references to trust in policy and media discourse leave many questions begging. Some concern what exactly trust is, and how it should be conceptualized. Others concern whether there is really a breakdown of trust in the north, and a history of gradually accreting trust in the south.

In terms of the concept of trust, a first problem concerns the highly generalized ways in which the term is often evoked in policy and media debate. Yet there are as many ways of defining the concept of trust as there are social theories in play (see Misztal, 1996), and each carries different analytical implications. For some, trust is a property of individuals; others see it located in social relationships, or a social system or culture more broadly, or as shaped in the interplay of individual action and structural conditions, acquired and reproduced through practice and habitus. Some see it as a cognitive concept, while for others it is emotional or behavioural. Some take a functional viewpoint, seeing trust as a precondition for social cooperation and the functioning of institutions; others associate it with rational interest promotion; while for others it has a moral dimension. In this mass of social science debate, a key distinction concerns whether trust is seen as people's expression (what they say) or their practices (what they do). Some see trust as a discursive concept that can be assessed – as polls and media often do – by asking people to identify who they do and do not trust. For others, trust is related to practical knowledge and has to be assessed through people's actions (O'Neill, 2002). Thus O'Neill argues that while people may express distrust when asked direct questions about technologies or public institutions, this is better interpreted as reflecting a 'climate of suspicion'. Trust needs, rather, to be assessed by whether, in their practices, people 'place their trust' in those institutions. For O'Neill, then, trust may exist despite suspicion. Walls et al (2004, p147) use the notion of 'critical trust' in a similar way to O'Neill's suspicion, to recognize that while publics may reflect critically on and suspect the motives, interests or performance of particular institutions, they may still continue to rely on and make use of them (Walls et al, 2004, p147).

As Hobson-West (2007) argues in the particular context of vaccination, if the concept of trust is to be analytically useful, it needs to be defined and dis-aggregated. Walls et al (2004) suggest that we need to do both these things to go beyond a monolithic view of trust. They suggest that people's judgements of trust in institutions involve a constellation of meanings and experiences, in which historical experiences of the institution, beliefs about the issues involved, and emotional dimensions may all be involved. Furthermore, non-disaggregated, generalized uses of the term trust can actually deter analysis. Trust and distrust become catch-alls, easy explanators that appear to say everything, so deterring further interrogation, while they actually say very little. In this, the concept deters more specific and perhaps awkward questions about the interests, performance or relationships with the public held by particular institutions.

Yet one can question how helpful the concept of trust is, however disaggregated and contextualized, in understanding relationships between the public, tech-nologies and institutions. Is trust actually the most appropriate descriptor of the meanings and experiences involved in such relationships, or can even dis-aggregated concepts obscure more than they reveal? Rather than consider a relationship with an institution in terms of trust or otherwise, it can be important to explore what people understand the institution to do, and what the nature of their relationship with it is. Thus rather than disaggregate the concept of trust into ever more specific types and contexts, we need to move beyond its shorthand, universalizing qualities, to an understanding of how people themselves consider their relationships with technologies and technocracies, in all their rich diversity and texture.

Nevertheless, several arguments describe and account for a so-called breakdown of trust, or for the emergence of greater public suspicion and critical trust. A first turns on the expansion of information in an emergent 'information age'. Thus O'Neill (2002) argues that new modes of public accountability with their emphasis on transparency, openness of information and audit – paradoxically set up to address a supposed crisis of public trust – have distorted professional practice and incentives in ways that are damaging to trust. 'The pursuit of ever more perfect accountability provides citizens and consumers, patients and parents with more information, more comparisons, more complaints systems; but it also builds a culture of suspicion' (O'Neill, 2002). However, can more information about how institutions operate really be assumed to be a problem in this way? In many settings, those who seek out more information are the most active in pursuit of their goals, so the distrustful, suspicious consumer might be re-read as the discerning consumer. Related arguments point to the mass of information made available through contemporary media and technologies. These, it is argued, make available ever more information, but also misinformation and disinformation, yet with no means to check its origins and sources. In such circumstances, people often 'and reasonably, withhold trust and suspend both belief and disbelief in favour of cynicism and half-belief' (O'Neill, 2002, lecture 4, p5). However, an assumption that the distinction between information and misinformation is so clear-cut – there to be made if only information declared its sources – is problematic as it assumes a singular framing and singular notion of expertise. Viewed from different perspectives, one person's biased, misinformation might be another's truth. Rather than contribute to uncertainty and suspicion, the proliferation of information might be read as the proliferation of available framings that make sense to people given their diverse circumstances and concerns.

A second set of arguments relates distrust and suspicion to the emergence of doubt and uncertainty as pervasive features of social life in late modernity (Giddens, 1991; Beck, 1992). Thus as Giddens (1991) argues, in the conditions of 'late modernity' public institutions have become both more diverse in their goals, and increasingly reflexive, continually reappraising and revising their assessments, knowledge base and practices. The increased fracturing of contemporary medical practice is often called upon as an exemplar of this, with elements of high tech and 'virtual' medicine juxtaposed with more biographical and holistic forms of healing in an increasingly pluralized marketplace. In these circumstances, whereas modernity implied a replacement of traditional forms of knowledge with the certainties of rational scientific knowledge, late modernity is characterized by increasing uncertainty and choice: 'doubt becomes a pervasive feature of modern critical reasoning, forming a general existential dimension of the contemporary social world' (Williams and Calnan, 1996, p1612).

To the extent that these meta-arguments that capture social transformations hold, do they really imply an 'age of anxiety' viewed in a negative sense, as analyses linking distrust and the emergence of a multiplicity of 'health scares' have done (Furedi, 2001; Fitzpatrick, 2004)? Others doubt this. For instance Williams and Calnan suggest in the context of medicine that what is emergent is a 'reflexively organised dialectic of trust and doubt' (Williams and Calnan, 1996, p1612). In this, different people's discourse and practices may show a mixture of antipathy and respect towards (different) aspects of modern medicine. What is crucial is to analyse these, in a way that sees people as 'critical reflexive agents who are active in the face of modern medicine and technological developments' (1996, p1613). While some lament the supposed end of the era of the passive, trusting recipient of modern technological developments, others celebrate this as ushering in a new, active scientific and technological citizenship, and challenge from the articulate consumer (Gabe et al in Williams and Calnan, 1996). They locate people's distancing from modern technologies and technocracies such as orthodox medicine as part of a process of reclaiming control over the body, the self and the wider environment (Williams and Calnan, 1996, p1617), in an emergent 'life politics' (Giddens, 1991). These arguments shift the focus from an emergent deficit of trust associated with the growth of anxiety in a negative sense, to the positive dimensions of anxiety, associated with goals and desires that people are striving for.

There are also problems with a linear view of history which presumes, perhaps romantically, that trust existed previously, only breaking down more recently. Others point to specific periods of public concern about and dissent from scientific and technological developments. Indeed, historical studies of public engagement with and responses to vaccination provide many illustrations of a non-linear history, in which both levels and expressions of concern are related to the social and political contexts of the day. Thus, in the British context, public worries about and dissent from vaccination technologies and technocracies were evident from the earliest instances. Durbach (2000) links dissent to smallpox vaccine in the 1880s with working class movements, although Porter and Porter (1988) emphasize greater social diversity in these concerns, even at this time. Some have suggested that the period of the 1950s and 1960s in Britain (sometimes taken as a baseline for the so-called breakdown of trust perceived to have unfolded since then) was in fact a high point of acceptance and positive engagement with the institutions involved in mass childhood immunization (Hardy, 2006), building from earlier periods of less easy acceptance. As Hardy elaborates, such trust emerged for specific reasons linked to the burgeoning of particular sorts of social contract, responsibility and expectation around vaccination, in the context of broader state systems and politics. It was neither a question of generalized 'trust', nor part of a state of trust that had existed since time immemorial. It is the trust of this period that needs explaining, not the distrust of others. In short, it is necessary to track the emergence and decline of particular vaccine anxieties historically, in relation to the broader political histories of which they are part.

This also applies to African settings, where political histories serve to qualify notions both that a generalized 'lack of trust' prevailed in pre-modern conditions, and that trust has accreted over time. Thus the long history of vaccine anxieties in Africa has involved suspicion of the motives of very specific state and global institutions, in ways that reflected particular political contexts and historical moments. White (2005) describes how in the early 20th century, 'many vaccine stories inscribe[d] onto vaccination the rich fears and concerns of colonial societies' (2005, p6) – fears of institutions of the colonial state and its global supporters. For instance, in 1913 an anti-colonial movement in western Kenya opposed vaccination strongly, seeing it as an extension of state power. In Madagascar, from the 1920s through the 1950s the popular belief that plague vaccines were designed to poison the population became part of nationalist rhetoric. In general terms colonial control over African societies and bodies was deeply entwined with the establishment and extension of public health regimes, including immunization (Vaughan, 1991). This – and the coercive means through which such programmes were often implemented – created a receptive context in which broader concerns about colonial authorities were linked to dissent from vaccination. White emphasizes, however, that the history of dissent has to be seen in relation to the history of the particular colonial states and their projects, which was varied and changing. Thus 'each vaccination program could be invested with new and topical meanings: vaccination was never routine' (2005, p7). Post-independence, political histories question any view that trust grew linearly with the transition to modern state systems. Instead, vaccine anxieties have arisen at particular times and places in ways that reflect shifts in local–national state politics, the political economy of neoliberal reforms, and the relationships between states, citizens and global institutions. Generalized notions of trust are inadequate to capture these relationships, as are linear notions of 'breakdown' and 'accretion' to capture their dynamics over time. In short, to understand vaccine anxieties we need to research them in order to understand conjunctures at which personal, social and wider political dimensions come together in particular ways.

Rumour and resistance

The notions of rumour and of resistance constitute a fourth set of concepts often evoked, whether separately or together, to explain controversies around issues involving science and technology, vaccination included. Rumour is most broadly defined as an 'unproved statement' or 'gossip or common talk'. In policy and media discussion, the notion of rumour is often evoked where people express worries about the negative effects of science or technology, about the political or economic motives of those promoting it, or about links between these and far wider processes, ranging from colonialism to capitalism, racism or religious politics. Rumours can be linked with resistance. Resistance implies that something must be being resisted. In some cases, people are seen to resist a technology or technocracy itself. In others, resistance to such things is seen as meta-commentary on some wider process, such as contemporary political economy.

There are several problems with these concepts, at least with the ways they are commonly deployed in commentary on anxieties around science and technology. A first critique concerns substance and framing, and applies to the many instances where describing concerns as 'rumour' serves to delegitimize their content, imaging them as grounded in doubtful or false allegations. This is the case where rumours are seen to be grounded in wrong, misunderstood or misconceived science – for instance in wrongly attributing negative health events to a vaccine cause (André, 2003, p594). A world is evoked of misled campaigners who mislead publics, in a context where only biomedical support for childhood vaccination is legitimate. An assumption is that rumours will abate with 'proper' biomedically oriented scientific education, yet the assumption of ungrounded rumour playing into public ignorance might mask what are actually struggles between differently framed 'sciences' and forms of knowledge and expertise. In the highly charged political field of debate surrounding new technologies, different framings and forms of knowledge are often linked to contrasting social and political concerns. 'Writing off' concerns as baseless rumours is highly problematic in deterring an analysis of what these are.

Second, while in much policy and popular discourse, rumour has become a shorthand for an idea that can be replaced with proper 'facts', this is a problematic distortion of the strict definition of rumour as an unproven statement; a status that should open up inquiry and reflection. Indeed it is in this vein that Geissler and Pool (2006) suggest that a key feature of rumours is that they can be spread with some degree of incredulity; 'rumours enable people to debate current events and concerns, and in order to do this it is not necessary that everyone actually believes them' (Geissler and Pool, 2006, p982). Used in this way, rumours are similar to urban legends and become particularly relevant in contexts of uncertainty, providing a mode through which people can reflect on the issues at stake in a wide-ranging and non-committal way.

Third, social scientists and historians have at times understood rumour to be 'about' other things. Two problems ensue: first, the difficulty of providing evidence of what they are really about, and second, taking analytical focus off their content. Explanation is by association rather than evidence, and there is often little attempt to relate the content of a particular rumour to its context. For instance, many anthropologists and historians have interpreted vaccine and blood- stealing 'rumours' in Africa as meta-commentary on the wider conse-quences of capitalism and globalization. In this view, rumours about sterilizing vaccines, blood stealing, cannibalism, and so on have often been seen as part of a realm of 'things occult', part and parcel of beliefs in witchcraft and sorcery that some have suggested are undergoing a resurgence in Africa (e.g. Comaroff and Comaroff, 1999). Allegations about nefarious uses of vaccines or blood stealing thus become linked with 'stories of zombies, cannibalism and head hunting ... [as] imaginative moral frameworks for making sense of wage labour, consumption, migration, productive regimes, structural adjustment programmes, development policies and the functioning of markets' (Moore and Sanders, 2002, p15). They become ways to comment on the mysteries of extraordinary acquired wealth that some have suggested is a pervasive feature of cultural reflection in Africa (Geissler and Pool, 2006). Thus:

The preoccupation with the occult ... at one level [is] about the desire to
plumb the secret of those invisible means [of rapid enrichment]; at another,

> *it is concerned to stem the spread of a macabre, visceral economy founded*
> *on the violence of extraction and abstraction in which the majority are kept*
> *poor by the mystical machinations of the few (Comaroff and Comaroff,*
> *1999, p293).*

Yet in such analyses, which see rumours as responses to a nascent modernity, it is difficult to discern among the different things that might be being resisted, or commented on (see Ortner, 1995). Broad issues that are apparently being resisted (such as capitalism) are not self-evident phenomena, but need to be understood in relation to how they are locally experienced. In assuming generalized responses to global processes, accounts such as those above overlook the specific social, institutional and political settings in which particular rumours arise. In contrast, works taking a more ethnographic or detailed historical perspective show how anything resembling meta-commentary on global forces is inflected by far more locally specific meanings and experiences (e.g. Musambachime, 1988; Weiss, 1998; White, 2000, 2005; Geissler, 2005). In these works vaccine and vampire 'rumours' become ways of interpreting political–economic processes which emerge and make sense in specific social and political settings. Yet in some instances, in failing to relate content to context, such analyses fail to discern why people should express wider political concerns through a technology, and why through a particular technology (among the many that are accepted without a problem). As we shall consider, worries about technologies are not just an 'idiom for' expressions of wider political concerns, as these things are more substantively related. What can seem like an idiom for something else to external eyes can within local framing be understood as a more substantive relation, between body and political economy.

Many of these same critiques apply to popular and policy arguments about the roles of pressure groups and media as key mechanisms for propagating and spreading rumours. These mechanisms are seen to be acquiring new and globalized force as the growth in global flows of information and new communications technologies creates a fresh capacity for 'rumours' to spread fast and pressure groups to network globally.

Forms of mobilization and movement that express concerns about technologies are often seen, in highly generalized ways, either as misguided (spreading baseless rumours), or as anti-technology in some general sense. The often-evoked notion of an 'anti-vaccination movement' crossing regions and enduring over time is a case in point. Yet this concept overlooks the specific, varied content of the concerns that can drive such mobilization, as well as the specific political contexts and processes in which they emerge (see Blume, 2006).

The relationship between movement content and political context has been a major preoccupation of theorists of social movements (e.g. Tarrow, 1998; Jamison, 2001; McAdam et al, 2001). Epstein (1996) proposes four possible ways in which social movements might engage with science: (a) by disputing scientific claims; (b) by seeking to acquire a cachet of scientific authority for a political claim by finding a scientific expert to validate their political stance; (c) by rejecting the scientific way of knowing and advancing their claims to expertise from some wholly different epistemological standpoint, and (d) by attempting to 'stake out some ground on the scientists' own terrain' by questioning 'not just the uses of science, not just the control over science, but sometimes even the very contents of science and the processes by which it is produced' (Epstein, 1996, pp12–13). Such movements are not simply anti-science or anti-technology, or resisting technology as an 'idiom for' resisting or commenting on something else; rather they are actively expressing anxieties around the content, methods and goals of specific scientific practices and their wider social and political implications.

The argument that media thus becomes a vehicle for spreading pressure group concerns and rumours is also problematic in several respects. It assumes a gullible public – that people take media stories at face value. Yet as Hall (1997) argues, media audiences can 'read' stories in oppositional as well as concurring ways, while this assumption overlooks the ways that media (like rumour, in Geissler's analysis) might provide a vehicle for debate, and for people to reflect on the inherent uncertainties in politicized scientific fields. Moreover, the media cannot be seen as a vehicle only for anti-technology sentiments, given that much coverage focuses on pro-technology arguments or on support to biomedicine or health delivery. Where there are many messages with conflicting views, a barrage of information flows can also become a vehicle for debate. How this unfolds will, as Hall (1997) reminds us, depend on how people read various media messages – positive or negative – in relation to their prior experiences and social relations.

Power, knowledge and vaccination

We have thus suggested that many 'off the shelf' explanations invoked to explain why people refuse vaccination (and the broader arguments about ignorance, misunderstanding of risk, breakdown of trust, rumour and amplification by pressure groups and mass-media on which they rest) can be more problematic than they might at first appear. They are certainly inadequate to capture the diverse ways in which people think about, engage with and struggle around issues involving science and technology amid specific sets of social and political relations. But rather than dismiss these concepts and arguments as inadequate, we need to see them in relation to the institutions to which they make sense and which produce them. Dominant arguments about ignorance, risk, trust and rumour, we suggest, embody the values and perspectives of powerful institutions involved in promoting vaccination technocracy.

Thus in relation to risk, risk statistics are only one representation of reality, and depend on the methods, institutions and cultures of the scientists that produce them (Wynne, 2005). Discourses about risk come so naturally to the institutions involved with promoting vaccination because they imply predictability, control and manageability. This is of fundamental importance given the large-scale, universal aspirations of mass childhood immunization, and the need for legitimacy of the state and international technocracies promoting it. Such endeavours dovetail nicely with justificatory discourses emphasizing the spread of benefits and the minimization of risks as defined by sound, biomedical science. Even where uncertainties are admitted, these tend to be framed as a temporary phase that will be overcome by further scientific research and the accumulation of evidence (Calman, 2002). The assumption is, therefore, that uncertainties can be turned into discoverable, measurable risks, and that controversies can and will be resolved through research that establishes and communicates 'the real facts'. Castel (1991) shows how regimes of concerted action in risk prevention are capable of extension into broader socio-environmental interventionism, as computerization and administrative rationalization begin to make possible forms of government of population which, by coordinating appropriate methods of expertise and assessment, are capable of identifying individual members of society who can be deemed to present a significant risk to themselves or to the community. Thus computerized child health databases in the north already identify non-vaccinated children.

In relation to trust, it seems that a technical, neutral state, and a singular body of authoritative technical science, may never have existed. Yet it is precisely this vision that the idea of a decline in or damage to trust presupposes. Discourses about loss of trust impose a normative vision of the state and of global institutions as technocratic, trustworthy and a-political. This justifies an appeal to greater levels of trust in a technocratically driven world. But have people ever had this vision, and hence the possibility of a decline in trust from it? Or has it always been a question of a politics and political economy and morality of science which people 'bought into' at some times, but at other times they have rejected or resisted? As O'Neill insightfully suggests:

> *Perhaps claims about a crisis of trust are mainly evidence of an unrealistic hankering for a world in which safety and compliance are total, and breaches of trust are eliminated (O'Neill, 2002, lecture 1 p5).*

Global and national desires to increase vaccination coverage often exhibit just such a hankering: for a world in which people comply with a technology that 'sound biomedical science' says is safe and in their and their children's interests. In this respect, discourses about trust and its breakdown operate rather similarly to discourses about risk. Both have a great deal of affinity with discourses about ignorance and rumours that delegitimize public concerns as unfounded.

It is striking how far dominant policy arguments construct public concerns about vaccination in negative ways: as ignorance, misinformation, rumour, media amplification, misguided or maleficient movements, and so on. A pervasive 'deficit model' is in play – whether the deficit the public are seen to have is of knowledge, of trust, of critical reflection on the media, and so on. This dovetails with a negative view of vaccine anxieties, emerging from and reflective of deficits, that fails to ask what positive desires and meanings the public might be bringing to bear when they question vaccination. As Wynne (2005) and others have argued, deficit models, by projecting 'the problem' onto the public, conveniently shore up scientific institutions and their perspectives as unproblematic, requiring no interrogation or adjustment.

Explaining why people and institutions understand things in the way that they do is the stuff of much bigger sociological inquiry. These questions have been addressed through a variety of traditions in the sociology of knowledge, from a Durkheimian tradition looking at collective representations linked to social structure, to structuralist traditions seeing understandings as reflective either of the hard-wiring of human cognition or of economic structures; or to post-structuralist traditions seeing in 'truths' the reproduction of relations of power, and looking beyond such truths into the experiential ways that knowledge emerges from everyday material and social interactions. Here we first consider the valuable contributions of post-structuralist perspectives on power and knowledge – especially those concerning 'biopower' – but then show how critiques of this concept suggest the need to integrate elements of other sociological traditions in the approach we take.

The relationship between the health sector and wider forms of power in society has been explored within debates on biopower, or forms of power exercised over people specifically insofar as they are thought of as living beings (Foucault, 1978). Foucault (1976) traced the emergence of biopolitics as a new kind of politics in the 19th century, in which issues of individual conduct as related to biology and life interconnect with issues of national policy and power. Biopower involves both disciplinary power centred on the body, optimizing its capacities and integrating it into efficient systems, through mechanisms linking science and disciplining institutions; and power centred on regulation of the biological processes that affect a whole population, achieved through techniques in fields such as demography, statistics and epidemiology (Foucault, 1978). Mass childhood immunization, with its integration of children's bodies into vaccination technocracies aimed at disease control in populations, can easily be seen as combining both dimensions of biopower.

Attention to biopower reveals how state and global institutions both articulate agendas, *and* discipline people into accepting science-based classifications of themselves and their behaviour, as part of the natural order of things. Thus governmental strategies achieve their effects by reshaping individuals who are the object of governmental regulation. A part of this more general governmentality through biopower is the so-called 'medicalization' thesis (e.g. Zola, 1975; Lupton, 1994), referring to the:

> *ways in which medical jurisdiction has expanded in recent years and now encompasses many problems which hitherto were not defined as medical issues ... the knowledge base of scientific medicine has encroached still further into defining the limits of 'normality' and the proper functioning, deportment and control of the human body (Williams and Calnan, 1996, p1609).*

Thus problems and subjectivities – such as around child wellbeing – which might have been defined in other ways become reshaped through biopower in conformity with biomedical concepts. Thus to analyse governmentality, one needs to attend to its foundation on a combination of (a) knowledges, (b) regulations based on these knowledges, and (c) practices that regulation seeks to govern, and (d) the transformations of subjectivities, or changes in conceptions of the self, that accompany the institutionalization of new strategies of power and regulation.

While valuable in expressing the operation of power–knowledge relations around issues such as vaccination, however, notions of biopower and governmentality have limitations. First, the image of a unified governmental discourse is belied by the realities of governance arrangements that involve multiple actors and institutions. Thus different parts of the state (different departments or ministries) may promote different and contradictory discourses. This plurality may be multiplying amid the plethora of international institutions, corporations, non-governmental organizations and networked connections in what many characterize as an increasingly multi-levelled, networked field of governance (Rhodes, 1997; Bache and Flinders, 2004). Thus not only government, but also international agencies, business and civil society organizations can contribute to the institutionalization of particular sorts of discipline and self-worry around medicine. Other modes of governmentality associated with non-biomedical therapeutic traditions – linked for instance with religious institutions, or 'alternative' medicine – further add to the cacophony. Around vaccination, such disjunctures between different discourses are often clear to see. How plural, competing forms of power–knowledge work out in governance takes varied forms in different countries, depending partly on what Jasanoff characterizes as national political cultures and civic epistemologies (Jasanoff, 2005), but also on questions of political economy and the relative material power of different institutions.

Second, the notion of biopower raises a range of questions about the relationship between biopolitical discourses and existing knowledge and experience. Analyses grounded in biopower often present people's 'alignment' with biopolitical discourses as somewhat unreflective, emerging perhaps through a combination of educational discipline and aligned practices of self-worry and self-perfection. Yet this begs questions about whether, and how, people experience and reflect actively on their relationships with powerful institutions; how, for instance, they might themselves relate their bodily experiences to wider political and economic experiences. This relates to a critique that notions of biopower deny people agency, which is not entirely correct, as the point of this theoretical tradition is that it is the very agency of people, harnessed through self-worry and its modes of expression, which makes us vehicles of power. Agency and power align. A more significant problem, however, is that people's experiences and reflections on them do not only emerge from the discursive truths of governmental, scientific, business or religious institutions, or even from an agentive self; they also emerge from the experience and structuration of everyday social and practical life. Social relations and practices themselves generate, transact and sustain vocabularies and concepts for reflecting on 'biological' issues. The identification of such forms of knowledge and practice can be assisted by other sociological traditions, whether those emphasizing the relationship between collective representations and social structure, in a Durkheimian sense (e.g. Douglas, 1966, 1992), or those giving more weight to the generative effects of interactions between social actors (e.g. Giddens, 1991; Long, 2001). These other sociological traditions help to identify and explain realms of public experience and reflection and action that are 'uncaptured' by biopower.

Such realms of public experience and reflection surely engage dialogically with biopolitical discourses, but in struggles that end up shaping both. Foucault himself never anticipated any kind of 'capture', arguing instead that modern biopolitics generates a new kind of counter-politics:

> *as governmental practices have addressed themselves in an increasingly immediate way to 'life' ... individuals have begun to formulate the needs and imperatives of that same life as the basis for political counter-demands. Biopolitics thus provides a prime instance of ... the 'strategic reversibility' of power relations, or the ways in which the terms of governmental practice can be turned around into focuses of resistance: or ... the way the history of government as the 'conduct of conduct' is interwoven with the history of dissenting 'counter-conducts' (Burchell et al, 1991, p5).*

Williams and Calnan (1996) further expose limits to the production of 'docile bodies' through biopower, and to the expansionist tendencies of medicalization. Public dissent from and questioning of vaccination, emergent from everyday modes of experience and reflection, can be seen as exemplars of just this kind of counter-politics. Yet public experiences and reflections, too, can become entwined with particular forms of authority and institutionalization, coming to operate as discourses that themselves suggest modes of appropriate behaviour, morality and sociality. In this respect, politics and counter-politics in a biopolitical realm involve not just 'poles' of knowledge that are opposed in perceptual terms, but encounters between different discourses and forms of governmentality. How these encounters play out and how the different discourses involved come to be shaped through them is a key question as yet little explored in work on biopower, yet of critical importance in analysing vaccine anxieties.

Vaccine anxieties – an analytical approach

This chapter has introduced many elements that we take to analysing vaccine anxieties in this book. It remains to draw these together into an analytical framework to facilitate an understanding of the unfolding of vaccine anxieties in a globalized world and, by extension, anxieties around other issues involving science and technology.

Anxieties, as we consider them, are forms of active reflection that are sometimes manifested in action and engagement (or disengagement) with a technology and technocracy. Anxieties can take negative forms – as worry, concern or fear – but also positive forms – as desire or striving. Analysing anxieties involves understanding what people are anxious about or for, their logics, and the ways these 'framings' translate into action. The configuring of anxieties involves the integration of bodily, social and wider political dimensions. These three dimensions form a tripartite framework, although with two further, crucial features: a focus on the ways that these three dimensions are integrated into people's thought and practice, and a focus on the dialogical ways that public experience, reflection and discourses, and those emanating from scientific and policy institutions, interact in encounters that shape both.

Here, we elaborate briefly on each of these dimensions, summarizing the areas of inquiry that they point to in relation to vaccine-specific anxieties, and literatures that are helpful in informing these areas.

Bodily dimensions

The first level of our analytical framework addresses how parents – in particular settings – conceptualize the bodily processes involved in keeping children well and enabling them to flourish, and how, in this context, they consider vaccinations and what they do. This involves considering people's located ideas about bodily processes, the concepts and metaphors they use, and the broader resonances these might have. It involves showing where these are congruent with or depart from diverse therapeutic traditions, whether they are those of biomedicine or other forms. Yet it is also necessary to expose people's wider ideas and practices concerning childrearing – different 'worlds of babies' (Gottleib and De Loache, 2000) – and the techniques they use to build children's qualities and to limit their vulnerabilities. This involves considering the ways that parents and carers observe and evaluate their particular child's health, and how this interplays with modes of reasoning that have wider salience.

Such a focus on bodily dimensions of technological experience can draw insights from medical anthropological works that address diverse conceptualizations and practices around health, disease and therapy, including vaccination (e.g. Nichter, 1995; Streefland et al, 1999; Samuelsen, 2001). It also draws on perspectives in science and technology studies that address the micropractices through which technologies come to have meaning in people's lives (e.g. Bijker et al, 1987; Latour, 1993; Mol, 2003). This enables us to consider not just how people think about vaccination in the context of their particular conceptions of the body, bodily processes and child wellbeing, but also how they might differentiate between particular vaccines and their effects, and how other trappings of the technology and the way it is delivered shape its meanings for people.

Social dimensions

The second level of our framework addresses how people's thinking and practices around vaccination become part of social relations and processes. Our emphasis here departs from traditions in quantitative sociology, including in the analysis of vaccination, that relate people's expressed health beliefs and practices to social categories such as class, level of education, degree of individualization, and so on. While attentive to these aspects of difference, we are interested in exploring, more dynamically, how social processes, talk and interactions shape people's ideas and actions, and how interactions and practices around vaccination in turn shape social relations more broadly – including the emergence of forms of social identity, difference and solidarity. Such an approach draws on the traditions of a more actor-oriented sociology (Long, 2001) as well as approaches in anthropology that emphasize performance and practice in the construction of social categories and relationships; for instance around gender, generation and community. Practice-oriented approaches in science and technology studies provide insights into the ways that technological practices are part and parcel of the shaping of social relationships, whether among those producing technologies or their users (e.g. Latour, 1987).

In analysing vaccine anxieties, we consider three main kinds of social processes and relationships. Our primary focus is on relationships among parents, family and community members. We consider, for instance, how parents talk and interact with each other, with their children and with other members of their families and neighbourhoods, around issues concerning child health and vaccination, and how such social relationships are implicated in vaccination decisions. We consider how people's engagements with each other over vaccines are shaping gender, generational and community relations. In this, we explore how science and technology are implicated in the construction of kinship and social worlds, involving particular forms of exclusion and differentiation, but also forms of relationality and solidarity.

Second, we consider social relationships and processes among health workers. Our focus here is on those involved at the 'front line' of vaccination delivery and research engagements with parents: doctors, nurses and fieldworkers. We are interested, particularly, in their perceptions, modes of talk and practice as they reflect on their publics, and how these forms of reflection create and reproduce particular forms of social and moral identity and community among them. This is important because it lays the groundwork for our third area of consideration of social processes: interactions between parents and 'front line' workers, considering the social relationships involved, as well as the substance of what is transacted. Attention to the social dimensions of these encounters at the interface (Long and Long, 1994) adds a crucial dimension to understanding parents' experiences of vaccination technology and technocracy, and highlights what are often key points in the shaping of vaccine anxieties.

Wider political dimensions

The third level of our framework considers how people's experiences of and reflections on child health and vaccination relate to wider political concerns. With a focus on those political dimensions that emerge in parents' discourses, whether explicitly or by implication, the latter may range from dimensions of wider state and governmental processes, to geo-political and inter-religious relations, to elements of transnational political economy. They may also include dimensions of governance more directly involved with vaccination, such as the politics and economy of healthcare regimes. Our approach here draws on insights from studies of biopower and governmentality to highlight how health technologies can become part of broader regimes of political control (e.g. Foucault, 1976;

Williams and Calnan, 1996). However, integrating insights from more actor-oriented sociological traditions and those addressing collective representations, we are particularly interested in the ways that parents draw such connections between vaccination and wider political issues, and how they represent them in ways that make sense given their more everyday experiences. Our approach to wider political dimensions of vaccine anxieties is also, at times, historical, paying attention both to particular, historically located dimensions of governance, politics and political economy, and to how people's representations of them have changed over time.

Integrating dimensions

Each of these levels is necessary to understand vaccine anxieties. Without attention to wider political dimensions, for instance, many of the factors that lead everyday technological and social practices around vaccination to erupt into instances of dissent are lost from view. Yet without attention to bodily and microtechnological experiences, analysis remains thin, and we cannot see why it should be through vaccines that people reflect on wider political structures in the ways that they do. Our framework therefore integrates these three dimensions, analysing how they come together in vaccine anxieties.

An important part of this integration involves attention to integrative concepts and metaphors that are significant in people's thought and practice. Here, Emily Martin's (1994) seminal work on the immune system in American culture is helpful, both in exemplifying a valuable genre of analysis and in providing particular insights that we draw on in later chapters. Martin describes how in the decades from the mid 1950s in the US, older notions of bodily protection centring on surfaces and their cleanliness gave way to a new view of the body as defended internally by a complex immune system, and as active, able to adapt and respond swiftly and flexibly to changes. Seeping from science into popular thinking and media coverage, Martin describes how the concept of an immune system 'moved to the very centre' of cultural conceptions of health (1994, p186), becoming a kind of currency in which people thought about and evaluated all kinds of health issues. She suggests, furthermore, that the immune system provided a much broader metaphor, extending to emergent forms of social and political–economic organization prevalent in the US of the 1990s. Notions of an innovative, agile body resonated with the ideals of innovative, agile firms that pervaded contemporary forms of business and corporate organization based on 'flexible specialization', in a world of mobile capital and intensified electronic communications. They also resonated with the notions of individual perfectibility – of lifestyle as much as health – in contemporary western society, to be achieved through personal training and self-improvement. In short, the emergent concept of an immune system served to integrate bodily and micro-technological experience, with wider social and political processes; the first three dimensions to our framework

Martin's analysis and others that have considered an 'age of immunology' in related ways (Napier, 2003) are important and particularly relevant exemplars of a long-standing genre of anthropology that considers the linkages between embodied reflection and the socio-political world. Our anxieties framework emphasizes the linkages between bodily, social and wider political processes in a similar way. However, these analyses of immunity as an overarching, configuring concept are exemplars from Euro-American contexts. In our analysis of vaccine anxieties in British and African settings, they invite us to consider how relevant immunity is as an organizing concept. But we need also to be attentive to the possibility of quite other organizing concepts. Works focusing on African settings are suggestive of some quite different possibilities, whether centred, for example, on the orderly flow of body fluids, people and trade (Taylor, 1992) or the strict separation of regenerative cycles (Gottlieb, 2001). Identifying configuring concepts that link bodily, social and political reflections in ways that make sense to parents in both British and West African settings is a central part of this book's analysis.

Interactions and dialogics

The final element of our analytical framework involves considering how parental framings around vaccine anxieties – including concepts that link bodily, social and political dimensions – interact with those emanating from institutions involved with vaccination and public health policy and delivery. To some extent, this is a false dichotomy. To portray parental and policy 'worlds' as if they were discrete, bounded entities risks overlooking the heterogeneity within each as well as the overlaps and flows between them. Boundaries are constantly crossed, for instance as parents work as health professionals, and as particular scientists and parents ally around particular causes. But while we are aware of these overlaps and blurrings, we are deeply interested in how what can appear as a deep gulf between parental and policy perspectives has emerged, and how it is sustained. We suggest that the construction of such polarity is a dynamic process, that needs to be understood as an ongoing outcome of the interactions between parental and policy worlds. In other words, dichotomies between parental and policy worlds should be seen less as pre-existing than as made and remade through interaction, and in our case studies we consider these dialogical processes.

This involves addressing, for instance, how parents interpret policy perspectives and advice in ways that sometimes reinforce their own, divergent conceptions. It involves addressing how policy makers interpret the behaviour and statements of the public, in ways that sometimes reinforce their framings of public engagement as driven by risk or ignorance. It also involves examining instances where parental and policy framings directly contest each other, and whether this serves to reconcile or drive them further apart. This element of our analysis takes a lead from studies of encounters at development interfaces that show how the lifeworlds of both developers and those developed are shaped in the process (Long and Long, 1994). But it also moves beyond this microlevel focus to address the interaction between parental and policy framings that integrate microtechnological with wider social and political experiences, and how this interaction shapes both. Such analysis of dialogics, we suggest, not only helps to explain how and why parental and policy perspectives on vaccine anxieties often become so polarized, but also offers clues as to how dialogue and deliberation could help to narrow these gulfs.

Conclusion

This chapter has moved from a consideration of what is currently being said about public engagements with and dissent from vaccination in British and African settings, to a critical consideration of the concepts of ignorance, risk, trust, rumour and resistance underlying policy arguments. Portraying public responses that do not conform with technocratic expectations in negative, deficit-ridden terms, these arguments, we suggest, cannot adequately explain parental thinking and practice around vaccination. Instead, we have proposed and elaborated a framework for analysing vaccine anxieties, both positive and negative, that integrates bodily, social and wider political dimensions, and explores the interaction of parental and policy perspectives. In the chapters that follow, we apply this framework to a set of cases in specific settings in Britain and West Africa, exploring how these different dimensions of experience are mutually configured in 'anxious' engagements between people and a variety of issues involving vaccines.

Using this framework to analyse a set of juxtaposed ethnographies in European and African settings should help to identify how far processes and social experiences are indeed common or different, interrogating the stereotypes that have so often presented Europe and Africa as 'two worlds' in relation to technologies such as vaccination. If Europe and Africa are not two worlds, they do not need two sets of theories. By building and applying a common framework, the book moves towards more integrative, globally relevant theorizing of changing science–society relations. As we show in the conclusion, this can unearth hitherto hidden commonalities as well as differences in the ways that parents in European and African settings are dealing with their children's wellbeing, each other, and state and global institutions in today's world.

Notes

1   *London Evening Standard*, 2003; *The Birmingham Post*, 2002.
2   'North Nigerian polio boycott unforgivable', AFROL News, www.afrol.com, 26 February 2004.
3   'Nigeria orders polio vaccine tests', CNN International.com, 29 October 2003.

3

Body, Body Politic and Vaccination in the UK

with Michael Poltorak[1]

Introduction

This chapter analyses anxieties around vaccination in contemporary Britain, at a time when one element of the childhood vaccination schedule – the combined measles, mumps and rubella (MMR) vaccination – became the focus of scientific and public controversy. How this controversy unfolded as certain parents mobilized, mobilized science and met a vociferous counter-mobilization from health institutions is the focus of the next chapter. Here, we are interested in how, against this backdrop, 'ordinary' parents considered the vaccination of their children.

During the late 1990s and early 2000s the MMR issue became a high-profile example of emergent problems in public engagement with science and technology, frequently dominating media headlines and editorials. In brief, certain parents had come to attribute autism-like symptoms in their children to MMR vaccination in the early 1990s (Mills, 2002). Arguably, their views gained credence from clinical studies (Wakefield et al, 1998; Uhlmann et al, 2002). Subsequent studies considering the incidence of autism in relation to MMR among larger populations claim not to show an association (see Miller, 2002). As we discuss in the next chapter, the debate turns, in part, on the significance attributed to epidemiological as opposed to clinical evidence, and on the status attributed to parents' own observations. As medical, popular and media debate unfolded from 1998, parental engagement with the MMR vaccination altered. Despite assurances of MMR safety in scientific literature and by the British Department of Health (DH), and despite information campaigns aimed at parents, uptake declined in many areas, and by early 2004, for children aged 24 months, stood at 79.8 per cent for the UK and 71 per cent for the city of Brighton and Hove

(Health Protection Agency (HPA), 2004). As some parents opted to have the measles, mumps and rubella components separately, a second debate emerged concerning whether these should be provided through the NHS, privately or not at all.

In this context, this chapter begins with a brief outline of how the delivery of childhood vaccination is organized in the UK today. We then consider bodily dimensions to vaccination, sketching out perspectives through which many parents think about their children's health and how vaccination plays into this. Essentially we explore here how 'immunity' is manifested in parental thinking and practice. We go on to address the relationship between parents' social networks and their vaccination practices, and how vaccination has become social. This social world extends to relations with health professionals. As we are exploring in this book, views of the body and immunity are not independent of experience and reflections on the social and wider political world, and we go on to address how wider social reflection and political experience interplay with parents' thinking about vaccination and child health, discerning how common metaphors and framings infuse and integrate bodily, social and political reflection. What this chapter reveals is how this complexity in parental thought and reflection encourages a concern with what it is that might distinguish one's own child from others. This is a set of concerns which lies at odds with a logic of vaccination among public health institutions premised on homogeneity. Crucially, the inter-actions configured by these contrasting framings have served to shape both. It is this dynamic, we argue, that lies at the heart of vaccine anxieties and problems in vaccination delivery in the UK today.

While this chapter draws on several studies and commentaries from around Britain, our principal evidence derives from ethnographic fieldwork in the city of Brighton and Hove in southern England, between March and June 2003, and a survey we conducted covering this town that probed further issues raised in the fieldwork.

Given that Brighton saw a particularly sharp decline in MMR uptake during the controversy, its health institutions were interested in this study. Also inter-ested, however, were the parents' groups that had mobilized in response to concerns with the MMR. Thus, apart from being the authors' university city, Brighton provided a good context in which to research vaccine anxieties. The city is in the relatively affluent south-east of the UK, and is popular both as a tourist destination and by commuters working in London. The census of 2001 reveals a relatively youthful and mobile population: of a total population of just under 250,000, 42 per cent are aged 20–44 (compared to the England and Wales average of 35 per cent). It is also somewhat peculiar in that the average household size is the smallest in the south east (2.09) and the fifth smallest in England and Wales (Chief Executive Policy Team (CEPT), 2004). The 60 per cent of adults defined as employed work predominantly in public services (27 per cent), financial and business services (23 per cent) and retail (14 per cent). At the time of our fieldwork, the local unemployment rate, 3.6 per cent, was a fraction higher than the national average of 3.4 per cent.

Our fieldwork focused on two contrasting areas of the city, Whitehawk and Fiveways/Preston Park. These areas conform to the stereotypes of a 'deprived' and a 'middle-class' neighbourhood respectively, and we chose them for this reason, as this is a distinction often highlighted in public debate over the MMR. The stereotypes are supported by the 'Overall index of Multiple Deprivation for 2000', which ranks these administrative wards 439 and 5,164 respectively (of the 8,414 wards in England, with 1 being the most deprived) (Department of the Environment, Transport and the Regions (DETR), 2000). Yet 'deprived' Whitehawk certainly covers some rather better-off pockets, and 'middle-class' Fiveways/Preston Park is not without poverty. Many Whitehawk residents feel that their area is unjustifiably stigmatized, and highlight its sense of community. Some parents there are long-term residents of Whitehawk, others have moved there because of its affordability, while others have been rehoused there from estates elsewhere (Netley, 2002). By contrast, the Fiveways and Preston Park neighbourhoods are characterized by commuters, families who have moved there in order to be in the catchment area of perceived good schools, and Sussex-based professionals including university academics.

We identified a focal general medical practice in each study area that served a significant proportion of residents, had more than one general practitioner (GP) and welcomed the research. Neither practice self-identified, or was known in local healthcare circles, to have a particular 'take' on MMR. In each practice, we interviewed the doctors (eight in total) and practice nurses (three in total). We contacted the Health Visitors' base serving each study area and interviewed six of the nine health visitors, going on to carry out follow-up interviews and shadowing the work of three. We contacted five carer and toddler groups – ranging from those organized by health professionals and community workers, to those operating as informal drop-in sessions coordinated by the National Childbirth Trust – a community centre supported by social-services and an organized physical activity/music class. These provided locations for short, informal discussions and much participant observation of 'MMR talk' among parents. We also convened group discussions at these, comprising between four and seven mothers who happened to be present on a particular day, without any advance warning. But as parents of young children, and residing in the study area, or nearby, participant observation extended beyond these contexts into the full gamut of everyday encounters. One member of the team recorded and transcribed 48 conversations, and 23 – evenly distributed between the two study areas – were developed into in-depth, repeat narrative interviews. The sample was opportunistic and was not intended to be statistically representative. The only selection criterion was having a child under the age of three and a willingness to be interviewed, either at the time or by later arrangement at home or another mutually agreed location. Mothers were contacted at the five different carer/toddler groups or introduced by one of six different health professionals. We spoke to only two recommended to us on the basis of their vaccination decision (one by a doctor as an interesting case of non-vaccination; the other by a mother as someone who vaccinated despite having an autistic child). The parents interviewed had a variety of social, demographic, educational and occupational backgrounds, and had made a

Table 3.1 *Vaccination decisions made by mothers interviewed in Brighton*

Vaccination category	Number
MMR, all children, on time	7
MMR, all children, but delayed	2
MMR for one child but not all	2
Single vaccines, all children, on time	0
Single vaccines, all children, but delayed	2
No MMR, but intention to vaccinate	3
No MMR, undecided	4
No MMR, intention to have single vaccine for mumps alone	1
No MMR, single measles vaccine alone	1
No MMR (nor DTP or other vaccines), all children	1
TOTAL mothers	23
TOTAL (have had MMR or intention to go ahead)	12

variety of vaccination decisions for their children, as summarized in Table 1. In the majority of instances, the interviewees were mothers.

Our survey is presented more fully elsewhere (Cassell et al, 2006b).[2] It was built from the ethnography, and explored the relevance to a wider population of a range of social and cultural issues raised by parents, and their relation with maternal demographic and vaccination decisions. It involved a postal questionnaire sent to the mother or guardian of a randomly sampled child (15–24 months old). It probed whether the child was a first or later child; parents' sources of information on parenting and immunizations; the early health of the child; parents' views on the risks associated with measles and the MMR; interactions with healthcare professionals and others in relation to MMR; and the process of decision making, including attitudes to public bodies and governments as sources of advice and influence. In addition, it offered a range of specific statements made by Brighton parents as part of the ethnographic study, for agreement or disagreement. On several issues it solicited free text comments. In this chapter, such statements are left unreferenced; they all derived from mothers in Brighton during March or April 2004. In contrast quotations from our ethnographic work and narrative interviews are referenced with the place and month of interview.

In the UK, vaccination is governed by the Department of Health, which manages vaccination policy and provides information. In most parts of the country, implementation involves GP's surgeries, their nurses and health visitors, who are either based at a large GP practice or have separate offices. Information about immunization is sometimes given at the various forms of state or private antenatal class and groups that parents may attend before the birth of their baby. It is health visitors who have the first formal opportunity – and official responsibility – to discuss immunization with parents, during the regular home visits that they are expected to make during the first few weeks of a baby's life. Parents then receive a series of official letters from the local health authority calling them for their baby's immunizations, with a time and place of appointment. This is often within the regular baby clinic sessions at GP surgeries where a practice nurse or health visitor gives the injections. If an appointment is missed, a follow-up letter is sent and this may be repeated several times. At the time of study, vaccinations for the combined diphtheria, tetanus and pertussis (DTP) (with meningitis and oral polio vaccine) were called at 2, 3 and 4 months, and at about 1 year old; the same procedure repeated for the MMR, which is officially due at 13 months. Both sets of vaccinations have pre-school boosters. Health authorities run a child health surveillance system that keeps track of which children have had which immunizations, and ensures that appointment letters are sent out at the correct time. In addition to this routinized system, GPs and nurses sometimes take opportunities at treatment and consultation visits to discuss immunization status and if parents are in agreement rectify it on the spot.

The DH has an 'Immunization Information' department that produces educational information for both parents and health professionals. As well as addressing the positive value of vaccination, in recent years its publications have also sought to allay fears about vaccine safety – especially over MMR – in the context of evidence of parental anxiety and falling uptake rates. At the time of our study, the DH also provided incentive payments for GP surgeries that hit certain vaccination targets, with GPs being paid a standard amount once 70 per cent take-up of the MMR vaccine is achieved and higher payments once take-up exceeds 90 per cent.

Bodily experiences and understandings

In our survey, 12 per cent of mothers claimed to be complete non-vaccinators, refusing all vaccinations for their child. The remaining 88 per cent did vaccinate – but reported a range of decisions over MMR. Thus 57 per cent of all mothers reported that their child had had the MMR according to the expected schedule; 11 per cent had decided to delay the jab until their child was older; 18 per cent of all mothers reported that they had chosen 'single jabs', (i.e. separate measles, mumps and rubella antigens, available only privately or overseas); and 3 per cent refused MMR altogether or said they were still undecided. Notably, while these figures suggest that only a small proportion refused the MMR altogether, the proportion failing to comply with the expected schedule as recommended by public health authorities was significantly higher. Notably too, in both the survey and in our ethnographic work many mothers who accepted MMR nevertheless expressed anxieties about it – a finding echoed in several other studies in the UK (e.g. Casiday et al, 2006). To understand this range of perspectives and practices, and the logics underlying them, we begin by considering bodily dimensions of parents' thinking and practices.

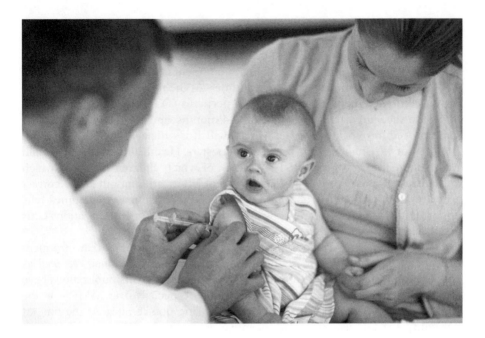

Figure 3.1 *A British baby receiving her MMR vaccination*

Personalized pathways of child health

Here, then, we want to sketch out some common ways that parents in Brighton speak about their children's health, the effects of vaccines, and the benefits and dangers they may bring. This cannot be comprehensive – it would be presumptuous to reduce the thoughts of a town so educationally, socially and culturally diverse to a few paragraphs. Yet drawing on our ethnography and survey, it is possible to discern some common themes.

To begin with, many mothers' narratives distinguished whether a child generally had 'strong' or 'weak' health depending on interactions of environmental, nutritional, inherited and other factors. They also indicated how a child's health depended on a particular, unfolding pathway of these influences, often extending back into family health history, birth, illnesses and other events. Many mothers expressed concerns about their child's sleep, allergies, eczema, asthma, dietary tolerances, character and behaviour in terms of such pathways; as part of the influences along the way, or as part of the outcomes. And many mothers talked about the particularity of each child not just through their different personalities, but also through the history of their weaknesses and strengths. This sometimes extended to an appreciation of how parental illness susceptibilities could be passed on to children. Thus in one instance, even the tuberculosis suffered by a child's grandparents was conceptualized as manifest in their constitution. Such personalized understandings of child health infused what, in the narratives, were often highly personalized views of how to keep a particular child healthy or promote his or her development.

Such personalized perspectives accord with current parenting advice in European and American contexts that promote active, child-centred, personalized approaches for improved child health and developmental outcomes. Indeed in many domains a new equation has come to be drawn between the good parent and the parent who, as the best expert on their own child, seeks to negotiate parenting advice with their child's individual particularities. This reflects a shift from earlier acceptance of more authoritative and generalized childcare regimes visible in, for example, the tenor of childcare advice books from the 1970s (e.g. Spock, 1976) to more individuated regimes adapted to the particularities of each child (e.g. P. Leach, 2003).[3] As we shall argue, particularistic thinking characterizes the ways that many parents now think about vaccination, evaluating the actual, or potential, effects of vaccination on their child in relation to his or her particular strengths or vulnerabilities. First, however, we consider the conceptualizations of the body which frame such thinking about vaccines and their effects.

Notions of immunity

When considering the effects of vaccines, the notion of an immune system emerged as important to the ways parents in Brighton conceptualize their children's health and their particular pathways of strength and vulnerability. In many parents' narratives, a child's strength was equated generally with the strength of his or her immune system. The immune system needs to be 'built' (trained?) through appropriate nurturing, nutrition and exposure to the world. As one mother put it:

> *The image I have is ... that ... for an immune system to work it has to come against something that's not good for you, this is the idea about letting them eat dirt in the garden, if I see that happening I think it's building up their immune system, I don't really understand how. You have to get ill sometimes ... my second child was healthier but the house wasn't nearly as clean – I just didn't have time for all that hoovering – but I figure you need dirt to build up the immune system (Mother, Whitehawk, April 2003).*

These concepts in turn shape the ways that parents consider the possible effects of vaccination. Some described vaccination working as part of this building or 'training' process:

> *That's how vaccination works isn't it, it's a little bit of measles, when the body gets it for real it goes 'I know what this is', fight it off (Mother, Whitehawk, April 2003).*

When encountering similar narratives in America, Martin (1994, p198) found that a dominant way of thinking about vaccines was as a form of education for the immune system, but describes how some people rejected this form of 'state education', preferring their bodies to learn to adjust to the environment for themselves. Such a notion – often put in terms of a distinction between 'natural' immunity, and 'artificial' immunity acquired through vaccination – emerged strongly in some Brighton parents' narratives. For a few, this underlay a rejection of all vaccinations, with a preference instead for building up a child's natural immunity through diet, lifestyle and hygiene standards. And in our Brighton survey, 43 per cent of mothers who rejected the MMR vaccination (whether or not their child had had other jabs) strongly agreed that it was better to 'get immunity naturally', compared with only 7 per cent of those who accepted it.

For some, exposure to small amounts of dirt and to what they consider as 'normal' childhood diseases constituted key parts of this process of building natural immunity. As a health visitor in Brighton commented:

> Why do you think some mums refuse to vaccinate at all?
> *I think probably because they obviously believe quite strongly in natural immunity and they actually think if the body is healthy and quite strong children are well nourished, sort of brought up in, sort of in not a dirty background, but in a non sterile, they're sort of exposed to dirt as they should be, their children will actually have a stronger immune system than if they're given the chemical, you know and they don't want to have chemical given to their children. Again it's sort of eating organic sort of thing. I think that's probably why (Health visitor, Brighton, March 2003).*

And as mothers put it:

> *My main concern is preserving my child's pure strong state of peak health, not disturbing her natural balance or immune system.*

> *I would rather he built up natural immunity by getting measles, mumps and German measles.*

> *I really feel strongly that some childhood diseases that people say can be quite dangerous are not dangerous – because it strengthens the immune system.*

The view of the immune system as an individual characteristic needing individualized health care, which emerged in narratives, was probed further in the survey. Most mothers agreed that each child's immune system was different (77 per cent of those who had rejected the MMR as scheduled, compared with 61 per cent of those who had accepted it). For some, whether or not vaccinations were appropriate depended on a child's particular strength, trajectory of immune-system building, and how effective 'natural' methods might be, given their home and lifestyle. For example:

Have you read a lot about the immune system?

A fair amount, and how to boost it naturally as well, with good nutrition and breastfeeding. I think as well if your child isn't well nourished it is maybe a good idea to go along that kind of route and have your child vaccinated to give them some sort of protection, but I think essentially if you've got a good diet and you're well looked after I don't think it's such a necessity (Mother, Preston Park, April 2003).

Some parents, however, expressed a view that vaccinations could actually harm the immune system, or prevent its effective development. For example as Brighton mothers said in the survey:

I am concerned about any vaccinations and whether they allow a person's immune system to develop or whether they do real damage.

I don't believe in vaccination. I don't deny they work but I believe they mess with our natural ability to deal with disease. They suppress as most modern drugs do.

I'm more worried about her immune system and what long-term damage we are doing to people's immune systems by suppressing them [with vaccinations]. My little boy has got quite bad eczema and again it's probably not related to anything but nobody in our family has ever had eczema, asthma, anything, there is no family history at all, and he has extremely bad eczema and I think well, why?

I think that children are given too many vaccinations – this causes them to be ill and develop unexplained allergies in the first eighteen months. The vaccinations cause unexplained illness that destroys routine and sleep patterns.

Some parents also expressed anxiety about the chemicals, preservatives and adjuvants that accompany the injection of vaccine into the body – especially those which were mercury-based. There was controversy in the US about this at the time, which eventually led to the withdrawal of mercury from vaccines.

Such findings support Fitzpatrick's (2004) observations that worry about threats to the immune system are now widespread in UK society, and that high on the list of potential dangers are immunizations, which some regard as damaging to the operation of natural processes of immunity. It is difficult to find any specific theory of how vaccines might do damage in our Brighton narratives. But as Fitzpatrick suggests, such an inquiry might be to miss the point. He suggests that such beliefs arise from a general feeling of vulnerability to a particular sort of danger that is widespread in contemporary times: danger not from 'nature' itself (in the way that people once feared infectious diseases), but from the products of human intervention in nature – such as through vaccines and antibiotics. The concept of a threatened immune system also provides a link with other syndromes that medical science, as much as publics, find difficult to explain, such as food allergies, eczema and asthma.

Heightened concern about threats to the immune system from outside also link with concerns about 'autoimmunity', which is another concept of growing significance both in medical science and popular thought. Ideas about auto-immunity have been invoked in some popular literature to explain adverse effects of vaccination, and indeed these figured in some Brighton narratives. For example:

> *We seem to be getting autoimmune diseases now and someone I work with, her daughter's got it and one of the beliefs is that because we are vaccinated against so many illnesses now the immune system doesn't actually get a chance to work and it does actually need to fight something, it turns on itself and that's where you get the autoimmune response (Mother, Preston Park, April 2003).*

Again, Fitzpatrick (2004, p54) links such reflections on the body to wider social reflections, commenting that the influence of such ideas may owe much to the contemporary appeal of the notion of human self-destructiveness. Thus we begin to discern that the understanding of bodily health through concepts of the immune system not only reflects a contemporary, individuated subject position (a flexibly adapted body in a flexibly adapted economy). It is also through the concept of immunity that broader anxieties and problematic experiences – such as social and self-destructiveness – are comprehended and experienced; refracted through this metaphorical context.

The notion that vaccines interact with the complex processes of building an immune system is also confirmed in two further ideas that emerged as significant in Brighton parents' evaluation of whether or not vaccination was appropriate for their child. One is the idea of the immune system 'maturing', as a child got older and stronger. This underlay some parents' preference to delay vaccination, especially the MMR:

> *to allow their immune system to mature a bit, mostly you know, they can see the sense of the vaccine, just a little bit uncomfortable about giving it too young (Health visitor, Brighton, April 2003).*

As other mothers put it:

> *I worry about putting too many diseases in vaccine form into a young child with an undeveloped immune system.*

> *I had to be confident that my child was big and strong enough to have the MMR. 12 months as in Brighton and Hove seems far too young. I will probably vaccinate my child when she is three years.*

Linked to such notions, and a reason why parents often expressed particular concern about the 'triple' MMR vaccination, is the idea of immune system 'overload'. Many of those concerned about the MMR suggested that three vaccines were too many for the immune system to cope with and could 'knock back' a child. In our survey, 86 per cent of mothers who did not accept MMR on schedule agreed strongly that 'the MMR is too much in one go' compared with only 22 per cent of those who accepted the jab. Such ideas have been noted elsewhere in the UK (Offit et al, 2002). As some Brighton mothers put it:

It's an awful lot to put into the immune system which has not developed.

I thought no, even if its the single vaccine which isn't as bad as the triple shot it's a lot easier on their immune system, it's still all these poisonous toxins going into their blood.

Complementary (or alternative) therapies

In Brighton, perhaps more than many parts of the UK, alternative therapies have a strong commercial presence, and appear to many to have increasing popularity. A question arises: how far do parents' ideas about vaccination – and especially its negative effects – reflect the influence of these therapeutic traditions? Certainly, many parents in Brighton are not just seeking treatment and protection for their children from biomedical practitioners, but are also visiting other therapists, ranging from homeopaths to herbalists, acupuncturists, ayurvedic practitioners, kinesiologists and many others who practise in the area. Several mothers suggested that more experience of alternative medicine might encourage rejection of the MMR. This was borne out in our survey findings where 33 per cent of MMR-refusing mothers had consulted a homeopath, in contrast with only 10 per cent of those accepting MMR. Complete non-vaccinators were also significantly more likely to have visited a homeopath; 68 per cent had consulted one about their child. Yet these associations do not reflect any simple opposition between biomedical, pro-vaccination views, and alternative, anti-vaccination ones.

First, this association may be reflecting a confidence to go against biomedical professional expectation, exemplified in consulting alternative practitioners and the camaraderie with other parents that emerges around this, rather than reflecting a clear bodily theory in alternative practice that would make rejection of vaccination logical. Indeed as we discuss later, the importance of parental confidence emerged as a key theme in parents' engagements with health professionals. Second, many alternative therapies share concepts of the immune system with biomedicine. So while many alternative therapists describe what they do as based on an entirely different viewpoint from biomedicine – such as a holistic view, one that denies biomedicine's split between mind and body, or which rejects the dominance of germ theory – many alternative methods themselves either encompass and aim to influence 'the immune system', or the conceptualizations that underlie the therapies can conceptually accommodate the immune system within various larger wholes (see Martin, 1994, p86).

Third, different strands of alternative therapy hold very different views of vaccines. Even within homeopathy there are several schools of thought. Some do not reject vaccination, although others do (see Schmidt et al, 2002). For example, a Brighton GP described how:

> *There are a group of people who won't immunize at all and who talk about 'I'm going to immunize the homeopathic way'. I don't even know if you can call it an immunization, I don't know enough to talk to them about what it does and there are also different schools of homeopathy and I understand that the short course that many GPs do, whichever group trained GPs, don't disagree with immunization (GP, Brighton, April 2003).*

Holistic practitioners, including those with some version of homeopathic expertise, forward diverse ideas about the negative effects of vaccines in relation to the immune system. As one mother described:

> *I have a friend who is a trainee homeopath – she has enlightened me re. the fact that vaccinations suppress illnesses which later on come out possibly as a worse illness (Mother, Brighton, April 2003).*

As another example, perhaps a particularly influential one for Brighton parents, a Brighton-based homeopath who has written pamphlets on the dangers of mass childhood immunization (Gunn, 1992) and who regularly gives public lectures on the topic, considers that:

> *Our immune system learns things; it isn't the same at one day old as it is at 18 months as it is at 5 years, it has to go through a process and there is stuff that you can't do when you are a day old that you can do when you are older. Now the problem with vaccines is that it is a really old model of illness...We vaccinated somebody because what we want are antibodies; now what we have done is single out one element of the immune response (Trevor Gunn, Interview, Brighton, July 2003).*

At a public lecture in Brighton in June 2003, Gunn claimed further that vaccines put toxins into the blood, so that the body cannot carry out its immune functions as effectively as before.

Alternative and holistic practitioners also elaborate connections between vaccination and health problems such as allergies, couched within the concept of immunity. For example writing in *New Vegetarian and Natural Health*, Hancock (2000) describes how:

> *Atopy is the tendency to allergies, manifesting as asthma, eczema, hay fever, etc, the most life-threatening being asthma. It is really no coincidence that atopy is more prevalent in the highly vaccinated Western countries and that its increase has paralleled the increase in vaccination intensity over time... Allergy is sensitisation, and it is very well documented in*

> *medical journals ... product inserts and even orthodox medical dictionaries,*
> *that sensitisation is the effect of vaccines... The injection of any foreign*
> *unwanted material is counterproductive... Firstly, it gives the material*
> *deep access to cause damage to ANY organ or system in the body. Secondly,*
> *immunity cannot develop. Rather, the immune system is stressed, derailed*
> *and confused (Hancock, 2000).*

Fourth, the influence of alternative therapeutic ideas may lie less in their specific theories about vaccines and the body than in the support they give to the ideas of personalized and inherited immune systems that we have found common among Brighton parents. Thus as one Brighton health visitor put it:

> *Some are quite influenced by homeopathy and homeopaths [and] have*
> *a different idea of immunity – one more particular to the person (Health*
> *visitor, Brighton, April 2003).*

And a father in Brighton:

> *It's just we've talked to a few homeopaths, and they've got a very interesting*
> *idea about the immune system – about how you can actually inherit a*
> *compromised immune system from previous generation, so you find some*
> *people that are very anti-vaccination because their family had TB and*
> *they say, 'we think our child is going to inherit that', and vaccination is*
> *even more dangerous (Father, Brighton, August 2003).*

This suggests an interplay between exposure to certain homeopathic ideas and discussion of them, and parents' own reflections based on experience and observation of their own children. Even parents who have not explicitly consulted a homeopath about their child are often exposed to such ideas, and these become part of the field through which they come to think about possible vaccine adverse effects. Reflections, however, turn on 'immunity', and again this metaphor (and with it vocabularies of sensitization, stress, derailment and confusion) enables social and bodily experience to infuse each other.

Reflecting on the possible effects of MMR vaccination

One of the most striking findings in our Brighton study was the personalized way that many parents reflected on whether or not their child should have the MMR vaccination, in the context of the public and media debate raging at the time over an alleged link with autism. This was encapsulated in a statement that recurred in mothers' narratives: 'MMR may be safe but not for my child ...'. What followed was often reflection on the various features of a child's particular strength or vulnerability, immune system characteristics, or family health history that underlay concern about MMR or vaccinations in general. Thus mothers evaluated any possible dangers (or indeed, lack of danger) from MMR not in general terms, but in relation to their assessment of their child's particular health pathway, and vulnerability (or not) to possible effects from the vaccine. The following examples from our survey illustrate this:

> *The issue for us was whether our son could cope physically with a dose of three live vaccines injected at the same time. He had suffered two previous febrile convulsions.*

> *My child suffers with severe eczema which only started after the first immunization; therefore I did not want her to have MMR when her eczema is still so bad, and make it worse.*

> *My first child has always caught chest infections from colds plus doesn't eat a varied diet. He is not particularly robust. We have a strong family history of very bad hay fever, eczema, asthma and food allergies.*

> *My first daughter had milk intolerance and was very ill for the first two years of her life. We didn't vaccinate her with MMR because she was quite weak.*

> *I am naturally worried about the whole autism connection, if you have a low immune system. Both Sarah and Tom[4] are very healthy babies, I prefer to wait and see. If they were allergic I would be more reluctant.*

> *I was more frightened of the potential side effects of measles should I decide not to get Luke vaccinated. Had he been a poorly sickly baby with allergies I might have considered single jabs.*

> *We think that as Callum is strong and healthy he can deal with the injections.*

For mothers who chose not to have the MMR, family health history was sometimes key to their decision. In explaining this further, seven mothers mentioned a family history of Asperger's syndrome; two mentioned autism in the family; three mentioned experiences of autism onset following MMR in the family; thirteen referred to relatives reacting badly to vaccines; ten referred to a family history of eczema, asthma or arthritis; five referred to a family history of irritable bowel; and several gave examples referring to neurological or autoimmune problems. For example:

> *My husband's sister had an extreme reaction to the whooping cough vaccine so that caused us to think about the whole vaccine issue.*

> *There is a history of allergies in my family and a cousin has a two and a half year old who developed regressive autistic symptoms and bowel issues after the MMR jab.*

Some parents raised the possibility of an unknown, undetected 'weakness' in a child, creating uncertainty about what effect MMR might have that in some cases was sufficient to deter going ahead:

> *I'm sure MMR is fine, but, there's a very, very slim chance [of serious adverse effects]. I think if there's a weakness in that child that gets it, the only problem is, you don't know, if your child has that weakness until it is too late, and I just thought, knowing how hard my son was ... (Mother, Whitehawk, March 2003).*

> *Not all the immune systems are the same and you don't know from a hundred children which one will get that and we didn't know if [my son] was going to be that one.*

Thus a particularistic view of child health and the immune system, manifest through family history as well as a child's own health pathway since birth, is highly relevant to the ways that parents think about and evaluate the possible effects of MMR and other vaccines.

The emergence of immunity

'Immunity' has not always been so central to health calculus in the UK. Indeed in public debate and dissent around smallpox vaccination in the mid to late 19th century, a rather different set of conceptualizations was apparent. Vaccination was made compulsory in 1867 but attracted considerable dissent (Durbach, 2005) – combining libertarian arguments with vaccine anxieties – and in 1898 compulsion was relaxed to allow for conscientious objection. This was a time when germ theories of disease were in their infancy, with an understanding that vaccines, like diseases, penetrated the body. Ideas of vaccines' efficacy turned not on an immune system, but more simply on their prophylactic power. Yet germ theory, and the prophylactic power of vaccines, was not universally subscribed to in a society where health (and public health) were strongly linked to upholding the moral virtues of cleanliness and civilization. In this context, Porter and Porter (1988) consider the beliefs which underlay resistance to vaccination in the 19th century, and identify a set of arguments cherishing 'natural' methods of treatment and 'sanitary' methods of prevention. This included the views of anti-contagionists, who denied theories of the specificity of disease, but linked ill-health to 'filth' in the environment and atmosphere which could only be addressed by a wider 'cleaning up' and 'civilizing' of environment and society. In this vein, Beck (1960) describes how the anti-vaccinationists' objections extended to all types of vaccination, and were linked to a worldview that included both the liberty of the individual, and a conviction that civilization consisted in strict adherence to nature's laws of cleanliness. Within these views, there was disbelief in the protective, prophylactic power of vaccination. Indeed vaccination was considered, in the words of one prominent spokesperson, Creighton, as a foul poisoning of the blood with contaminated material. Indeed, many parents were concerned that vaccination would endanger their children's health through the introduction of infectious material into their blood.

Other theories were also in play. Some of those following germ theory were concerned that vaccines would propagate other diseases, arguing, for example, that the lymph used by Jenner was a source for the transmission of syphilis (Porter and Porter, 1988, p237). Some combined religious arguments (that vaccination interfered with the ways of God) with humoral theories, that smallpox should be encouraged because it 'relieves the system of humours that ought to be carried out of it' (cited in Porter and Porter, 1988, p237). The hydropathic healer John Gibbs, a key proponent of resistance to compulsory vaccination in the 1850s, also argued that removing one disease through vaccination simply allowed others to take their place, maintaining a constant level of disease in society (Porter and Porter, 1988).

Across these debates, then, anxieties turned mainly on the idea of infectious material entering the body through vaccination, rather as diseases did. And such vaccine scepticism made sense in a world in which sanitary and moral living was considered the main defence against disease.

As Martin (1994, p25) documents in the US, the notion that the most important defence against disease was cleanliness and the strict prevention of germs entering the body endured into the 20th century. By the 1940s and 1950s it had taken such hold that enormous attention was devoted to maintaining the cleanliness of bodily surfaces, and to hygiene in the home and at large. As she highlights, this fitted a period of heightened domesticity, at least for the middle classes, in which women were forced out of jobs they had held during the Second World War, and emerging lifestyle and commodity values were geared to the 'good' hygienic home maintained by a housewife. 'From inside the safe and clean home, the world outside looked dangerous and hostile' (Martin, 1994, p31). Martin makes the case that such images of domesticity inter-animated with images of a body whose best defences against disease were its surfaces, as barriers between inside and outside. Indeed, during the Cold War, it was not only the body and the house but also the nation that had to be defended. To help the body, parents purchased malt, cod liver oil, rose-hip syrup, the curiously-named 'radio malt' and iron that were all advertised as helping to make children strong.

From the mid 1950s, alongside these notions, some attention began to be paid to health protective and defensive processes inside the body, and the idea that the body produced antibodies in response to the invasion of disease germs (or vaccines) began to circulate in media images and popular consciousness. Martin finds that, especially from the 1970s, a radical shift took place in which emerging views came to see the body as defended internally by an active, complex immune system able to adapt and respond swiftly and flexibly to changes.[5] These shifts in thinking partly reflected transitions in the science of immunology, which by the late 20th century conceptualized:

> *a body that actively relates to the world, that actively selects from a cornucopia of continually produced new antibodies that keep the body healthy and enable it to meet every new challenge (Martin, 1994, p37).*

But the concept of an immune system also seeped from science into popular thinking and media coverage. By the 1990s, Martin found that in the US, while people might not name and understand its components and processes exactly as scientists did,

> *they readily and vividly convey their sense that the immune system is a complex system in interaction with other complex systems inside the body, a system that changes constantly in order to produce the specific things necessary to meet every challenge (Martin, 1994, p80).*

Martin thus argues that the immune system has 'moved to the very centre' of cultural conceptions of health (1994, p186), becoming a dominant field in which people think about and evaluate all kinds of health issues. She documents a widespread process during the 1980s and 1990s through which in medicine, media and popular thought, a wide variety of health conditions, from cancer to allergies, were reinterpreted as immune system dysfunctions, and the effects of environmental factors came to be understood as mediated through the immune system. In this, popular and media portrayals also underwent a further shift from the use of military metaphors, in which the body defends itself from external attack, to more holistic notions of the body as a complex regulatory system within a larger world order. Martin suggests, furthermore, that the immune system also provides a much broader metaphor, extending to emergent forms of social and political–economic organization. Notions of an innovative, agile body resonate with the ideals of innovative, agile firms that pervade contemporary forms of business and corporate organization based on 'flexible specialization', in a world of mobile capital and intensified electronic communications. They also resonate with notions of individual perfectibility – of lifestyle as much as health – in contemporary western society, to be achieved through personal training and self-improvement. Yet the sense that everything about an individual's health is connected to everything else, and that it is one's personal responsibility to manage and control these interactions, also leads to what Martin (1994, p122) terms the paradox of 'empowered powerlessness': 'feeling responsible for everything and powerless at the same time'. Similarly for the UK, Fitzpatrick (2004, p51) argues that popular concepts of immunity reflect what he identifies as a 'prevailing sense of individual vulnerability in an age of anxiety'. Among Brighton parents, as among others in contemporary western societies, such understandings of immunity, along with ideas of strength and weakness, have become pervasive terms in which people think about vaccination for their children.

Vaccination talk: the social world of anxiety

Vaccination is not something that parents only think about for themselves, or speak about with health professionals. When considering vaccination, parents interact with a much wider social world. Of particular importance are discussions with other parents. As a group of young mothers in Whitehawk put it:

Figure 3.2 *A setting for MMR talk: Mothers and babies in a post-natal support group in the UK*

What information have you had apart from the newspapers?
(Mother A) You probably get more information from talking like this, as a group, if [my friend] comes around we talk about different things, maybe I'll try that with Kayleigh .... you get more of an idea.
(Mother B) You feel that you can ask, you can't actually go to the doctor and say, look I've got a real big problem, life is really hard, I cannot cope, but you can say to your friends, 'she's a nightmare, have you got anything I can try'.
(Mother A) Everyone's been through exactly the same.
(Group discussion, Whitehawk, February 2003).

It is the rare mother who has not been drawn into discussing vaccination, and MMR in particular, given prevailing uncertainties about it, along with other issues of concern with their children's health and wellbeing, whether it be sleeping, feeding, behaviour or childcare arrangements. Such discussions take place in a variety of settings. Some are with acquaintances in the organized groups and carer-toddler sessions that many mothers participate in with their children. Some strike up informally in the park or the school playground. Some are with closer friends in informal gatherings at home. 'MMR talk' has become a social phenomenon in Brighton, as it has in Bristol (Evans et al, 2001), Birmingham (Petts and Niemeyer, 2004) and presumably the country over.

Talking vaccination, constructing community

Many mothers in Brighton described such interactions as their most valued and useful in the difficult process of thinking about MMR. But this was not because they are a source of definitive advice. Rather, 'MMR talk' seems to have a particular style and ethos that mothers find supportive. The parents we encountered value the informal, friendly and above all egalitarian quality of such conversations. Little heed is paid to people knowing more than others, by having done more research or by having older children. Given that many parents are thinking about MMR in relation to the particular characteristics of their own child, more dogmatic advice from peers is less appropriate. Rather, the ethos of MMR talk centres on a sharing of experience and views which can open up or support the process of 'making one's own mind up'. Little sense emerges of anything resembling peer pressure to vaccinate or not. What does emerge is a sense of taking other parents' concerns seriously and respecting them, and of acquiring confidence in one's own position through listening to other's views. This is clear in the following quotations from mothers:

> *My friend asked me what she should do and I say whatever is right for you. I don't say, 'oh don't do that', I'd tell them how I feel but 'you may have other reasons to feel how you feel' and she did have the MMR done. I didn't say 'oh you stupid' whatever, it was like 'Ok is the baby fine? Good'. You can't put your highly opinions on them, otherwise if they did what you did and they did catch something they could blame you, couldn't they? (Mother, Brighton, April 2003).*

> *Half the mothers I spoke to were for it. Half were against. No-one really influenced me. I made the decision by myself.*

> *I found it reassuring talking to parents who'd given their child MMR vaccination and their children were fine.*

> *Talking to people whose children had already had MMR with no problems gave me more confidence.*

> *It is good to talk about your concerns – but this just helped to confirm my decision.*

> *I talked a lot to other mothers I know well. As their views varied a lot I felt stronger in my own position.*

> *Talking to friends who hadn't gave me more information and confidence to do what I thought was right.*

At the same time, styles of MMR talk also seem to favour a questioning of vaccination over any blind acceptance of official pro-vaccination advice.

Camaraderie among mothers rejects any denial of parental right to choose. However scientifically informed a mother is, the powerful association between talking about MMR and fomenting relationships with other mothers means that failure to question assurances of MMR safety often seems to threaten newly established and valued relationships. Equally, strong identification as a mother makes it difficult not to relate sympathetically to the accounts of mothers (first-hand, or through social networks, internet or media) who noticed a dramatic change in their children's behaviour after vaccination. In short, to ignore concerns about MMR, one has to distinguish oneself as a mother from other mothers. Expressing sympathy with MMR anxieties is part of a process of constructing community.

MMR talk among networks of mothers is significant across the social spectrum, and among mothers who end up deciding for or against MMR. Only a few – 14 per cent – agreed with the survey statement that 'I tend to avoid talking to my friends about the MMR issue', and this did not correlate with any particular vaccination decision. In slight contrast, 25 per cent of the complete non-vaccinators agreed, which suggests that total non-vaccination might be a rather different social issue. Many mothers who do not vaccinate at all appear to feel defensive and sensitive about their more extreme position and are more reluctant to engage in conversation about what they find a highly emotive issue except, perhaps, with others whom they know share their views. Sharing of positions around total non-vaccination thus tends to be part of the construction of more narrowly defined communities of parents, with non-vaccination talk often taking place in focal, rather than general settings, such as around public lectures by anti-vaccination campaigners and alternative therapists.

For some mothers without established social networks with other parents, the social relations of parenting – including vaccination – are structured some-what differently. For instance on Brighton's Whitehawk estate, some of the newly settled mothers we met from low-income groups lacked established com-munity relations. Their parenting relations were structured more through their engagement with health and social services. In this vein, four newly settled single mothers expressed how their sense of isolation from peers overwhelmed their ability to make what they regarded as an informed choice for the DTP.

> *Had all of the baby jabs done. Because being on my own, as I said my mum wasn't down here and I hadn't established a group of friends down here, I felt really vulnerable. The responsibility of looking after him was extremely overwhelming (Single mother, Whitehawk, April 2003).*

In this account, a feeling of vulnerability was a reason for handing over judgement about vaccination to health professionals.

This is a rare case, however. In our survey, no one specified a conversation with a health professional as having particularly influenced what they planned to do about MMR. It was largely conversations with peers that parents found most valuable, along with conversations and advice from other relatives. In some cases, those taking vaccination decisions seek out relatives or neighbours who also have some specialist medical training. In others, discussions and advice about MMR take place in the context of ongoing kin relationships that parents find valuable and supportive. The role of a child's grandparents is important in some cases. In Whitehawk, especially, some mothers are living with extended families nearby, and day-to-day interactions with grandparents are part of everyday parenting. For those living far from their parents, whether or not they discuss MMR with them is much more varied, and depends on personal relationships.

One might expect grandparently advice to emphasize alignment with the state and authority, reflective of an era when grandparents themselves were parenting, and when parenting and engagement with health services was less a matter of individual choice, and when polio vaccination eradicated this devastating childhood disease. Yet, most grandparents are also of a parenting generation that pre-dated MMR vaccination. While some have personal experience of severe complications from mumps or measles, many recall these as the relatively commonplace diseases of childhood that they were for most, and of taking children to mumps parties to ensure that they caught it before puberty. Moreover, other factors have altered their views, giving rise to a generation of what one might term 'post-modern grandparents' in relation to vaccination. Many grandparents are now of a generation that has experienced public questioning of vaccination as well as other aspects of science and technology – for example through firsthand experience of the pertussis controversy in the 1970s (see Baker, 2003) – and are strongly in tune with contemporary debates around such issues. Thus grandparents' part in 'MMR talk' is now just as likely to dwell on MMR concerns in relation to mild childhood diseases, as it is on the importance of vaccination. For example:

> *My mum thinks that in the past when there were no midwives and health visitors they just got on with it. Mum thought she didn't think it [vaccination] would work for us, she thought if we were ill we would be ill (Mother, Whitehawk, April 2003).*

> *Talking with my mother and mother-in-law influenced my views on MMR. Both have friends whose children became autistic after MMR.*

> *My parents felt that giving my baby the MMR could be dangerous to him so they offered to pay for single vaccinations. I accepted their offer.*

The encouragement to research (or 'to look into it') and then make up your own mind is a pervasive theme in MMR talk, and in parents' narratives about the process of deciding. Indeed vaccination seems to have become a subset of expected personal research into parenting options and advice of all kinds, encompassing health, diet, sleep, behaviour and other issues. That some parents are implicitly defensive of not looking into vaccination in more detail is evidence of this. Personal research is encouraged by other parents, as well as by health professionals. It variously involves searching for recommended books, contacting parents' groups for advice, and surfing the internet. In this, parents often have to balance the dramatic claims of individual mothers, the perspectives of anti-vaccination campaigners, serious work on the history of science and public health, and relatively inaccessible texts on immunology.

Through these processes of research, parents' social networks around vaccination are extended to encompass people met at talks or lectures, and those contacted through websites. Indeed, several organizations that aim to provide vaccination-related information and advice to parents run online discussion fora to which parents contribute questions, share experiences and respond to others. These range from those aligned with governmental, pro-MMR positions, such as the British National Health Service Website, to those offering highly open fora, such as the BBC website, to those largely questioning vaccination, such as 'JABS' and 'The Informed Parent'.[6] They include parents sharing stories of what they suspect might be vaccine damage to their children, and other one-off contributions asking for information, for example about single vaccines, or where they might obtain advice. These dedicated discussion boards are joined by a range of other online fora, including both websites for general baby chat and care tips – which have become sites for 'MMR talk' among other topics – and temporary electronic fora set up to coincide with, or follow-up, specific media events. By participating in these, parents join and help to construct 'virtual communities', extending MMR talk into them. This is the vaccination-specific version of what Madge and O'Connor (2006) refer to as cyber-parenting. MMR engagement is thus linking people in virtual networks which in turn link localities both within and outside the UK, forging aspects of solidarity and common identity in the ways that Melucci (1996) and Castells (1997) see as typical of contemporary 'network society'.

The process of deciding

Perhaps not surprisingly, given the range of views and arguments they encounter, most parents do not find that MMR talk or research leads them logically to a particular decision over MMR. Indeed the relationship between processes of discussion and decision is usually somewhat indirect. For some, exposure to diverse perspectives magnifies confusion:

> *I don't feel we have enough information. I sway one way then the other. Single vaccinations concern me too. Confusion really. When I do do it, and I probably will, it will be closing my eyes, running and jumping. (Mother, Brighton, April 2003).*

Many parents we talked to had participated in the agonizing of other parents, had heard stories of 'vaccine-damaged' children, talked conspiracy, and expressed belief in many of the DH's list of 'MMR myths', yet still went on to vaccinate. While this could be attributed to 'trust', several mothers emphasized lack of confidence or lack of knowledge as explaining decisions to vaccinate.

I'd have to be a lot more knowledgeable not to have it (Mother, Brighton, April 2003).

I'm not confident enough to go down the non-vaccination route (Mother, Brighton, May 2003).

This positive relationship between confidence and a sense of knowledge, and MMR refusal, was borne out in our survey. Here, 70 per cent of those who accepted the MMR according to schedule felt they would have liked more information to make a decision, whereas only 44 per cent of those who refused, delayed or sought single jabs felt this. In other words, more non-acceptors felt that they already knew enough.

Even among parents intending to vaccinate, the final decision to vaccinate may be postponed for logistical or familial reasons, including household gender relations. Our survey indicated that 23 per cent of Brighton mothers said the final MMR decision had been theirs alone (an equal percentage for those who decided for and against MMR), whereas 76 per cent said the decision had been made jointly with their partner or the child's father. Only in 1 per cent of the cases (all in favour of MMR) did the partner decide. Making the decision jointly perhaps implied a desire for shared parental responsibility. Yet there are cases where a child's parents disagree on the best course of action, or one parent feels more certain than the other, and decision making becomes a process of negotiation shaped by other aspects of their parenting relationship.

Thus a decision to vaccinate does not necessarily reflect resolution or acceptance of the safety of the MMR. It may on occasion be an outcome of intra-familial negotiation, or a more contingent, spontaneous or professionally encouraged decision on the spur of the moment, when in the doctor's surgery for other business. The difficulty of dealing with the wide variety of social and economic factors, pressures, uncertainties and implications for parental responsibility are captured well in the narrative of a 21-year-old single mother from Whitehawk who had postponed the MMR vaccination for about six months.

Do you ever get to the point when you can decide?
She's going to have it. I've been told. Her dad's told me he wants her to have it and it's a strong thing that he wants her to have it, so he's going to take her to have it, and I'm ok with that. I don't want to take her to have it, really.
Do you feel because it's his decision, because he took the responsibility, takes the pressure off you a bit?
A bit yeah. I do feel like it's a lot of pressure and I do think she should have it, really, realistically. I just cannot pay for single ones. If I could afford it, I would have single ones. Why should your child's development maybe suffer, we don't know yet, because you can't afford it... That's not really fair is it?
How come your partner is so sure that it's right?
Well, ... hmm ... she needs to have something done. I'm weighing up the

pros and the cons of it, for her to have it, she could become autistic then that's the chance you are going to take. If she doesn't have it, she could get very ill, she could die. Then realistically I'd rather she be autistic. It sounds really silly, maybe, I'd rather take that option, if she's still here with us, and I would still love her, she is still my child, rather than thinking to myself I'm putting her through all that illness, for nothing, you know, when really I could vaccinate against that. It's probably less chance of her becoming autistic than there is of her actually getting ill. Even if she didn't get really poorly she'd still get ill, she'd still get it, she's having it now, (laughing...) I'm not quite sure but she's having it. (Single mother, Whitehawk, March 2003).

While many studies have treated MMR as a single decision, then, our research suggests this may misconceive parental engagement. Actual outcomes depend not on a singular deliberative calculus and the information, education and social characteristics that inform it, but on contingent and unfolding personal and social circumstances in an evolving engagement. The MMR issue has taken on a social life, and understanding parental engagement with it requires us to understand how 'MMR talk' and anxieties unfold amid relationships between parents, and with the diverse worlds of official and complementary health delivery. Parents 'talking MMR', are not merely expressing their reading of science, but also what they regard as valued parenthood, their sense of responsibility to their child, their views of institutions, how they place themselves among their friends, and so on. How parents read or react to different information sources (whether pro-MMR DH publicity or health professionals' advice, or information from anti-MMR pressure groups) depends on when and how, in these social processes, they encounter them – questioning the central significance of information in itself emphasized in many studies.

Neither social engagements with MMR, nor personal reflections on its implications for a particular child's health, stop with the act of vaccination (or without it). In the immediate weeks after vaccination, parents may be aware of possible side effects and express relief that nothing serious happened. Even long after vaccination, when reflecting on problematic aspects of their child's development, the unnerving worry remains for some that the MMR might be responsible. Future children may not be vaccinated with the MMR even if previous children were. Whatever the choice, the process of learning about MMR continues and plays a role in future vaccination decisions for future children.

You've got to hope and pray that the decision that you made was the right decision, yours and your own (Mother, Brighton, May 2003).

Nonetheless in our survey, ex post facto, 95 per cent of those who accepted MMR on schedule and 93 per cent of those who did not, who delayed or chose single vaccinations, said they felt certain they had made the right decision.

In remembering and communicating their decision to other parents in MMR talk, some issues, such as the importance of choice, appear to become a safe idiom through which to verbalize more ambiguous experiences. Parental choice emerged as an important value for all, regardless of their particular decision. Indeed very few mothers strongly agreed that it would be easier if the decision were made for them.

> Do you think you think about it differently now post event than the way you were thinking about it then?
> *Possibly, I think, I don't think I would change my mind and have the MMR but I don't necessarily think the MMR is a bad vaccine, that there is a problem with the vaccine. I just think there should be a choice for a parent to, you know, so that you can make the decision yourself. Unless something comes out that there is absolutely no link with autism, it is completely safe, I think the choice element should be there and that's how I felt at the time that I wanted to make that choice and that's what I chose for my children. But I just think the choice should be there for all parents (Nurse and mother of two children both vaccinated with single vaccines, Brighton, April 2003).*

Assuming personal responsibility

A strong theme which emerged in parents' discussions of their MMR thinking was a pronounced sense of personal responsibility, and assumption of personal blame, for any harm that might come to a child either through disease or through vaccination adverse effects. 'I couldn't forgive myself if ...' (my child got autism/measles) was a common refrain. Survey responses confirmed this sense of personal responsibility, although unsurprisingly those who had opted for the MMR expressed their personal responsibility more in worry about measles than about possible MMR side effects. Mothers in a study in Birmingham also emphasized that as mothers they had a burden of responsibility to make the right decision for their children, and that this sense of responsibility had heightened in the context of uncertainty over MMR (Petts and Niemeyer, 2004; Petts, 2005).

Both political discourse and sociological analysis suggests that the importance of personal responsibility – in this case responsibility for a particular child – has become a major societal value in recent decades in Europe and the US. This is seen to be linked to processes of individualization and a shift from direct government to an agenda emphasizing citizens' own rights and responsibilities (e.g. Beck, 1992; Rose, 1999; Beck-Gernsheim, 2000; Beck and Beck-Gernsheim, 2002). In what Beck (1992) calls 'risk society' publics must shoulder much of the burden of risks that institutions of government cannot control. Individual responsibility for health is claimed to be 'a major value of the modern age' (Beck-Gernsheim, 2000, p131). To some extent our findings resonate with this theme. However, a sense of individual responsibility does not suggest that people are simply thinking and acting as atomized individuals; rather, it goes along with the forging of social relations and forms of community among parents, through MMR talk. Moreover, our findings do not conform with the view in some health literature that the importance of individual responsibility and choice is more important to higher socio-economic groups (e.g. Lindbladh and Lyttkens, 2003). These values were emphasized by mothers in Preston Park and Whitehawk alike, and across the class spectrum in our survey. Thus reflection on the uncertainties around MMR is not confined to affluent groups, leaving behind an unreflective poor; rather, people's practices and the social processes of MMR talk that shape them seem to be a more general phenomenon of modern parenting. In shaping people's varied engagements, pre-defined social groupings and classifications are less significant than issues of personal history, reflection on a child's personal health and strength, genetics and health of children, experience of other mothers and their children, and issues of confidence – fields which are part of and are shaped by MMR talk.

In stressing personal responsibility and choice in the context of MMR, it can be argued that parents are overriding longer-established social norms around vaccination. It has been argued that most parents have their children vaccinated because it seems 'the normal thing to do'; attending when called is a habit. Moreover the norm is not just a non-reflective act, but also involves moral judgement: vaccination seems the 'right' thing to do, given the social benefits from herd immunity as well as the benefits to the individual (Streefland et al, 1999). Thus as Petts (2005, p793) puts it, 'vaccinating children is "right" and the habit of taking your own child for vaccination serves to reinforce both the individual and the collective notion of normality'. Social routinization of vaccination, in this view, is thus part of reinforcing one's sense of membership of a collective, of society. To some extent, such norms applied in the days of the UK's immunization programme prior to the uncertainties around MMR, and they still hold, for many, for the other vaccinations in the schedule – many parents just turn up as expected for the DTP. Yet people do not adhere to social norms unreflectively, and the impression of 'habit' overlooks the variation and active forms of reflection – anxieties both positive and negative – that will have shaped how different parents arrived at their vaccination appointment. Moreover however important 'routinization' has been, it is clear that for MMR, such norms have been overturned. MMR is a matter of intense reflection, and little routinization.

How then, in the context of MMR, do parents balance the potential conflict between individual responsibility for their own child, which might suggest in some cases not having MMR, and collective responsibility to contribute to the social good through having MMR vaccination? In health policy circles it has sometimes been suggested that parents are acting selfishly in refusing MMR, flouting broader societal responsibility and morals. However the high sense of personal responsibility evident in mothers' responses suggests that the MMR issue has become so important that personal parenting concerns are paramount, leaving less space for wider social considerations. Nevertheless around 60 per cent of mothers claimed, when asked in our survey, that when deciding about MMR they did consider possible benefits to other children. And more still – 67 per cent of those having MMR on schedule (although only 37 per cent of those not) felt it was right for health professionals to push this social message. Parents are thus engaged in a tough balancing act of personal and social responsibilities.

Some feel that if they must prioritize their own children, then responsibility for upholding collective morals should pass to the state. Parents' own statements convey both a strong awareness of these conflicting responsibilities, the poignancy of these dilemmas and varied ways of resolving them – in ways which often make reference to a child's personalized immune system:

> *I did think about benefits to other children, but it makes me so angry when parents blame others if there is an outbreak of measles. The choice over MMR is so difficult.*

> *I did think about benefits to other children but it was very much secondary to what was best for Molly – with so many children un-immunized it was even more important to protect her.*

> *I believe my child's immune system to be good due to having a healthy diet and holistic healthcare and I intend to build on this. I also believe that having the MMR will compromise her immune system. Thus I only see benefits to other children.*

> *I believe that herd immunity is vital – as the number of immunized children drops the risk of epidemics increases and I would feel a responsibility in that if I did not have my child immunized.*

> *I realise that if my child was vaccinated this could protect weaker children who can't be vaccinated from the disease. However this didn't make me vaccinate her as she is my responsibility and how do I know at age one how strong she is?*

Finally for others – including complete non-vaccinators – doubt in the efficacy of mass vaccination or a conviction that it is damaging means that the moral position collectively, as well as individually, is to reject vaccination:

> *The rationale for mass vaccination is protection of the weakest who cannot have the vaccines for health reasons. I am not prepared to risk my child's health when I am not convinced that vaccination works as stated by the health professionals and government.*

> *If mass immunization really works (and I'm not sure) that is great. But why risk the health of my child in the future for something which might not protect him or other children – it doesn't always work.*

> *The long-term health of all our children is being severely threatened not just by MMR – but by all immunization.*

> *I believe I have a responsibility both locally and globally to consider others but … I do not regard vaccination as the best choice for health.*

Thus in the contemporary British context, MMR has joined other parenting issues as a matter for much personal reflection, responsibility and a desire for choice. Decisions about vaccination involve balancing diverse anxieties and notions of responsibility, within an ultimate sense that one only has oneself, as a parent, to turn to. Yet at the same time, through vaccination talk social relations and a sense of community among parents in their dilemmas are being created.

Social relations with frontline health professionals

Parental encounters with health workers at the front line of vaccination delivery – GPs, nurses and health visitors – provide formal occasions for giving advice, but they are also social encounters. At the same time, vaccination is just one of many issues around which parents and health workers interact. As our discussions with and survey responses from parents confirmed, these broader relationships – whether between parents and a particular health worker, or with their institution – shape the kinds of interaction which take place around vaccination itself.

Our interviews and discussions with doctors, nurses and health visitors suggest that many find their role as brokers between national policy and parental views extremely challenging. As people and often as parents too, health workers have not only expert knowledge but also personal experiences around vaccination which inevitably influence how they approach this role, and their encounters with parents. Several were uncertain about the MMR issue themselves. They were more comfortable when giving a range of information from which parents could make choices.

The social nature of interactions with health professionals becomes apparent in who parents choose to discuss vaccination with, as well as in what actually happens in those discussions. The majority of the GPs we interviewed feel little involved in most parents' MMR decisions. They find that very few parents consult them. Moreover, most of the parents who do, have already made up their minds and seek support rather than advice.

Indeed many mothers confirmed that they did not raise their questions with GPs. They see them as time-constrained and probably partial in their advice, not least because of their perceived financial gain from meeting vaccination targets.

My GP encouraged the vaccine but I feel that GPs are bound to do so.

I found it hard to get unbiased views so I chose the middle ground. I felt doctors told me what they had to say and didn't support me with their concerns so I didn't trust them.

I didn't trust the doctor, I thought she was just trying to get her quota up. The health visitor was neutral.

As a result of our 'choice' regarding vaccination the children have been removed from the GP list as the practice will fail to meet its targets and thus lose financially. The practice has stated that it will continue to treat the children until they can go back on the list in one year's time. However it places us in a rather vulnerable position re. healthcare and does little to counter a view of a politically engineered health system.

Such comments would tend to qualify the popular view in the UK that doctors are a highly trusted 'expert' group, and indeed there are studies that find this (e.g. Tarrant et al, 2003). Clearly, it depends not just on the nature of people's interactions with their GPs, but also on the issue at stake.

Some mothers from our more deprived study area, Whitehawk, were also worried about appearing ignorant in voicing questions that a doctor might find 'stupid'. Some feel patronized or intimidated in engagement with health professionals, and thus do not ask questions. This can be read (mistakenly) as passive acceptance (compliance). Thus to quote one GP:

I think the majority of Whitehawk are not having to make those decisions, because they are allowing us to make those decisions, because they are quite happy to hand that over, that responsibility over, they don't want to have to think about that, hopefully because they trust what you are doing or don't have the space to put thought into it, I don't know (GP, Whitehawk, February 2003).

However, that same GP, in relating one particular case, appeared highly aware of how such institutional relations influence their encounters. As she related her encounter with one particular mother for example:

She won't even come back and talk to me. She is not as educated, she finds it really threatening to talk about the details, and that [information] pack is very technical, which is one of the reasons that I wanted to see her again.

Parents' interactions with health professionals are thus shaped by broader relations of power and authority. These can have real social and material implications. For instance, a health visitor working in a deprived area of Brighton suggested that in a setting where social services treated the completion of infant immunization schedules as one among other indicators of adequate parenting, mothers were reluctant to voice any anxieties about vaccination for fear of attracting the authorities' attention. Seen in this way, seeming compliance may reflect reluctance to question more than an informed realization that MMR is 'safe'.

Nevertheless, there is great variation in health professionals' personal approaches, and in the personal relationships that parents might have built up with them. In some cases, this meant that a GP's advice was highly significant. For example:

The decision was made with our first child and I talked it through at length with my doctor who was very supportive either way – others in the health profession were very pro-government, pro-vaccination and it was a bit of a brick wall.

My GP is very supportive and takes time to explain anything I don't fully understand. I discussed it with him and felt it was best to have the vaccine than be at risk of measles-mumps-rubella.

Turning to health visitors, most of those we interviewed were strongly appreciative of parents' dilemmas, and did not wish to compromise carefully built relationships through anything that might be perceived as a heavy-handed advocacy to vaccinate. Moreover, vaccination is not the immediate priority for health professionals working with parents who are perceived as deprived, with many related health and social problems. As one professional described her work in Whitehawk:

I think your role is much more, damage limitation. Sometimes they have so many illnesses and so many risk factors, that you take the worst one and try to deal with that.

Vaccination is, however, a usual topic in the visits mothers have from health visitors in the period after birth, and in baby clinics for weighing – and it is part of a health visitor's role to make it so. Health visitors vary in how they play this. Most see their role as supporting a parent's own choice-making process about vaccination, while aware that this does not always lead to the outcome being vaccination acceptance.

Some health visitors are themselves confident in the safety of MMR and are comfortable in passing on government advice and documentation to parents. Others are themselves uncertain or have had personal experiences which make them question MMR safety. Their approach is often to offer a diverse range of information and options, balancing the DH leaflets with those from parents' support groups such as JABS and The Informed Parent, and from clinics offering separate vaccines.

I was thinking of not giving it at all. My health visitor was very supportive in advising to look for other options. She gave me a telephone number to look for single vaccines.

Our survey explored how mothers experienced or imagined health professionals' reactions to different vaccination decisions. Of those who had decided in favour of the recommended MMR schedule, it is not surprising that virtually all felt their doctor and health visitor would approve. However of those who had decided to delay or seek single vaccinations, responses were not only negative: 30 per cent considered that their doctor would disapprove of their choice, while 21 per cent considered that he or she would either 'approve' or 'wouldn't mind'; 46 per cent considered that their health visitor would disapprove, but 47 per cent believed that he or she 'approved' or 'wouldn't mind'. The image of health professionals universally conveying a pro-vaccination line and disapproving of those who do not accept MMR thus does not hold up. Rather, parents experience and regard health professionals' judgements in more varied ways, and often as supportive of or flexible about parents' own choices (and right to choose) even when this conflicts with vaccination policy.

Health professionals often report parents asking what MMR decision they made or advised for their own children or relatives. Indeed, several parents' narratives singled this out as a crucially influential piece of information:

> *The practice nurse said she has a grandchild herself and she would not encourage her daughter to vaccinate if she did not feel it safe.*

> *When I spoke to my GP he put my mind at rest immediately. He gave the MMR jab to his three children (recently) and gave me statistics as well as telling me about other studies that have been carried out on MMR overseas and in the UK.*

> *The practice nurse was very helpful. She said she had been convinced of the safety of the MMR since joining the practice and had had her own daughter vaccinated.*

Whether or not professionals choose to divulge – and some do not, on principle – it seems that for many parents, such lines of questioning usefully shift the interaction to a more personal register. The discussion comes to be about real, actual children, rather than the 'dry statistics' and 'whole populations' that some complain dominate professional advice:

> *The medical profession takes a wide view of the issue along the lines of public health. My decision was about my own children's health.*

This more personalized framing of interaction is, perhaps, one which better allows parents to voice and discuss their particular concerns about their individual children – concerns which as we showed earlier are central to parental framings of vaccination safety. Indeed, it may be this desire for more personally focused discussions, as well as for reliable advice, that leads many parents to seek out and value advice from health professionals who are also relatives or friends. Thus examples such as the following were strikingly common in parents' responses:

> *I spoke to other mothers with jobs in medicine. They happily immunized their sons.*

> *We talked to people we believed to be informed – a relative who is a nurse, our GP – as well as reading as much as we could.*

> *My next door neighbour is a doctor and she makes a point of telling other Mums that her son has had the MMR. I think this would work. Real people who know their stuff telling others as examples.*

A friend is a midwife and she provided me with an informative study article documenting the experience and use of MMR worldwide. I felt much better giving the injection knowing it was in use in Scandinavian countries and the USA over many years.

One wonders whether the article mentioned above would have been so trusted had it been given out by a GP or health visitor who was not also a friend. These examples show how the source of advice can be more significant than its evidential content. A 'medical expert' who is also a friend or relative is experienced as more approachable, and 'on one's side'.

When talking about their interactions with both health professionals and others (peers, family) that they might have consulted about MMR, 'supportive' and 'unsupportive' were words that cropped up frequently. Support in the difficult process of thinking the issue through, or support in sticking to and carrying through a decision already made, are particularly valued by parents regardless of whether their tendencies lean towards MMR acceptance, rejection or delay. Some mothers actively choose between health professionals, seeking out those who will support their particular perspective on vaccination. Such an egalitarian engagement premised on common concerns is often highly valued. For some, with less firmly held views, having a supportive health professional lends momentum to the process of research, of coming to a decision and of acquiring confidence in one's judgement.

Parents' interactions with alternative therapists, too, often seemed to be as important for such confidence-building, as for the content of the advice offered. In mothers' survey responses concerning homeopaths, it is the process of support for a decision that is paramount, whichever way that decision eventually goes:

My homeopath provided me with lots of information giving ongoing support and advice which instilled confidence in me to further question the issues surrounding MMR and make the right decision for my child.

Discussions with a homeopath about vaccinations gave me confidence about the course of action taken.

My homeopath confirmed my thinking.

In short, frontline health workers are not simply acting as conduits to communicate national vaccination and public health perspectives to parents. Rather, their situations as brokers are far more complex, involving negotiations of their own uncertainties and institutional imperatives, with the diverse parental worlds they encounter. Parents relate to, and sometimes actively seek, health professionals in ways that are shaped both by broad relations of power and perceived hierarchy, and by kinship and personal relations. Encounters with professionals sometimes involve knowledge and information about vaccination – whether biomedical or not. Yet it is often less the knowledge dimensions of an encounter, than the way relating to a professional builds or undermines confidence, which shapes parental decisions about vaccination for their child.

Vaccination and changing political philosophies

We have highlighted, then, ways in which views of the body, its immunity and the impact of vaccinations are not independent of experience and reflections on the social and wider political world. To understand further the nature of current anxieties about vaccination, it is important to consider how transformations in political traditions are playing into parents' thinking about vaccination and child health – while contrasting with technocracies of public health.

The emphasis on individual choice in relation to vaccination that pervades parental narratives has, we suggest, been co-produced with a wider political context in Britain that also emphasizes active choice – and a shift towards a liberal politic of choice, extending far beyond health care into other domains of life. This attention to personal choice is accentuated by the highly personalized perspectives on a child's particular immunity, in contrast with earlier perspectives on pubic and social hygiene, and moral virtues of cleanliness and civilization. The lens of immunity thus enables the person to become a liberal subject in body as much as mind.

Yet the technocracy that plans, organizes and delivers vaccination has its roots in an earlier ethic of public health, and in more assertive social planning. Moreover, as a technocracy, it must continue to emphasize 'the herd'. This contrast is resulting in a clash of discourses of governmentality. As one health visitor jokingly lamented:

> *We are constantly pushing active, decision-making parenting, sometimes against the odds – yet for vaccination, we sometimes wish people would just passively comply! (Health visitor, Brighton, February 2003).*

Public health regimes were important to the ways in which nation states developed in the 18th and 19th centuries, bolstered in their capacity to address infectious diseases such as cholera and smallpox, and undergird the civic infrastructural revolution (Porter, 1999). The political vision of an organizing government continued on in Europe and the US into the 1920s and 1930s, somewhere between its extreme forms of socialist command economy, and fascism. It extended into wartime and colonial planning that itself extended on into the 1950s. As discussed earlier, metaphors of strength and protection aligned with discourses of strong, protective states. Hardy (2006) argues that the period when mass childhood immunization was introduced on a large scale in the UK, in the 1960s, shortly after the founding and building of the National Health Service, coincided with this mood of confidence in public institutions involved with health delivery. There was, at this time, a sense of 'contract' in which people could expect their own and their children's health to be safeguarded, and that in turn they would uphold the collective responsibilities involved in adhering to public health programmes such as immunization and blood banking through gift. In this respect, in having a child vaccinated, individuals contributed to a mutually constituted social as well as a private 'good'. Hardy argues further that in this period 'the therapeutic revolution ushered in by penicillin, and the extension of mother and baby clinics under the new health service arrangements, also contributed to make Britain a society that accepted immunizations' (2006, p5). Thus it was not just the efficacy of the polio and other immunizations, but a sense of public, collective responsibility associated with it, that provided a receptive context for the introduction of mass childhood immunization. It is this conjuncture that enabled vaccination to become a 'routinized' part of normal parenting.

While these political assumptions endure for some areas of society and government, other political philosophies have emerged as government cedes to governance and an acceptance of and adaptation to more individualized desires. Political ideals of localized, deliberative democracy, and social ideals of multiculturalism contrast strongly with those of the UK at the height of its empire. A world of jobs-for-life has ceded to ideas of every individual's life as an enterprise in which one is continually employed, re-skilling and taking 'care of the self' in relation to work, associated with a new psychological culture emphasizing self-realization, self-awareness and performance (Gordon, 1991, p44).

Moreover in the UK since the 1990s, reforms in the health sector have been advocating greater individual decision making and patient choice, as part of the wider consumer-choice agenda promoted by the 'New Labour' government. Notions of individual responsibility, risk awareness, legal recourse and insurance (values central to the 'risk society' (Beck, 1992)), have been actively promoted as part of the moral framework for this agenda. The government has sought to promote these values at the expense of more 'traditional' sources of authority – notably in the professions and civil service – drawing in sociologists such as Anthony Giddens and Ulrich Beck as part of their advisory networks. Moreover, as Fitzpatrick (2004) argues, politics in Britain itself focused more on personal issues, encouraging the politicization of health, lifestyle, family relationships and childrearing practices. The same is true of the media. And around these issues, the state is increasingly encouraging 'responsible' citizens who self-govern their health, behaviour and lifestyles (Barry et al, 1996).

In this context, the emphasis on vaccination to maintain health at the population level has come to exist in tension with the citizen's individual right to pursue their own health (or that of their child). As long as vaccination is deemed by a parent to be in their child's best individual interest, then there is little conflict between these perspectives, but should a vaccine become associated with potential harm, then these principles diverge. The MMR issue, and instances where parents believe that because of their child's particular constitution a vaccine would be damaging to them, brought this fundamental tension between individual and public health objectives into sharp focus.

This tension has become all the more apparent for other reasons. First, medical science is discerning ever more the importance of individual variation and medical interactive effects in determining the efficacy and side effects of medications. Such emphases have been amplified in the media, and in the many popular lifestyle and health books, magazines and supplements that exist to help craft individuals' health. A person is not the public writ small.

Second, another often cited reason for these shifts in the relationships between individuals and the state over public issues involving science is that 'command' technocracies have proven both fallible and compromised in their links with the private sector. Some major scandals, such as the case of the emergence of Bovine Spongiform Encephalopathy (BSE) and the recognition in 1996 that it could be passed to humans in the form of 'variant' Creutzfeldt-Jakob Disease (CJD), have fuelled suspicion of government and scientific institutions more broadly. As Van Zwanenberg and Millstone (2003) have shown, in the BSE affair the Ministry of Agriculture, Fisheries and Food (MAFF) appeared to the public to have been intentionally misleading them. They held to a technocratic narrative that the knowledge and science surrounding BSE/CJD was undoubted and not clouded by uncertainty; one which supported their core economic and political agenda of shoring up the viability of the British beef industry. Being locked into this narrative made it difficult for MAFF to revise its views as challenging evidence emerged: 'Low cost steps ... were avoided, partly to avoid damaging the competitiveness of the meat trade, but also to sustain the illusion of zero risk' (Van Zwanenberg and Millstone, 2003, p34). So when the UK government finally acknowledged the dangers of BSE to human health in 1996, MAFF appeared to have been lying to the public.

Yet in our interviews, many fewer parents than we anticipated mentioned the controversies over BSE – or others, such as over genetically modified foods or mobile phones – in the UK as influencing their worries over MMR. Indeed several actively denied any link:

> Have you been worried by any of the scandals about food that were reported in the papers?
> *No, no (affirmatively), BSE! I was told that I was a mad cow anyway. It doesn't bother me (Mother, Brighton, April 2003).*

Views of government and the ways it handles scientific issues thus came over as less relevant than mothers' personal confidence in their decision-making process. In short, parental celebration of informed choice appears predicated on a form of personal responsibility that implicitly takes governmental fallibility into account. This acceptance of personal responsibility is manifest in the recurring statement 'I couldn't forgive myself if my child became autistic'; or inversely, '... if my child developed complications from measles'. In short, people's contemporary anxieties about state-led technocracies reflect the emergence of individuated perspectives and political philosophies surrounding health, lifestyle and choice that are rooted far more deeply than are a few instances of government reputational damage.

Conclusions: the dialogics of engagement over MMR

When reacting to the decline in parental uptake of the MMR vaccination, the UK Department of Health established an information campaign which focused on 'sound science', the 'social good' and a true appreciation of the balance of risk. These values were expressed in a suite of publications and web-based information aimed at parents and health professionals (e.g. NHS, 2002a, 2002b, 2004), and later at both combined. Yet the 'sound science' and the balance of risk were expressed in relation to population-level epidemiological studies, and were thus of little use to parents who were assessing the risk in relation to 'their child'. Equally, arguments concerning the 'social good' highlighted reasoning in relation to 'the herd' – although publicity also highlighted how certain children could not tolerate vaccination, and only herd immunity could protect such children from these diseases. The publicity thus found limited traction with large sections of the public who conceptualized vaccination risk in more personalized terms, and wanted to make personalized choices about it.

In as much as people appeared not to follow advice, the public health reaction was often to presume that the public remained ignorant or misled about risks, and to pursue education campaigns with greater force. In this, the DH was encouraged by the findings of its own attitudinal surveys, that it regularly commissions in random locations across the UK. Focusing narrowly on parents' perceptions of the benefits and risks of immunizations, and sources of information about these, these surveys at the height of the MMR controversy seemed to suggest that the DH approach was working. Thus interpreting the survey findings, Ramsay et al (2002) indicated that 67 per cent of mothers perceived the MMR as safe or to carry only slight risk. They concluded that:

> *the fall in MMR coverage has been relatively small, mothers' attitudes to MMR remain positive, and most continue to seek advice on immunization from health professionals. As the vast majority of mothers are willing to have future children fully immunized, we believe that health professionals should be able to use the available scientific evidence to help to maintain MMR coverage (Ramsay et al, 2002, p912).*

Pareek and Pattinson (2000) surveyed attitudes and beliefs in a similar way, with similar findings and conclusions. Such studies helped to support an interpretation of parental demands for 'choice' as selfish freeriding, set against the public good of vaccination. Public discourses minimized and marginalized those who did not comply with the expected MMR schedule, characterizing them as newly irrational middle classes, misled by inappropriate media coverage and amplification. A view was taken that once the media quietened down, the MMR controversy would blow over – a view that drew on the historical resurgence of parental uptake following the controversy over pertussis vaccine in the UK in the late 1970s (e.g. Yarwood, 2007). Such arguments tended, overall, to reinforce the idea of a compliant mass, and the logic of a public health model that relies on this.

Yet as publicity campaigns unfolded, parents' rather different views in Brighton, at least, appear to have become reinforced. The generic information on science and risk was read as too abstract and coarse to relate to particular children, and as insensitive to parental perspectives. Hence the tendency was to withdraw from this into further personal research in other arenas, heightening a sense of personal responsibility. Many parents found the public health technocracy to be too inflexible to accommodate their interests. The DH was, in effect, promoting and reinforcing a view that 'there is one system, and we'll stick to it', in a world where 'one size fits all' approaches were considered with suspicion. The withdrawal of access to single vaccines so that parents could only seek these privately (and as we have seen, many did – although this did not show up on government child health records), and the DH's refusal to offer either these or flexible vaccination schedules, was interpreted by parents as reflecting a technocracy that was out of touch, and pursuing other political and economic interests. Issues that emerged in critical public discourse turned on the financial logics of an uncaring state (exemplified in the financial incentives that doctors receive when vaccination thresholds are achieved), and the shadowy world of pharmaceutical companies, their influence on medical research results and penetration of government departments.

Thus what emerged was an unfolding 'stand off', or indeed, a dialectical widening of the gulf between parents and the DH as the arguments of each, premised on conceptually incompatible framings, played out in articulation with each other. Views central to the science of public health are written into a particular version of government, and a particular view of society (of social immunity) and of the body (of vaccines with generic effects on the body, suggesting a person as population writ small). These now encounter a very different, but equally embedded set of views which conceptually coordinate across views of government (decentralized, responsive), of society (of respect for individual choice and responsibility) and of the body (of personal immunity). Crucially, the interactions configured by these contrasting framings have served to shape both. It is this dynamic, we argue, that lies at the heart of vaccine anxieties and problems in vaccination delivery in the UK today.

Certainly, parents remain deeply anxious for the health of their children in ways that can and often do encompass positive evaluation of vaccines and their effects. Such positive anxieties are often framed in relation to ideas of a child's strength, vulnerability and personalized immunity, and as part of a repertoire of personal health and parenting choices that might encompass alternative medicine and nutrition as well as biomedicine. Such evaluations emerge from parents' experiential expertise – in this case that knowledge that comes from daily observation and interaction with particular children on whom parents and everyday carers are clearly, in many respects, experts. In the context of parents' knowledge and expertise – gained and maintained in interaction with a diversity of other experts – those who do not accept prescribed vaccination schedules should be seen neither as ignorant, nor, necessarily, as 'resisting' in a negative sense. Rather, such parents are often following positive, informed strategies geared to the health of their child; strategies which sometimes include vaccination but wish it timed differently, or which understand its effects in personalized ways. In short, vaccination, as a technology, acquires different meanings when framed as part of personalized pathways of child health, than when framed as part of the technocracy of mass childhood immunization. Yet it is such meanings, as this chapter has tried to show, that are crucial to understanding parents' practices and desires.

Notes

1   Michael Poltorak played central roles in the ethnographic fieldwork and survey in Brighton, and was lead author of an earlier joint article (Poltorak et al, 2005) on which this chapter draws.

2   The sampling frame for the survey consisted of all children aged 15–24 months listed in the Child Health Dataset held by South Downs Health NHS Trust as resident in the catchment of Brighton and Hove City PCT, in early March 2004. Children were categorized into those who had and had not had an MMR immunization recorded, and of the 1800 children eligible, a sample of 1000 MMR uptakers and non-uptakers in a ratio of 1:1 was randomly drawn, using the statistical programme STATA™ Version 8. All the 135 registered children who had had no vaccination events recorded were also sampled. A postal questionnaire addressed to the mother or guardian of each child was sent in March 2004. This contained a questionnaire for the mother, and also one to be passed where possible to the father of the child. A follow-up letter with a second questionnaire was sent after 3–4 weeks to non-responders, with the exception of children who had had no vaccinations recorded, due to late receipt of the data needed for sampling.

3   This shift is by no means total. Indeed in the early 21st century advocates of highly generalized, strict, routine-based childcare regimes (e.g. Ford, 2001) have enjoyed a renewed popularity, perhaps in the context of the pressures that many parents now feel to regularize childcare routines around contemporary work demands.

4   These are pseudonyms, as are all other parents' and children's names cited in this book.

5   The term 'immune system' was first used within science only as late as 1967, when it was introduced as a way of holding together two contending strands of immunology: that emphasizing the action of specialized cells (lymphocytes) in fighting off infection, and that emphasizing the role of antibodies (Moulin, 1989).

6   JABS (Justice, Awareness and Basic Support, www.jabs.org.uk) and The Informed Parent (www.informedparent.co.uk) are both organizations claiming to offer 'objective' information, advice and support to parents in making decisions about vaccination. In practice their emphasis is as fora and channels for much information and discussion that questions vaccination, as well as support to parents who think their children have been damaged by vaccines – as we discuss further in the next chapter.

4

Anxieties over Science: Arguing MMR in the UK

Introduction

This chapter focuses on the dynamics of the controversy that formed the backdrop for the previous chapter. The debate which raged in the UK from the 1990s over whether the measles, mumps and rubella (MMR) vaccine was linked with autism has become a high-profile exemplar of a recent vaccine controversy in the European context.

According to many commentators, the MMR controversy was instigated by the publication of a scientific paper (Wakefield et al, 1998) which led to suggestions in the media of a link between MMR and autism. This, and subsequent supportive scientific work by Wakefield and others, has been labelled as bad or 'junk science' (Fitzpatrick, 2004). Yet, so the account goes, it has been taken up by an avid 'anti-MMR' campaign of parents of autistic children, desperate for an explanation for their children's acquired autism. They wrongly and misguidedly link it to the MMR vaccine, confusing a concurrent onset of symptoms with a vaccine-related cause. To some (e.g. Collins, 2004) these 'MMR mums' exemplify an ignorant public pursuing an ill-founded cause that ignores the 'truth' shown by epidemiological studies purporting to show no link between MMR and autism. That their campaign has had a major impact on parental thinking, it has been argued, is because its messages have been overblown by the media (Hargreaves et al, 2002). Furthermore by the 1990s, publics in Britain are seen to be living in a 'risk society', already distrustful of government and receptive to being misled into exaggerated worry about health risks (Fitzpatrick, 2004).

Such accounts of the controversy put into play many of the concepts that in Chapter 2 were shown to dominate contemporary analyses of vaccine anxieties in European contexts. They rely on notions of ignorance versus science, and of rumour exaggerated by pressure groups and the media. They have led health policy makers to assume that once 'good science' prevails over 'bad', media and pressure groups will quieten down and the controversy will cease.

In this chapter, we explore the understandings and practices of parents at the heart of the controversy: those who claimed that their children had been damaged by the MMR vaccine, and who mobilized around these claims. By looking at their perspectives a rather different story emerges. This is one of a struggle between opposed forms of knowledge – differently framed sciences – linked to different social and political concerns. We show how parental perspectives linked bodily understandings – of their children's symptoms, and their possible links with vaccination – with the building of solidarities among themselves and with certain scientists who took their views seriously. We also explore the wider, and linked, political issues that the parental mobilization raised. These parents challenged established perspectives and institutions in both biomedical science and public health policy. They faced what increasingly came to be a vociferous counter-mobilization from scientists, policy makers, health professionals and journalists questioning their claims. In examining the dynamic interactions in what emerged as two distinct sides of the MMR debate – interactions played out in ways that linked science, politics and media processes – we will illuminate both how the controversy became so polarized, and why it has been so difficult for the MMR debate to reach closure.

There has been a great deal of writing about the MMR controversy, from many different viewpoints. The argument that we develop in this chapter is based on material from a range of sources. Central among these are interviews and informal discussions held with the spokespeople and members of a parents' support group for vaccine-damaged children in Brighton, south-east England. This led to a series of email exchanges and participation in the circulation of documents among members of this group, and other similar groups across the UK. While this cannot be considered as a detailed ethnography of these mobilizing parents, it did enable an understanding of their perspectives, motivations and relationships that could not be discerned from media and policy commentary. To complement these sources, we also attended and observed several national events around MMR; reviewed the web-based and documentary publicity materials of key organizations involved in the controversy, and closely followed the prolific media, policy and internet debate about MMR, especially during 2001–2004.[1]

Bodily understandings and the origins of MMR anxiety

Parents who mobilized around MMR locate the origins of concern in their own intimate observation of and experiences with their children; in their knowledge and experiential expertise of their individual children's health. They describe how from the early 1990s several noticed dramatic changes in their children who, from a developmentally normal infancy, regressed suddenly from around the middle of their second year. They describe how the children became withdrawn, with symptoms later diagnosed as part of the autistic spectrum, along with severe and painful bowel problems. As time went by, such children often developed other symptoms such as excessive thirst, loss of language, allergies, respiratory problems and food intolerances.

Reflecting on the timing, a number of parents came to link the symptoms to MMR vaccination. Some describe how it had been obvious to them that a serious reaction had occurred just a few hours after vaccination. For others the link emerged when they searched back through family photographs and child health records. One mother described, for instance, how after the MMR jab her son:

> *went pale. I took him home and he slept for an hour, but when he woke, he started screaming. He was clearly in terrible pain. The look on his face terrified me... All the next week, he was very sleepy and I couldn't establish eye contact with him... He never recovered. I'd watched the life go out of him. Afterwards, he started having horrendous temperatures. He became aggressive, hyperactive and out of control, but the doctors insisted there was nothing wrong.[2]*

In conversation, this same mother described how as health professionals refused to listen seriously to her, she 'began to do her homework', and to suspect vaccines.

These parents began to come into contact with each other through chance encounters, existing networks such as autism support societies, and a snowballing of email and telephone communication. As parents shared, compared and made causative associations between their children's symptoms and MMR through informal networks, so a form of popular epidemiology emerged. From the early 1990s, this acquired a greater degree of formality as one vaccine-damage support organization, JABS, organized an ongoing web-based survey, and analysed the patterns it suggested (Fletcher, 1995). What emerged can be considered as a veritable example of 'citizen science', in which publics orchestrate their own scientific investigations and pose their own research questions – often as a basis for engaging critically with the scientific perspectives of 'expert' institutions (e.g. Irwin, 1995; Fischer, 2000).

Parents have pursued a number of further lines of inquiry. These have included identifying and confirming common symptoms, leading them to the conclusion that their children have not just 'autism' but a 'novel syndrome' linked to MMR vaccination. Parental research also focused on the timing of the onset of symptoms. This led them to argue, against government views, that MMR vaccination and the onset of autistic symptoms could not just be a coincidence of timing since 'degeneration in affected children always follows immunization with MMR or measles-containing vaccine regardless of the age of the child' (Thrower, 2002). And acknowledging that it is only a small proportion of a wider population of children affected in this way, parental research began to ask about the 'co-factors' which might make particular children vulnerable. Here, an emergent set of questions turns on family history. For instance the JABS survey claims to have:

> *highlighted a number of common allergies in the families: asthma, eczema, hay fever, antibiotics or a history of febrile convulsions, fits or epilepsy. Is*

it possible the child has some allergy element and has an allergic response
when presented with several viruses at once? (Fletcher, 1995).

These questions reflect an intimate parental focus on the bodily processes of individual children, acknowledging that each is particular. These are features which, as we discussed in the last chapter, are in line with the concepts of the immune system and personalized immunity that now pervade parental thinking about child health more broadly in the British context. The notion that the particular constitution and immune system history of certain children might make them vulnerable to the MMR vaccination became a key framing concern among mobilizing parents. In asking questions such as: how do combination vaccines actually interact with each other and with the genetic and illness history of particular bodies? Might there be sub-groups of children who are vulnerable to a vaccine that for most is safe? Parents entered areas that scientists themselves acknowledge as little-understood and replete with uncertainty (Moulin, 2007).

Social dimensions of mobilization around MMR

These common experiences and reflections on the bodily processes in their children created grounds for emerging forms of solidarity that developed among parents. Bodily understandings thus became linked with social relations, helping to create and consolidate them. As we discuss here, these took multilayered forms. Emergent social solidarities among parents involved localized parental support groups; national organizations and networks; and a wider field of supportive networking and discussion among sympathetic publics. As we go on to show, however, relations between parents and certain scientists were also key to the way that mobilization unfolded.

Social relations among mobilizing parents

In some localities, parents who believed that their children had been damaged by the MMR vaccine established support groups. Their common experiences helped to forge and maintain a sense of common identity. One such group in Brighton, for example, included about 20 members who met once a month in a community centre. Participants describe equality and common experience as the factors binding them, across differences of class and gender: 'we were all equal and together'; 'we were discovering similar symptoms – it was an amazing insight into not going mad'. Through conversation, affirmation of common experience and identity was combined with emotional support. As members recall: 'We laughed, cried, and became very close', and 'it was like a family'. The sharing of practical information about diet, treatment options, entitlements to support, and so on contributed to this.

At least in the account of its founder, the Brighton group and its various activities also became a means through which parents empowered themselves, acquiring the vocal skills, knowledge of organizations and networks, and familiarity with scientific vocabularies that some would employ elsewhere as part of what became a wider activist movement questioning the MMR vaccine (see Leach, 2005). In this way, local support groups did not just forge a common identity but also laid the ground for strategies of the kind explored later in the chapter.

Co-existing and interacting with such local support groups, there emerged a variety of national organizations and networks. These had overlapping aims and memberships, but also significant differences in the details of their agendas and framings. Most came to use the internet as their major means of publicity and coordination, as well as contributing to the media and public events. Important examples are JABS (Justice, Awareness and Basic Support – an information and campaigning organization concerned with vaccine damage) and ARCH (a campaign concerned with acquired autism).[3] These came to focus on the MMR issue. JABS, founded by one of the first mothers to voice public concern over what she saw as MMR-damage to her child, was originally established to provide a helpful support network for parents of vaccine-damaged children. As time went by, however, JABS found other parents looking to the organization as a source of information and advice on vaccines, as an alternative to both the pro-vaccination stance of official government advice fora and more extreme anti-vaccination websites. JABS came to be the most high-profile organization claiming to represent parents' concerns in the national debate over MMR. However its founders emphasize that it is not 'anti-vaccination' nor indeed 'anti-MMR' as is often claimed. Rather, they claim they are anti the giving of MMR to vulnerable children who might be damaged by it, and anti the lack of dialogue that has come to pervade the debate and deter investigation of the causes of vulnerability. They have campaigned for more research into vaccine effects, for compensation for vaccine damage, and for the rights of parents to choose vaccination strategies for their children, such as the choice of single jabs instead of MMR.[4]

While social mobilization around MMR centred on the social solidarities of parents forged through experience, and the organizations that emerged to represent their claims, the social relational field also extends further. Many 'ordinary' parents in thinking about whether to have their own children vaccinated with MMR, as we saw in the last chapter, draw on the internet and media materials of the parental mobilization to inform their own reflections and discussions with each other. And many find themselves in sympathy and support, not least because their bodily and wider political understandings of vaccination through the concept of personalized immunity find resonance with the framings and questions of the parental mobilization. In this respect, the concerns of the parental mobilization and the reflections of parents more generally have inter-animated with each other, united by a broadly common conceptual field. Pointing out this interrelationship, however, is not at all the same as suggesting that parents were led (or misled) by a pressure group in a one-way sense, as many commentators around vaccine anxieties have suggested (e.g. André, 2003).

This supportive social field for the parental mobilization around MMR has been created and sustained in several ways. The 'MMR talk' among mothers that we considered in the last chapter is important, given its tendency to provoke sympathetic listening to stories of vaccine damage. It is also sustained through sympathetic readings of pro-mobilization articles in the media, and through the internet. For instance the electronic discussion boards of campaign organizations such as JABS are central means for the forging of such broader social fields of support. Contributions to these tend to draw together at least three sorts of participant, thus exposing them to each other's perspectives: the 'core' mobilizers engaging in ongoing discussion over vaccine science and policy; parents sharing stories of what they suspect might be vaccine damage to their children; and other one-off contributions asking for information, for example about single vaccines, or where they might obtain advice. Parents also use Usenet groups, blogs and chatrooms to talk about the MMR issue and its science and politics, actively engaging in conversation (Richardson, 2005). In these ways the mobilization questioning MMR came to link people in virtual networks that extended across and beyond the UK, forging aspects of common identity in the process (see Melucci, 1989, 1996).

In terms of the central role of the internet, MMR mobilization illustrates a kind of 'cyber-politics' that Bauman (1999) and others see as becoming a dominant form in late modern societies with high internet access. But while Bauman considers cyber-politics as too disembodied to produce effective social and political solidarities, as it relies on and creates further fragmentation, this does not seem to be the case for MMR. Strong solidarity among parents has been generated partly by the strong sense of shared experience and conceptual framings as parents have communicated through cyberspace, and partly because cyber-networks have been reinforced through other practices – of face-to-face encounter in support groups, campaign events and in other practices and strategies.

Social relations with scientists

Conversations among members of the Brighton support group would often dwell on experiences with health professionals, in a style which simultaneously served to construct solidarity among an 'us' versus an unsympathetic 'them'. Thus several members spoke of health professionals' disbelief when they described their children's symptoms and their view that they were caused by MMR. They speak of being dismissed, and told that their children 'just had toddler diarrhoea', for instance; of 'being made to feel tiny' and of being called a 'bad parent' for questioning vaccination. Several also report being accused by health professionals of having either caused their children's autistic symptoms, or having invented them in a version of Munchausen's syndrome by proxy.

These parents also describe how they came to learn about medical specialists who might take their experiences seriously. Key among these was Dr Andrew Wakefield of London's Royal Free Hospital, whose work was already suggesting possible links between measles virus and the development of inflammatory bowel disease (Wakefield et al, 1993, see also Ekbom et al, 1994). Parental networks forged specific links with Wakefield's research group. This was sometimes through their children becoming patients and research subjects (the parents of several of the twelve children in Wakefield's 1998 study became founders and core members of parental organizations), but it was also through other forms of communication, meetings and reading of materials. Thus parental science developed in active engagement with the network of scientists and research groups in the UK, Ireland and the US who were pursuing research on different elements of the biological processes that might be implicated in their children's syndrome, and its possible links to MMR. Several of these scientists explicitly presented themselves as exploring questions raised by parents.

Indeed, that Wakefield's 1998 paper presented no evidence for an MMR link except the experience of the parents attracted furious criticism from government agencies and other medical scientists. Yet Wakefield justifies this as an important and legitimate stance:

> *It wasn't my hypothesis; it was what the parents said. We acknowledged this did not prove a causal association... It's not my job to censor the parents' story. If we censored that history, how would we enable people to test it? The parents said to us: my child has bowel disease. Unequivocally they had bowel disease which the medical profession had played no part in diagnosing... So when the parents say they believe this happened after vaccination, we are not in any position to say, you are wrong. We must say instead we will investigate your history to the best of our ability.*[5]

This emphasis on hypothesis-building from clinical case histories, and on the scientific analysis of data gathered from detailed individual medical examination, is a uniting feature of research that, by the early 2000s, involved diverse medical specialists – paediatricians, gastroenterologists, pathologists – in at least eleven institutions. Their clinical investigations sought to unravel the bodily processes and histories of the children, to see whether there were factors that might have made these particular children vulnerable, and whether MMR might have interacted with these predispositions (see for example Sheils et al, 2002; Singh et al, 2002; Wakefield, 2002; Wakefield et al, 2002; Wakefield, 2003; Bradstreet, 2004).

This evolving research and interactions around it involved a constant interplay between parents and medical experts. Their shared concerns, and the mutual processes of 'expertification' and 'layification' at work as each came better to understand the other's perspective, contributed to a breaking-down of established boundaries between lay and expert knowledge, and indeed to some extent of the social identities of parents and medical experts. What emerged was a parental–clinical scientist alliance that was social as well as scientific, drawn together in a solidarity created by shared concerns with the wellbeing of a particular group of children, and shared questions as to what was going on in their bodies.

Arguing science and politics over MMR

The claims of this emerging parental–clinical science alliance, and their media reportage, were of serious concern to scientists and policy makers concerned with public health and vaccination in the UK. They saw questions about MMR safety as risking a decline in vaccine uptake, a drop in social immunity to measles and the return of epidemics, and an undermining of public confidence in the UK vaccination programme as a whole. The government reflex was thus to suppress these claims, rather than enter into discussion of them (Stilgoe et al, 2006). Thus the then prime minister Tony Blair, reflecting on dealing with Wakefield's hypothesis, stated that: 'My worry was that if we gave it even a prima facie credibility, before you knew where you were people would have assumed it was credible'.[6]

As the government sought to counter the parental claims, the MMR controversy became extremely polarized, with the perspectives of the parental–clinical science alliance, and of the policy makers and scientists who opposed them, at times appearing irreconcilable. The dynamics of interaction between these groups both helped to create and consolidate them as two emergent 'sides', and to confirm their particular framings in ways that often served to drive them further apart. A key feature of these dynamics is that both parental and policy worlds used remarkably similar strategies in developing and promoting their arguments. Here, we consider how such polarizing interactions unfolded in three overlapping arenas: in producing knowledge and science; in exposing the political economy of science and in debate through the media. In each of these arenas, arguments very often integrated bodily understandings of the effects of the MMR vaccine with wider social and political concerns. Scientific and political dimensions of the controversy were thus intimately linked, but in different ways among mobilizing parents, and in the policy world that they encountered.

Producing science and knowledge

In response to the parental mobilization, the DH and related policy and scientific agencies engaged in several strategies which directly involved science. The first was to engage critically with the content and methods of the science of the parental mobilization – for instance arguing that Wakefield's 1998 work drew on a very small self-selected sample – thus discrediting its relevance to a wider understanding of any relationship between MMR and autism. The second was to commission expert scientific reviews ostensibly to settle the issue (e.g. Committee on Safety of Medicines (CSM), 1999; Medical Research Council (MRC), 2001). The third was to produce new scientific research. So it was that from the late 1990s, numerous epidemiological studies considered the incidence of autism (and in some cases, bowel disease) in relation to MMR among larger populations, and claimed not to show an association (e.g. Taylor et al, 1999; DeWilde et al, 2001; Fombonne, 2001; see Miller, 2002 and Jefferson et al, 2003 for reviews). The volume of such studies soon enabled government, scientific and professional organizations to claim that the weight of scientific evidence was strongly against an MMR–autism link.

Parents' organizations responded to these studies, in part, by critiquing them on their own terms, engaging in detailed criticism of their data sources, methods and reasoning, publicizing such critiques on their websites. The most systematic of these critiques was by a parent, David Thrower, and occupied centre-stage on the ARCH website during 2002–3 (Thrower, 2002). Thrower's study reviewed about 70 of the most pivotal, or most frequently quoted studies and papers, concluding that that 'there has not been a single credible study that can robustly refute the claims of the parents that their children's acquired autism has been caused by MMR or related vaccines'. Each apparently refuting study, the review suggested, was either flawed in design or ambiguous in results. In this respect, parental strategies paralleled the strategies used by pro-MMR science-policy networks to critique Wakefield's work, producing a storm of critique and counter-critique at the level of scientific methods, data and reasoning.

However, major differences in the framing of each side's science became apparent. Fundamentally, whereas the science supporting parents' concerns was grounded in clinical case histories and the medical and biological processes in individual children, the opposed science-policy networks largely drew on statistical analyses of the medical records of wider populations. This contrast between individual/clinical and epidemiological/population work was, parental groups argued, fundamental, with these population studies being wrongly framed to pick up on their concerns. As one Brighton mother put it:

> *If I drop a ring on the floor and I see it rolling in one direction and I tell you it is in the other direction, you won't see it. They are not looking in the right place, so they won't find it. They are not looking at our children (Interview, Brighton, March 2002).*

This was echoed in Thrower's review for ARCH:

> *The medical establishment has repeatedly asked itself the wrong question. It has asked itself 'Is MMR safe?', hoping for an affirmative answer. In contrast, researchers and parents have asked two very different questions: 'What is wrong with this child?', and 'Why did this child change from being healthy to being autistic?' It is answering these latter two questions that should be the key issue (Thrower, 2002).*

More specifically, parents argue that population-level studies are 'too broad brush' to pick up rare adverse events from MMR that may affect only a tiny proportion of children.

These contrasting individual versus population framings can be seen to reflect each side's social and political concerns, within this politicized scientific field. Whereas parents were primarily concerned about what they saw as the vaccine-damaged health of their individual children, government policy makers and their supportive scientific networks had institutional commitments to the continued integrity of the UK vaccination programme with its public, population-level imperatives, and mass-focused technocracy. Tensions between scientific framings thus spoke directly to fundamental tensions in public health policy, and in citizen–state relations. In the controversy, those adopting these different framings tended to speak past each other. Little explicit attention was therefore given to the moral question of whether it was justifiable for the health of a few children to be sacrificed in the interests of maintaining population-level herd immunity. Nor have pro-MMR science-policy networks paid much heed to the parental mobilization's attempts to resolve this particular dilemma, by claiming that their aim was to determine scientifically which children were vulnerable to the MMR vaccine, so that they could be screened out of population-level vaccine programming.

Further, related contrasts in framing are also evident. First, whereas the parental movement claimed to be investigating a 'novel syndrome' in affected children, with a particular set of symptoms, the opposed science-policy networks largely frame their concern as with 'autism in general'. Second is a contrast between framing in terms of risk versus uncertainty. Pro-MMR science-policy networks have tended to treat the issue as one of risk. Population studies are thus designed to determine the risk of developing autism from MMR (and have generally claimed that this is negligible). Risk has also been the key theme of government communications to the public on the MMR issue, using quantitative comparisons of the relative risks of developing autism from MMR, developing serious complications from measles, and other health risks in an attempt to shore up public confidence that MMR is safe (e.g. Health Promotion England, 2001). Whereas the concept of risk presupposes that there are calculable probabilities between known outcomes, those involved in the parental mobilization have tended instead to frame the issue as one of uncertainty or even ignorance, given the many unknowns about the effects of MMR, and to advocate a precautionary principle in holding back on MMR use.

Despite these distinctions, there are also some commonalities in the ways each side has sought to bring 'closure' to the scientific debate in their favour. Pro-MMR science-policy networks have successively framed reportage of their studies as 'settling the issue', claiming to show that MMR is safe. Several practices have been important in this creation of closure and black-boxing of uncertainties (Latour, 1987). These include, when scientific studies are reported in policy and media contexts, not acknowledging caveats made by the scientists themselves, and omitting from the final reports of advisory reviews the incertitudes and demands for further investigation noted in earlier drafts. Parents and supportive journalists suggest that this applied to both the MRC and the CSM reviews (CSM, 1999; MRC, 2001).[7] Further, claims that MMR is safe have relied on re-casting absence of evidence as evidence of absence. Thus as Dr Peter Fletcher, a former assessor to the CSM, protested in a letter to a clinical periodical: 'The readers of this journal may ponder the curious turn of events which has now led to the Department of Health, the Medicines Control Agency, the Committee on Safety of Medicines and other eminent bodies citing negative studies as absolute evidence of safety'.[8]

Mobilizing parents have equally sought closure in 'proving' the link between MMR and their children's disease. Despite the multiple pathways of investigation being pursued by the different scientists supporting them, sometimes following quite different hypotheses, and despite their frequent claims that more research is needed, their communications in the media and through website reviews have tended to portray the building of an increasingly large and coherent body of evidence which is gradually filling in the pieces of a jigsaw puzzle, telling a coherent and plausible story. Like the governmental counter-mobilization, the parental mobilization can thus be seen to construct a strategic 'rhetorical science' which is coherent. That the overall debate has not reached closure reflects, at least in part, the incompatible framings of each side's scientific stories, despite their similar strategies.

Exposing the political economy of science

While each side in the MMR controversy has thus sought to critique the science and knowledge of the other by exposing flaws in its content and methods, and in its framing, mobilization strategies have also gone further, attempting to expose the political–economic interests underlying the opposition's position, and thus to delegitimize their claims. As both sides engaged in such strategies, so each appeared to construct its own science as 'objective', discrediting the other's as conflicted and biased.

Therefore, evident in MMR-concerned discussions among parents, on the internet and in media coverage is much reflection, and critique, concerning the personal, institutional and political–economic biases to statements about the safety of MMR. These portray a perceived alliance between the government and its DH, a range of medical scientists and official advisory bodies, and interested pharmaceutical companies in promoting a message that 'MMR is safe', and silencing detractors. This alliance, parents argue, is intended to avert any challenge to childhood vaccination policy, as a revered cornerstone of public health policy, and to protect the political–economic interests claimed to be entwined with vaccine manufacture and sales. The parental mobilization, in this sense, links its concern with MMR to a broader commentary on the political economy of the state and of technology.

These specific concerns over biases in MMR science echo a strong theme in the broader literature questioning vaccination. Several prominent writers (e.g. Coulter, 1990; Coulter and Fisher, 1991; Scheibner, 1993; Cave and Mitchell, 2001) adopt an explicit strategy of 'exposing' the biases in what they term the 'orthodox' medical science which supports large-scale childhood vaccination. They do this both by drawing on other bodies of evidence (e.g. parents' experiences), and by arguing that evidence in published scientific works which apparently supports vaccination can and should be reinterpreted, read between-the-lines and against-the-grain, as confirming the ineffectiveness and adverse effects of childhood vaccines. It is such reframing of established scientific evidence that enables Scheibner, for instance, to subtitle her book '100 years of orthodox medical research shows that vaccines represent a medical assault on the immune system'. She suggests that doctors, medical scientists and policy makers have been blinkered from seeing this by working within a medical system which is 'totalitarian', 'highly politicized' and dominated by 'big business' interests (1993, p262).

However, pro-MMR science-policy networks were quick to counter these accusations by pointing to the commercial interests and biases among the parents' advisors and publicists. Thus Mike Fitzpatrick, the GP and commentator who dismissed Wakefield's and related work as 'junk science', argues that:

> *Anti-MMR campaigners have frequently disparaged doctors and scientists who refute the MMR-autism link for their links with the drug companies that manufacture vaccines...Yet there are substantial commercial interests involved in the promotion of junk science to which these same journalists remain oblivious (Fitzpatrick, 2002).*

Among these political–economic interests, he claims, are lavish trips and hospitality offered to journalists by pharmaceutical companies; profits to be made from selling expensive laboratory tests, medicines and dietary products to the parents of claimed MMR-damaged children; profits made by private GPs and clinics from selling single vaccines, and legal aid fees collected by lawyers supporting parents to pursue their MMR-damage claims through litigation. In February 2004, the pro-MMR lobby made claims that Wakefield's original scientific work was mired in a 'fatal' conflict of interest. An exposé in the *Sunday Times* claimed that at least four of the children in his 1997 study were part of a legal class action against the manufacturers of MMR vaccine, and that Wakefield had received funding from the Legal Aid Board 'to assist their case by finding scientific evidence of the link'.[9] This disclosure was subsequently used by journalists, government spokespeople and top politicians as a basis to discredit Wakefield's work, style of operation and the parental campaign more broadly.

In this to-ing and fro-ing, then, both sides of the controversy have claimed that theirs represents the 'objective' view, whereas the other's is biased by economic, political, personal or commercial pressures. Each side has reacted to the other's claims by further claims, in a remarkably similar set of strategies. This echoing of strategy – and the increasing sophistication of strategy use by each side in the controversy – has arguably helped to drive them further apart, contributing further to non-closure of the debate.

Dialogue and debate in the media

As preceding sections have made clear, much of the MMR controversy unfolded publicly through the the UK print and broadcast media – even while it also rolled on in academic journals. As we saw in Chapter 2, some commentators have cast the controversy as the creation of an irresponsible media that gave voice to an ill-founded scare. However a closer look denies this image, suggesting instead that the mass media became integral to the controversy, as each side enrolled sympathetic journalists into its networks, and as particular forms of coverage fed the debate, requiring reaction. The media and its journalists were not fully controllable. Nevertheless, it is worth considering some of the particular media-related strategies used by the parental mobilization and its critics. Linking science and politics, these were central to how the dynamics of the controversy unfolded.

From the outset the parental mobilization gained a great deal of media coverage, with stories putting forward their claims of damage from MMR – often misreported as a link between MMR and autism-in-general – significantly outnumbering those denying this (Hargreaves et al, 2002). The mobilization benefited from the fact that personalized stories of alleged vaccine damage were appealing, especially to tabloid newspapers and television. So, too, were 'David and Goliath' stories which counter-posed the struggles of Wakefield and parents against 'the establishment' (Science Media Centre, 2002), and which portrayed parents as victimized (Fitzpatrick, 2004). The tendency for news framings to represent debates as having two sides with apparently equal evidence also played into the parental mobilization's interests, appearing to amplify the weight of 'scientific' evidence in their favour (Hargreaves et al, 2002). Thus a study by the King's Fund (of health reporting by the BBC, the *Daily Mirror*, the *Daily Mail* and the *Guardian*) treats MMR as a case *par excellence* which has lent itself to the dramatic stories that give good news value, thus acquiring disproportionate and (they claim) amplified coverage of the risks involved, as compared with other risks that might have a statistically greater impact on health.[10] The parental mobilization lobby also enrolled key journalists who wrote major investigative features sympathetic to their perspectives. Major examples were a special issue of *Private Eye* by Heather Mills (Mills, 2002), and a major three-part investigation by Melanie Philips in the *Daily Mail* (11–13 March 2003).

In seeking to counter both these claims and the growing public anxiety around MMR, the opposed science-policy networks also used media strategies. The DH publicized its claims that MMR is safe through a major leaflet and television advertising campaign, while journalists wrote supportive news articles. Key strategies involved framings in terms of both science, and of risk. Thus epidemiologically framed science in academic journals was cited to support claims of MMR safety, while Wakefield was dismissed as a charismatic maverick whose work was 'bad', or 'junk' science, not to be taken seriously. Regarding risk, the government attempted through the media to counter the 'MMR scare' with the risk of disease (Fitzpatrick, 2004). The DH emphasizes that it avoided competing with tabloid newspapers by duplicating their florid language and dramatic imagery. In their own communications about the MMR issue, for instance in booklets for parents and health professionals, they were deliberately measured and factual in tone (Yarwood, pers. comm.). Yet journalists often competed for them. Thus dramatic stories about measles outbreaks appeared, presaging a breakdown of social immunity and a return to epidemics, as well as personalized stories of children damaged by complications from measles, mumps or congenital rubella. These stories in some respects paralleled the parental movement's personal stories of vaccine damage, and could be expected to have similar popular appeal.

This media coverage was not constant over time. Rather, particular events – including media events – in the political process of the MMR controversy would spark anew rounds of media 'feeding frenzy'. One such round of media frenzy erupted in 2001, sparked by controversy over whether or not the Prime Minister's son Leo Blair, who would have been due for his MMR vaccination around this time, had received it or not. Another was provoked in February

2002 by a BBC *Panorama* television broadcast on Wakefield's research and a simultaneous outbreak of measles in south London. Another took place in late 2003, provoked by the broadcast of Channel Five television's docudrama *Hear the Silence*. Yet another emerged in early 2004, coinciding with the claimed exposé of funding conflicts in Wakefield's work. During each of these episodes of heightened media attention, each side would take opportunistic advantage to advance their broader claims.

Each side also invoked 'science' in its media strategies. Yet in the translation of complex, diverse strands of scientific inquiry into media soundbites, nuances were often lost. Thus the media staging of scientific debate tended to reduce it to a battle, either between the establishment and the lone maverick or between science-as-epidemiology versus worried parents – i.e. between reason and emotion. With a few notable exceptions, little media coverage dealt in any detail with the clinical science underlying parents' claims.

In certain episodes of media coverage, the themes of consumer choice versus public policy, and of the respective rights and responsibilities of citizens and the state, came to the fore – often submerging explicit consideration of scientific dimensions of the controversy still further. This is the case, for instance, for media episodes which focused on the question of single vaccines. Thus the DH used the media to publicize and affirm its refusal to make single vaccines available. It justified this position through the claim that the triple vaccine was safe; that no scientific evidence differentiates the effects of single measles vaccine from measles in MMR; that single vaccines would leave children vulnerable to infection in the gaps between vaccines or where parents did not complete the course; that damage to population immunity would result, and that there are significant supply problems with single vaccines. The parental movement used the media to counter with the claim that the government was withholding single vaccines to 'coerce' parents into having MMR, reinterpreting supply problems as a conspiratorial ban on imports of single vaccines.[11] It also cast the government stance as going against the 'patient choice' agenda that the NHS advocates in other arenas, and as representing inappropriate interference by a 'nanny state'. Thus as Bill Welsh of Action Against Autism argued:

> *The present policy of 'MMR or nothing' is unsupportable and epitomises the arrogant attitude of 'doctor knows best'. Choice is the keynote of the government's NHS policy, so why can't we have choice with MMR?*[12]

Intriguingly, MMR-concerned mobilization has been able to gain support and media coverage from various parts of the UK political spectrum, by emphasizing variants on its messages. Thus the *Daily Mail*, a tabloid newspaper with a predominantly working class readership and right-wing reputation, has been highly prominent in supporting parents' perspectives, as has the right wing *Sunday Telegraph*. This, to some extent, reflects a casting of the MMR issue as a question of the individual against the establishment; of parental choice versus a 'nanny state'. This libertarian pro-individual framing of the movement sits in some contradiction with its alternative framing in terms of demands for public inclusion, social justice and participatory debate about technological risks and consequences; themes which have emerged more strongly in conventionally left or centre-leaning broadsheet newspapers such as the *Guardian* and the *Independent*.

Pro-MMR science-policy networks have similarly mobilized support from diverse corners of the media-politics nexus. Left-leaning media have been supportive in putting across messages in support of government vaccination policy as a public health measure, pursuing wider social benefits at the population level. As Monbiot (2003)[13] identified, others on the right have also promoted a corporate and pro-technology agenda, undermining consumer and environmental campaigns, and dismissing public anxiety, critique and demands for dialogue, for instance over GM foods, as well as over MMR (e.g. Science Media Centre, 2002; Fitzpatrick, 2004).

The question of debate and dialogue, whether it should take place and what it should be about has been a further recurring theme in the MMR controversy. Mobilizing parents frequently claim that they are seeking 'open discussion', and wish 'to be listened to'. And their discussions, whether in local groups, on national organizations' websites, or in the media, turn frequently on what they see as defensive denial of this by those opposed to their cause. They claim that their requests for meetings with senior public health officials and politicians have been shunned, and that the DH has refused to entertain proposals for an independent, off-the-record dialogue and sharing of scientific evidence. Indeed one of the reasons why many parents were so keen to pursue their claims through the legal process, in the class action against the three pharmaceutical companies manufacturing MMR vaccine that solicitors prepared through the 1990s,[14] was because they saw the court case as a vital opportunity for open, public debate, in which each side could present its evidence, and have it listened to and arbitrated in an open, neutral manner. This dimension became increasingly important as the controversy unfolded and, as parents saw it, the government's counter-campaign denied opportunities for open dialogue in any other domain. Those in pro-MMR science-policy networks tend to justify their positions on the grounds that there is nothing to debate; that parents' claims are spurious and that they have already reached scientific closure on the safety of MMR – the task is just to communicate this to the public. In this context, there have, as a senior DH official put it, been 'encounters' between each side in the controversy, but little real dialogue. Frequently taking place through the media and at public events, such encounters have tended to contribute to further polarization of positions, sharpening further the stand-off and non-closure that has come to characterize the controversy.

Conclusion

Rather than see the MMR debate as 'parental ignorance versus science', as it has been represented in much policy discourse and related commentary, attention to the perspectives of the parents involved suggests that the MMR controversy is better seen as a controversy that arose between differently framed sciences (clinical/personal versus epidemiological/population). These are grounded in different conceptual and political worlds: the world of parents, intimately concerned with their own children, their personalized immunity, and their sense of personal responsibility and need to choose for their children's health, versus the world of public health policy makers, emphasizing the societal good and political importance of mass vaccination. A feature of the controversy is the way these two – potentially highly compatible – 'worlds' came to be pitched as separate and opposed. At the same time, each side has used very similar strategies in the controversy – and this similarity has arguably helped to drive them further apart, contributing to difficulties in establishing genuine dialogue and reaching closure on the debate. In critiquing population-focused vaccination science and policy, parental campaigners were also critiquing the broader political economy of science and technology in which this is embedded. In campaigning for the right to choose vaccination pathways (whether or not to have MMR, and when; whether to have single jabs) the campaign was making a substantive connection between an evaluation of child health and technology grounded in experience and personalized immunity, and a policy context that would enable that experience to be acted upon.

Given its distinct framing, social structuring and political strategizing, the parental mobilization around MMR is, in some respects, usefully seen as a social movement in a way that the parental thinking and practices we discussed in the last chapter are not (see Leach, 2005; also discussion in Blume, 2006). As the dialogical stand off between it and the DH unfolded, it animated the vaccine anxieties among ordinary parents discussed in the last chapter. Whilst alone, the parental mobilization may not have caused these emergent anxieties, its framing evidently chimed with many parents' conceptualizations of bodily and wider political processes in terms of personalized immunity.

This chapter has, then, explored a dialogical dynamic between health services and parental framing, seeing how each is shaped in relation to the other, and not only according to its own internal logic. But this has also been a dynamic which suggests that understanding and moving towards resolution of the controversy requires both sides to become more appreciative of the partiality of their own position, and of the conceptualizations of their opponents. Horton (2004), in a major reflective review by an involved science editor, emphasizes that the MMR debate 'has reiterated the need to strip away the mystique from science, throwing open its doors to public scrutiny'. In parallel, this chapter would suggest, parental science and claims need the same degree of scrutiny, understanding and appreciation by pro-MMR scientists and policy makers.

Notes

1   A longer account drawing on this research which explores the MMR mobilization in relation to ideas of social movements and citizenship is given in Leach (2005).
2   'Suing the drug companies', *Daily Mail*, 17 October, 2000.

3   www.jabs.org.uk; www.autism-arch.org

4   The suggestion that giving measles, mumps and rubella as separate, temporally separate injections would avoid the problems claimed to be associated with the triple vaccine can be traced back to a remark by Dr Andrew Wakefield at the press conference around his 1998 paper. Despite the prominence this has assumed as a theme, it is also the case that neither his nor subsequent work have properly distinguished between the supposed effects of measles vaccine when given as part of MMR, or when given singly.

5   Melanie Philips, *Daily Mail*, 12 March, 2003.

6   Tony Blair, interview with the *New Scientist* (2 November 2006), full text available at www.number10.gov.uk/output/Page10326.asp (accessed 15 November 2006), cited in Stilgoe et al, 2006.

7   Melanie Philips, *Daily Mail*, 12 March, 2003.

8   Cited by Melanie Philips in 'The MMR controversy: An investigation. Part one', *Daily Mail*, 11 March, 2003.

9   Brian Deer, *Sunday Times*, 22 February, 2004.

10   http://news.bbc.co.uk/1/hi/health/3110490.stm, Media 'distorts risks to health', accessed October 2003.

11   'Is there a third way?' The *Independent*, 1 August, 2003.

12   Murray Ritchie, 'Bill would allow right to free single jabs for MMR', 17 December, 2003, www.theherald.co.uk/politics/6483-print.shtml, accessed December 2003.

13   George Monbiot, 'Invasion of the entryists', The *Guardian*, 9 December, 2003; see also 'Reds under the bed', www.gmwatch.org/profile1.asp?PrId=141, accessed December 2003.

14   By the early 2000s, several thousand families had signed up to be part of this, although the case itself would centre on eight test cases, including several children who had been part of Wakefield's 1997 study. The case was scheduled for October 2003, and then delayed until April 2004, and eventually dropped when legal aid funding was withdrawn on the grounds that the class action had insufficient evidence.

5

Body, Body Politic and Vaccination in West Africa

Introduction

We now turn from the UK context to West Africa, examining people's anxieties with childhood vaccination in settings in The Gambia, Guinea, Nigeria and Sierra Leone. Our focus is on the 'routine' vaccinations given to infants as part of the national immunization programmes in these countries. In the following chapter, we focus more specifically on anxieties with vaccine research.

As we begin with a brief outline of how immunization delivery is organized in these countries, it becomes clear that in several cases problems with vaccine supply and delivery have emerged amid struggling health systems in economically impoverished conditions. Yet childhood vaccination coverage depends on far more than questions of supply. We consider how many parents have come to value vaccination very highly amid the ever-present dilemmas of keeping children well. In particular, vaccinations are seen to contribute in important ways to bodily strength and fluid balance; central notions in conceptualizations of health which have resonance across much of the West African region. Yet we go on to show that as bodily understandings intersect with social and political dimensions of vaccination, anxieties sometimes arise that deter uptake. We then shift from bodily to social and political concerns. We consider the social dimensions to vaccination attendance: in relations with family and community members at home and in clinic settings, and with the nurses and vaccinators encountered there and the difficulties these present for some mothers. And we consider how anxieties around health and vaccination implicate broader relations with the state and international agencies. Again, we are attentive to common concepts that configure understandings of bodily process, social and political experience in similar ways, providing insights into the ways vaccines play into each. There have, we suggest, come to be major gulfs between these conceptualizations and the concepts and assumptions that drive vaccination technocracies in West Africa. It is the interactions between these framings, whether playing out in encounters with frontline vaccinators or in larger scale campaigns, that both perpetuate these gulfs, and that help to explain recent 'failures' of vaccine uptake and instances of mass refusal in the region.

Literatures have addressed several of these issues in various West African settings. In this chapter we draw on the few focused studies of social aspects of vaccination in West Africa, as well as wider literature on health in the region. Yet to explore the bodily, social and political worlds of vaccination and how they intersect and unfold, we focused our own fieldwork in two countries, and contrasting locations within these. Thus in Guinea, we carried out ethnographic studies in a group of rural villages and urban locations in each of two administrative divisions (prefectures),[1] Kissidougou and Dinguiraye.[2] This involved informal conversations and observations in households, compounds, fields, markets and clinics, as well as narrative interviews – child health and vaccination biographies – with 1550 mothers (see Millimouno et al, 2006, for full methodological details). In The Gambia, we carried out a focused ethnographic study in the settlement of Sukuta in the rapidly expanding peri-urban fringe of the capital Banjul in Western Division, and in the rural village of Marikunda[3] in Upper River Division. In both sites, our main focus was on speakers of Mandinka, one of five main languages in the country. We explored the wider relevance of issues emerging through observation, conversations and narrative interviews in these sites through a questionnaire survey, in which a team of local researchers interviewed a random sample of 1600 mothers, 800 in each focal Division (see Cassell et al, 2006a).[4] We also supported other researchers focusing on these issues in Sierra Leone (Kamara, 2005) and Nigeria (Jegede, 2005; Yahya, 2005, 2007), and we draw on their work here. Thus this chapter tacks between detailed ethnographic examples derived from site-specific fieldwork, and discussions of what we discern to be more widespread regional framings. This enables us to consider both some generalized framings of health and political issues across the region, and also how they play out amid specific health delivery and social settings.

Delivering vaccination in West Africa

In West Africa, vaccination provision is largely the responsibility of state agencies. Building on the legacy of mass vaccination programmes carried out in the colonial period, from the 1960s and 1970s government Ministries of Health began to build routine childhood vaccination programmes into their work. And with acclaimed success in reducing childhood diseases such as measles, mass childhood immunization became integral to the work of state public health regimes.

National programmes have from the outset interacted with a variety of forms of support and intervention from the international community. Thus routine childhood immunization programmes generally aim to deliver the standard schedule recommended by the World Health Organization's Expanded Programme on Immunization (EPI): BCG (ideally at or soon after birth); combined diphtheria, tetanus and pertussis (DTP) with oral polio (three doses, ideally at 2, 3 and 4

Figure 5.1 *A group discussion among mothers during field research in rural Gambia*

months), and measles (ideally at 9 months), with boosters of DTP and polio ideally given at 18 months and five years. Many governments have, over the years, received funding and logistical support through UNICEF and WHO for procuring vaccines, and maintaining the cold chain and other infrastructure to deliver them. Currently, many governments are negotiating for support from other international agencies, such as the Gates Foundation's Global Alliance on Vaccines and Immunization (GAVI). This offers support in bringing new vaccines such as for Hepatitis B – whose costs would be prohibitive to governments alone – into existing schedules, and following arguments that this would be unsustainable without broader support to delivery infrastructure, support to those existing schedules (Brugha et al, 2002; Heaton and Keith, 2002). In some settings, a variety of donor agencies and international NGOs also support immunization programmes, whether through broad sector-wide support to healthcare systems and their financing, or by placing health agents in community settings to assist with vaccination delivery and information, often alongside other aspects of health care. The technocracy that has built around childhood vaccination in West Africa is, then, a thoroughly internationalized one, although as we explore below, parents do not always experience it this way.

Today, these conditions involve at least two further trends. A first is the renewed international attention to running top-down immunization campaigns, as the prospect of the eradication of diseases of global importance looms. Thus alongside such routine vaccination provision, international organizations support campaigns for polio, through the Global Polio Eradication Initiative of the WHO. Campaigns have also been run for measles and in the case of outbreaks, for meningitis and yellow fever. Such global campaigns are generally manifested in-country in the form of National Immunization Days (NIDs). These involve massive publicity and mobilization exercises in which international agency staff work alongside national and local health workers taken out of their normal duties, and, often, a further mass of local volunteers recruited to go door-to-door to vaccinate children. There is often enormous political support for such campaigns that are high-profile exercises separate from routine state activity.

A second important trend is the breakdown of conventional distinctions between state and 'traditional' medicine as an array of private, informal and hybrid providers (e.g. state employees dispensing privately) multiply, making available both biomedical and naturalistic treatments and services (Bloom and Standing, 2001). Such trends have most direct effect on the use of curative services. Even where people seek treatment from many different providers, the public sector remains the key provider of preventative services such as immunization (e.g. Institute for Health Sector Development (IHSD), 2004), and there is little evidence of vaccines being sold by private providers or of their leakage into the commercial sector for resale. However, there are important indirect effects of pluralization in other aspects of health-seeking and delivery on vaccination, for instance as alternative services draw parents away from the state-run clinics that provide vaccination services.

The four countries we consider in this chapter exemplify different variants on these generalities. In each, a slightly different set of practices for organizing vaccination delivery – and its associated challenges – prevails. The Gambia is internationally recognized for relatively high rates of vaccination coverage in the African context. The country's small size and strong state investment in primary healthcare infrastructure over several decades, as well as the support of international agencies including the UK's MRC, contribute to this. Although there are debates at the national level about how sustainable this situation is, given broader national budgetary problems and fluctuations in donor support, with the exception of a few particularly isolated areas, vaccination delivery problems are relatively rare. A system of Infant Welfare Clinics (IWC) at health centres (usually weekly, sometimes twice weekly in busy urban areas) and by mobile teams at health outreach posts (usually monthly) ensures that vaccination is generally available to all. Immunization is integrated with other aspects of mother and child health (weighing infants, giving health advice, antenatal care) on these infant IWC days, which tend to be held on the same day each week or month. Women commonly attend en masse, so that the event takes on something of the character of a group outing – with crowds of best-dressed women and their infants, and often long queues.

In some respects, Guinea faces greater challenges in getting vaccines to its populations. Size and general economic decline play a role, but so too do particular dynamics in the financing of health services at the local level. Vaccination is supposed to be integrated with routine mother and child health care (curative as well as preventative) through the country's Programme Elargie de Vaccination integré aux Soins de Santé Primaires et Médicaments Essentiels (PEV/SSP/ ME), which operates through a system of health centres and outreach posts. Given policies of financial self-sufficiency (Camara, nd), vaccines themselves are officially supplied free of charge to health centres but since the mid 1990s they have been expected to finance other aspects of delivery (cold chain maintenance, transport, and so on) for themselves. In particular, it is expected that user charges for curative services will be used to finance (free-to-consumer) preventative services. Several linked problems have emerged. Nationally fixed user fees for curative services have failed to keep up with inflation and escalating costs, so that health centres have had difficulty in raising money from this to support vaccination delivery (fuel, refrigeration, vehicles). Local personnel often 'informally' charge for vaccination services. Health centre revenues have also declined as local populations, discouraged by the lack of drugs and drawn to the growing range of private pharmacies and itinerant drugs traders, have eschewed health centres for treatment. These trends have combined to undermine the capacity of health centres to maintain their vaccination programmes.

Guinea's immunization delivery relies on several different organizational strategies. The main form is the 'fixed strategy', where infants are brought to the health centre in accordance with an appointment scheduled at the previous visit or when the child is first registered. Individual mothers thus attend according to their particular appointment, rather than as part of a group visit day. Second is the 'mobile strategy', where a mobile vaccination team delivers immunizations at a grouping point, usually a large village, to which children from surrounding areas are brought, according to a calendar pre-established between the health workers and local administrative authorities. Third is the 'missed opportunity' strategy, in which curative consultations are used as an opportunity to check and if necessary rectify a child's vaccination status. Health agents are also supposed to consult health centre records and actively seek out at home those children who have missed vaccinations, or who live in isolated communities. Mobile, missed opportunity and seeking-out strategies, in particular, have all been severely challenged by health centres' financial and administrative difficulties. Finally, on National Immunization Days (usually two per year), vaccination agents – both government health staff and specially recruited assistants in this more vertical component of the programme – move from house to house to deliver oral polio vaccine and Vitamin A supplements.

In Nigeria, routine immunization coverage is, according to official statistics, the lowest in the region and said to be declining. National coverage rates for full childhood immunization have been on the decline since the 1980s with current rates as low as 13 per cent. A dramatic resurgence of measles occurred in 2004, while crises in the uptake of oral polio vaccines in the northern part of the country during 2003–2004 were linked to a resurgence of polio in what was one of the few remaining countries in the world where the disease was endemic (see Yahya, 2005, 2007). Nigeria faces many challenges of vaccine supply and delivery. Problems of finance, vaccine procurement, cold chain maintenance, staffing and management in the National Programme on Immunization (NPI) and its local implementation are linked to what is argued to be a wider collapse in Nigeria's primary healthcare system (FBA, 2005). Moreover, since 1988, NIDs and sub-NIDs focused on the eradication of polio have become a centre of attention for the NPI. The enormous human and financial resources consumed by the polio eradication initiative have taken their toll on the already limited capacity of the NPI and wider primary healthcare system (FBA, 2005).

Vaccine supply and delivery problems appear greatest in isolated rural areas and in the country's northern states. Here, people must often travel great distances to reach the nearest vaccination posts for routine immunization services (Dunn, 2005). Some central and southern regions appear not to experience the same degree of supply and infrastructure problems reported for some other parts of Nigeria (Jegede, 2005), but especially in rural areas, low attendance often leads to inefficiencies (e.g. wastage of opened vaccine vials). Immunization is generally organized through designated routine immunization days either at primary health centres, or at mobile immunization assembly points. In the few areas where attendance is high – more often in urban and peri-urban settings it sometimes becomes a group social event, associated with singing, dancing and social networking. But in other areas 'only a trickle' of mothers attend on these days (Jegede, 2005). This low attendance contrasts with the mass mobilization often achieved for national immunization campaigns, although in some cases – as in the OPV controversy in 2003–2004 – these have met with equally widespread mass refusal.

The fourth country we consider in this chapter, Sierra Leone, has had a programme of routine infant immunization since 1982, implemented through community health workers (mother and child health aides) operating through a network of primary health centres and outreach clinics. With the launch of the EPI in 1986 and major reorganizations and inputs of donor funds, by 1991 Sierra Leone had attained over 75 per cent coverage of children aged 12–23 months with the full set of WHO-recommended antigens. However between 1991 and 2002, civil war in the country caused massive destruction of health facilities and services. Over 75 per cent of rural health centres were destroyed, and virtually all health staff were displaced or became refugees. Routine health services including immunization came to an almost total standstill. Notably however, national immunization days – primarily for polio, in the context of the global polio eradication initiative – continued. Through the mediation efforts of UNICEF, the various fighting factions sometimes allowed government-employed personnel to extend such vaccination campaigns behind rebel lines (Kamara, 2005).

Sierra Leone's current major challenge, then, is the rebuilding of its war-torn routine immunization infrastructure and system, in the context of the rehabilitation of the health sector more broadly. This has been assisted by government commitments and a wide assortment of foreign donors, local and international NGOs. The result has been a massive renewal of facilities. Solar refrigerators have replaced the kerosene ones that were deployed before the war. Staff members have received new rounds of training and supervision has been strengthened, resulting in a more efficient cold chain. In this renewed supply context immunization coverage increased to 52 per cent by 2004, and the upward trend continues (Kamara, 2005). Nevertheless, challenges continue in reaching more isolated areas given the poor roads and transport facilities. Immunization sessions, conducted on designated mother-and-child health clinic days in primary health centres and outreach posts, do not cover all villages. Vaccines are not always available during the sessions. Informal charging for formally free vaccination services is common, levied by primary health staff to meet the costs of transporting drugs and vaccines, conducting outreach clinics, and paying fees to 'volunteer' assistants.

These four countries are by no means fully representative of vaccination delivery systems and their challenges in contemporary Africa. Nevertheless, they exemplify a range of variations on some common themes. In particular, the challenges of maintaining vaccine supply and delivery systems in economically constrained health systems; the intersection of routine immunization with strongly contrasting campaign-style delivery on national immunization days, and the spectrum of delivery styles – from 'group' clinic days with varying levels of attendance and crowds (in The Gambia, Nigeria and Sierra Leone) to individual appointment systems (in Guinea) all, as we shall see, have an important bearing on how parents experience and engage with vaccination. We begin our exploration of parents' experiences by considering their bodily dimensions.

Bodily dimensions of child health and vaccination

There are many different ways in which people understand and seek to protect their children's health in West African settings. In this section, we will focus on our studies in The Gambia to draw out and illustrate some core themes in the ways people conceptualize child health. These, as we show, are important to seeing how people understand vaccination. While this material is from particular Gambian settings, however, it is illustrative of a set of linked themes in parental concern that are echoed both in the other countries and in literature across the region, albeit with various specific manifestations.

Health and strength, fluids and flow

A first theme is the importance of building strength in an infant, in relation to the multiplicity of uncertainties that he or she will face. As many of our conversations with Gambian parents suggested, there is a sense in which parents consider giving birth to and raising an infant as being fraught with hazards. Some of these are physical, related, in people's understanding, to the effects of rain, wind and soils in the landscapes in which they live, and the 'disease seeds' (*kuran keso* in Mandinka, a local conceptualization of bacteria/viruses) that these can bring. Some are related to the will of God, or Allah. Some derive from the rather capricious actions of the djinn spirits with which humans share their landscape. And others relate to imbalances in prevailing socio-ecological and spiritual orders which can result if people break important moral and behavioural codes; issues also of significance elsewhere in the region (e.g. Fairhead and Leach, 1996; Gottlieb, 2001).

As people in the Gambian village of Marikunda describe, these hazards begin at the foetal stage. For example, they consider that a foetus's growth and development can be damaged not only if a pregnant mother falls ill, but also by djinn spirits, making it inadvisable for her to go out in early afternoon or at dusk, when these are thought to roam freely in the winds. Sexual intercourse with the father can be beneficial, however, at least before 7 months when a woman becomes too tired and heavy, as this is thought to help eventual delivery and gives the baby strength. Some elderly women emphasized that 'men's fluid' (semen) adds substance to the foetus. Similar ideas are echoed in Guinea, where mothers describe how during a woman's pregnancy, her female relatives and friends will advise her on correct conduct and on the proper practices to observe at each stage: how to tie her clothing, types of work to avoid, and so on, to avoid damaging the foetus. It is said, for example, that wearing a skirt or pagne across the stomach can provoke abortion or a difficult labour, while washing oneself at night risks turning the baby into a djinn spirit.

People often consider the period immediately after birth as one of particular vulnerability. Thus many parents in The Gambia tie a piece of cloth around a newborn's wrist as a sign that it is part of the human world; otherwise a djinn spirit might come and tie its own cloth, to claim it as one of its own. People consider that neonatal deaths, and repeated neonatal deaths, can simply be the will of Allah, or they can be due to a djinn spirit or in Islamic perspective, a 'devil' in you that 'does not like children'. Our conversations and narrative interviews in The Gambia revealed that the wide variety of illnesses, with different causes, that can afflict a baby as he or she grows and develops are variously attributed to physical happenings, the agency of djinn spirits or 'bad people', events which disrupt socio-ecological orders, or to Allah. Several mothers described how the state of being ill (*kuranta*) can be both hastened by, and further encourage, weakness (*sembo doya*).

Gambian parents therefore orientate many practices towards ensuring that an infant has the strength or power (*sembo* in Mandinka) or bodily protection (*balakanta rango*) to withstand such hazards. It seemed from our narrative interviews that parents understand each child as having a particular history and health status, shaped by a particular interaction of hazards and circumstances. Some of these particularities relate to the social, economic and geographical circumstances of a child's upbringing: housing, a mother's work, and a family's ability to afford certain kinds of food or clothing, for instance. Other particularities relate to events that may have befallen a mother, child or wider family: an attack by djinn spirits; breaking of a moral code, or a family health trait, which manifests itself in a particular child's health. As we shall see, such a particular history often influences how parents think about vaccination for that particular child. That so many of these factors are either inherently uncertain or outside human control underlines the importance, in people's strategies for child health, of building strength – resilience – against hazards.

A second theme concerning health and strength are relationships drawn between strength, growth, breastfeeding and sexual intercourse. Thus in The Gambia, people speak of how with the nourishment of breastmilk, a baby grows and accretes strength through a series of stages: from a scrunched up newborn to a baby that can stretch out; through a punctual moment of 'putting on flesh' (*balo subuduno*) at 2–3 months which 'opens up' the body to receive and benefit from more milk, to a phase of subsequent steady, gradual growth. Several older women explained that a baby will often be restless and feverish at this time, and a first-time mother might be worried, but if she consults an elder, they will reassure her that 'oh, it is just more flesh coming'. The later stage when a baby can hold its back and head up ('neck straight', *kantilindo*) signifies the stage at which it can be carried on its mother's back, and also the moment when a woman might be considered available again for sexual activity (see also Bledsoe, 2002). This is a negotiated length of time, because while husbands might press for it earlier, women are strongly concerned about possible damage to their baby's health by resuming sex too early. This is because of the widespread belief that if a mother has sexual intercourse while breastfeeding, the man's sperm enters the milk and can lead to the child having diarrhoea and being malnourished. The baby will lose strength. Some – from a Koranic perspective – insist on abstinence for a minimum of forty days after birth. Whatever the precise reasoning, as an elderly woman in Marikunda put it: Generally, 'a baby of a good weight is an indication that one has abstained' (Interview, elderly woman, Marikunda, 5 May 2003).

Conceptualized links between strength, breastfeeding and sexual intercourse are also manifested in what, in Mandinka, is referred to as *timparo*. People describe how if a mother falls pregnant again while her baby is still breastfeeding, the state of *timparo* is likely to result, causing the breastfeeding child to become sick, weak and thin, sometimes with vomiting and diarrhoea. Some interpret this as simply due to the double load of a mother attempting to nourish two children at once. Others, however, attribute it to fluids from the developing foetus, including residual semen, entering the breastmilk. Avoiding *timparo* is another reason for avoiding sexual intercourse during breastfeeding, and one of the reasons why women are so interested in birth spacing (and some use contraceptives to this end – see Bledsoe, 2002). Within these conceptual understandings, how strong and plump, or how weak and sickly, a baby is become very much linked with moral and social issues concerning the timing and appropriateness of sexual activity, in ways which, as we shall see, can have important bearings on mothers' social experiences of vaccination clinics.

A third theme concerns the importance of blood to health and strength. This turns on the importance of maintaining the quantity, quality and proper circulatory flow of blood, and its separation from other body fluids. These conceptualizations are by no means unique to this area. Indeed, blood calculus is important in understanding strength and health throughout much of the West African region and in the Islamic world more broadly (e.g. Cros, 1990; Fairhead and Leach, 1996; Fortier, 2001). Gambian villagers insist that maintaining health, for an infant as for an adult, requires in particular the quantity and flow of two sorts of fluid to be maintained in the body: blood (*yelo*) and 'white blood'. Each has its distinct circulatory system in vessels (*faso*) and illnesses are caused by a crossover of these, and by blockages to them. White blood links the brain, spinal cord, kidneys, male and female reproductive fluids and breastmilk, underlying the interactions and health effects described above. As for (red) blood, people talk of its quality – of 'good' or 'strong' blood – as important to health; something that certain foods and medicines can help. Flow is important: people consider that if blood flow is blocked, indicated perhaps by bruising and swelling, the body becomes very hot and sickly. And quantity is important: if blood levels diminish (*yelo doya*), people consider the body to lose strength and become weak, with headaches and dizziness. This is both life-threatening in itself, and renders the body more vulnerable to other problems such as disease.

Understandings of vaccination

These ideas about the quantity, quality and flow of blood and other bodily fluids are important to people's understandings of how vaccinations work. We found that in all the study countries, people generally do not differentiate between vaccinations and other injections, using the same term for both. People often value injections because they are seen to be strong, and to go straight into the blood. Thus for example parents in The Gambia spoke of vaccinations/injections – both *penko* in Mandinka – in positive terms as being a powerful *poisono* – using the term for 'poison' to connote a strong substance – which goes directly into the blood. Once inside, as people expressed to us in The Gambia, the injection substance/vaccine is understood to act on the blood in various, somewhat related ways.

First, people describe vaccines as 'chasing out' illness. As one Gambian mother put it: 'it ensures that all the illness that is, or may be, inside a baby's body disappears.' And as another described: 'I think the children may look healthy

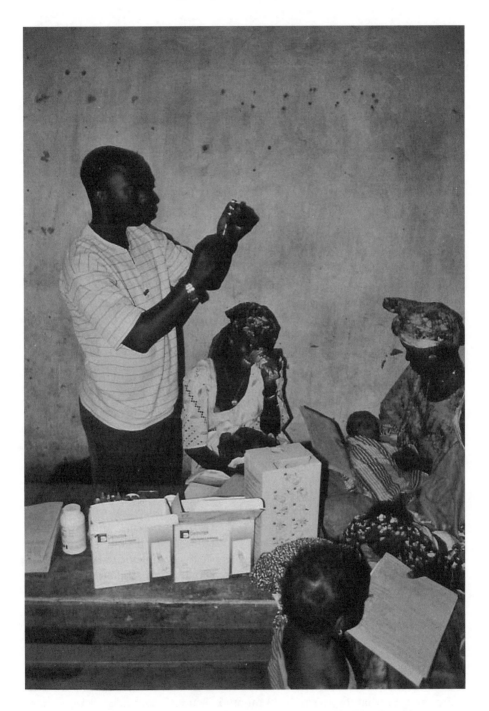

Figure 5.2 *Vaccination during a mobile infant welfare clinic, The Gambia*

while they are having problems; that's why injections are given to them, to treat those sicknesses'. In a similar way, a mother in Kissidougou, Guinea described vaccinations as 'cleaning the blood'. Second, people appear to have a notion that the vaccine itself, within the blood or body, provides a physical barrier to illness substances; a kind of internal wall. This is suggested, for instance, by several Gambian mothers' descriptions:

> *The injection 'medicine' scatters in the child's body and protects the child from illnesses.*

> *It serves as a wall or a mechanism for defence against diseases that might have attacked them.*

A group of Sierra Leonean mothers, in similar terms, expressed how 'Immunization is like a fence around the farm to prevent animals from entering and eating the crops'.

Third, many mothers claim that vaccines have attenuating effects should a disease manifest itself in the body. This is the case in The Gambia. Mothers in a group discussion in Beindou, Guinea similarly recounted how:

> *Vaccination makes a curative fight in the sense that it stops or reduces the illnesses found in the body ... without vaccination one becomes vulnerable to all the bad symptoms.*

This notion of attenuation, coupled with the use of a single term for vaccination/ injection, suggests that the biomedical distinction between vaccinations as preventative and other medicines as curative may not reflect people's experiences and conceptual worlds. As Samuelsen notes similarly in Burkina Faso, villagers (and in this case a local healer practising a scarification technique) use the term 'vaccination' for both preventive and curative incisions, in contrast with healthcare personnel who distinguish clearly between injections as vaccine and injections for treatments (Samuelsen, 2001, p170). In parents' understandings, therefore, injections of all kinds, covering both those given routinely to infants or taken when a problem strikes, can be seen as playing complementary and unified roles, helping to strengthen the body to cope with or stave off illness.

Fourth, some people describe vaccinations as actually building the child's bodily substance and strength – in ways that allude to perceived connections between blood, plumpness and strength as discussed above. Thus, as one Gambian mother put it: 'The injection strengthens the health of the child. It gives the child good body. It also protects her.' And another: 'They also "nourish" the child. I believe the injections have something in them that helps children grow well.' This provides one interpretation of why Gambian women attach particular importance to what they term the '3 month injections' (*karo saba penko*) – those which in health professionals' terms are given at 2, 3 and 4 months for DTP. These are given at what Gambians understand as *bala subunduno* – the period when a baby most rapidly 'puts on body' – and the injections complement and boost this phase of growth. Such reasoning also interplays with people's experiences of vaccination delivery and its technological and organizational practices. In many infant welfare clinics in the Gambia, it is standard practice for the routine of weighing to precede vaccination; mothers are expected to join first one queue, and then the other should vaccinations be due. Some mothers have come to interpret weighing as a screening procedure to evaluate an infant's strength, and hence the need for injections that day. As one mother put it, for example: 'The child is weighed and the nurses will know if he has power or not. Then he is injected if seen to be weak.'

Such understandings among West African parents of the positive roles of vaccination in bodily processes thus rest on the notion of the vaccine as a substance that, going into the blood, either builds its strength or builds in the blood defences against disease. These notions do not conform to those of contemporary biomedicine, with its grounding in notions of an immune system. What is clear, though, is that such ideas about the impact of vaccination as a substance on blood/fluid quality and quantity have been sufficient to ground great appreciation of vaccination – anxiety for it – among parents throughout the West African region, whether in The Gambia or in Guinea (Millimouno et al, 2006), Sierra Leone (Kamara, 2005) or Nigeria (Jegede, 2005). In many areas parents actively value and seek vaccination for reasons that are framed in these strength-fluid-substance terms.

Given this, it is not surprising to find that the relation between specific vaccines and specific diseases, so central to biomedical framings of vaccination and the scheduling of vaccination programmes, is not part of the reasoning of many West African parents. For example in our Gambian survey (see Cassell et al, 2006a), of the two-thirds of mothers who listed 'protect against disease' among the things they thought immunizations could do, some categorized the type of disease as either 'small illnesses' or as 'those transferred from one person to another'. Only a very few mentioned specific diseases, or made statements such as: 'I think every disease has its own injection.' When asked to list the names of diseases that they thought vaccinations could protect against, 29 per cent of urban and 48 per cent of rural mothers reported no diseases that were 'correct' according to the formal immunization schedule. Many of those reporting 'correct' diseases also mentioned others, such as malaria, diarrhoea, fever, stomach problems, rashes, common cold and eye problems. Notably, mothers tended to identify illnesses by symptom rather than disease name, so that apparently 'incorrect' diseases could in fact be a 'correct' symptom of a 'correct' disease. However, the naming of many symptoms also corresponds with many mothers' belief that vaccination protects generally against the multiple 'small illnesses' that afflict children. Perhaps most tellingly, mothers with more formal education named more diseases, but also more 'incorrect' ones. It is certainly the case that throughout the region, government and NGO health education programmes emphasize the links between particular vaccines and particular diseases, and it may be the case that women with more formal education are better able to assimilate these. But this evidence from The Gambia suggests that the result may be greater ability to list disease names, in ways which leave conceptualizations of the roles of vaccination little touched.

This set of West African notions that injections given in infancy strengthen a child in a general sense (rather than preventing particular illnesses) does not square with the views of healthcare personnel and most scientists. Notably, however, it does correspond with certain strands of scientific debate that emphasize the non-specific effects of childhood vaccines, and the limits to specific effects (Aaby, 1995; Aaby et al, 2001).

Nevertheless, our studies also revealed instances in which people understand certain categories of illness as unable to be addressed by vaccinations or injections, or which are even incompatible with them. This can relate to the aetiology, or causative pathways, for particular diseases. Thus for many Hausa people in northern Nigeria polio is caused by a spirit, Shan-inna, who consumes the limbs of human beings. 'Traditional' healers often promote this view, going to elaborate means to prevent and treat the affliction through procedures that begin by attempting to appease the spirit (Yahya, 2005). Given this, polio is not thought to be amenable to vaccination. Yahya (2005) relates how this bodily understanding was a significant factor in the rejection of oral polio vaccine in northern Nigeria in 2003–2004, since if, in local understandings, the vaccines could not cure polio, it was logical to suspect them of having other bodily effects. As one northern resident expressed this:

> *We have to be very careful when the White man comes with medicine and claims to cure a disease like polio. It is easy for us to believe that these vaccines are in fact meant to cause infertility because from my experience, you cannot cure polio with drops in a baby's mouth. It is all pretence to cover up what they are really trying to do (Man, Kaduna, July 2005).*

There are also ailments for which injections are considered dangerous, as these two examples from mothers' narratives in Guinea indicate:

> *At her sitting stage, my daughter suffered from an illness called basibaa or yikoro-fen [a sort of chronic anaemia]. This same illness had also much affected my two previous children. To treat the girl, we always gave her the leaves koyabere, yamun and kurumbu fira, because the elders have told me that it is an illness which must not be treated by injection. And that is the reason why I avoided taking her to hospital (Mother, urban Dinguiraye, 2004).*

> *At his sitting stage, Robert had a swollen shoulder and left hand. We took him to the health centre. They prescribed some medicines which we bought but despite taking these there was no improvement. The doctor had prescribed quite a lot of antibiotics and certain injections whose names I forget. As there was no improvement, I consulted a healer who saw the state of the child, and told me that this is a problem that one cannot treat at the hospital, only with naturalistic medicines. This illness is called linda in Kissi. He treated it with leaves that I prepared and washed him with black soap (Mother, rural Kissidougou, 2004).*

In these examples, the ailments which are deemed to be incompatible with injections concern qualities and quantities of fluid and blood in the body. The same is true of a further condition termed *fonyo*, characterized by swelling and linked to imbalance and blockage of fluid in the body. People in Guinea are clear that this should not be treated by injection or the patient will die. This phenomenon appears to be common also in The Gambia, and within the wider region (e.g. Bierlich, 2000). However, whereas Bierlich attributes this problematic effect of injections to the inappropriate use of a 'white people's' medicine to treat an 'African' disease, a linked interpretation is possible. That is, by adding fluid directly to the blood, injections can aggravate medical problems themselves linked to blood blockage and quality.

Vaccinations thus exemplify a biomedical therapy which West African parents interpret in terms of building infants' strength. Yet it finds its place amid a range of further practices to enhance infant strength that are less biomedical from the outset, and which in their use similarly cut across any divide between 'biomedical' and 'traditional' practice, and indeed any divide between 'medicine' and everyday care. Practices to give strength and protection range from the use of amulets such as small leather pouches containing Arabic script, belts and anklets, horns, seeds or cowrie shells, to incantations and herbal washes, to particular clothing, foods and forms of cleanliness. The ways in which parents often integrate these diverse forms of protection with vaccination are illustrated in the following narratives from Guinea:

> *He received his first vaccination the day after his birth. To protect him against wind and illness, his father bought him clothes as a means of protection, and we tied a string to his right hand to stop him getting thin, because he was very fat. When a child is born we tie this string, made with Koranic writing, because when certain people praise the baby, he can start to have health problems (Mother, Kissidougou, 2004).*

> *The child's father bought many syrup medicines. There are also leaves with which my mother washes him. We also tied a cord around his kidneys against the effects of undesirable weaning, caused by someone who would have had sex and who would come and take the child without proper cleansing (Mother, Dinguiraye, 2004).*

As in these Guinean examples, then, a logic of child strength-building and protection unites what might otherwise be seen as very diverse practices and technologies. It also underlies the strong, and overt, complementarities that people often draw between these other practices and vaccination; complementarities that recur, in slightly different manifestations, across the region. Thus Imperato and Traore (1969) found that Bambara parents in Mali in the 1960s saw immunizations as 'like amulets', offering generalized protection which, in this case, was thought to require periodic renewal. Mende mothers in Sierra Leone in 2005 described charms in the form of horns, cowries and Islamic pouches (*lassimoi*) as working with vaccination to give 'double protection' (Kamara, 2005). Many Mandinka parents in The Gambia describe amulets (*safe*) as for 'protection' (*balakanta rango*), saying that amulets and injections 'both go together' in this respect. For some, this complementarity is direct: for example 'It is for protection just like the injections given to children at the clinics'; 'The amulet the child has on is meant to protect the child against transmittable diseases like measles and yellow fever.' Others consider that amulets protect a child against other threats for which vaccination is not effective, such as certain local categories of disease, 'witchcraft' or the harmful 'bad medicine' of others. Moreover, Gambian parents emphasize that life is uncertain; you don't know what will happen or bring a problem to your child, and both these forms offer generalized protection. Those who claim not to 'believe' in amulets frequently put them on anyway, perhaps due to kin or peer pressure, a husband's pressure, or simply 'just in case'. In our survey (see Cassell et al, 2006a), 57 per cent of urban and 51 per cent of rural children were wearing an amulet. Of those without, some mothers explained that they simply had not bothered, but a few rejected amulets as counter to their religious beliefs or modern outlook, saying, for example, 'We do not like amulets; we believe in Allah, and scientific knowledge.'

It is certainly the case that health professionals shun the use of amulets as a remnant of outdated tradition, at odds with the use of 'modern' forms of health care such as vaccination. But that some Gambians have assimilated this and reject amulets on the grounds of their incompatibility with modern biomedicine-seeking does not mean that they view vaccination in modern biomedical terms. Many of these same parents expressed views about vaccination that saw it as building generalized strength.

Interpreting adverse effects of vaccination

People's understandings of how vaccines work also underlie particular views of the adverse effects, or reactions, that they can sometimes bring. A number of public health oriented studies in Africa have suggested that parents' fears of common effects such as fever, swelling and – especially – abcesses, which have been all too frequent, are important factors that discourage parents from having their children vaccinated (e.g. Cutts et al, 1990; Statview, 1999).

The parents in our Gambia, Guinea, Sierra Leone and Nigeria studies were all well aware of effects such as fever and swelling. Many find vaccination-related fevers tiresome to cope with, especially in babies who must be walked long distances in the sun after vaccination because the clinic is far from home. However, most consider such effects as a valued indication that the vaccination is strong and effective. As one urban Gambian mother put it:

> *My babies experienced swollen arms, which I would massage with shea butter and mentholatum, and fever, for which I would use paracetamol or leaves. At times I was tempted to stay away on clinic day for fear of high fever or swollen injection site, but my husband would say that it is the strength of the injection (Mother, Sukuta, March 2003).*

Figure 5.3 *Twins in rural Gambia wearing their protective amulets*

Several people expressed views that the power and strength of the injection substance, and the severity of the reaction, are related. Thus for instance one man, noting more severe reactions in his sixth child compared with his first and second, concluded that 'modern injections are stronger'.

Even abcesses can be interpreted as signs of the effectiveness of the vaccines in the body. Commonly, Guinean mothers, for instance, theorize that an abscess is the physical manifestation of an illness that might have been 'hidden' – not showing any symptoms – being expelled from of a child's body by a vaccine. As one explained: 'Once the abscess bursts and the wound heals, it is finished; the baby once more enjoys good health.'

Nevertheless, there are cases where mothers perceive their infants as having unusually severe adverse effects. They frequently relate this to the particular constitution of the child. The particular pathway through uncertainties that certain infants find themselves taking can render them particularly vulnerable to adverse effects. It is such particular children that may not be taken back for subsequent vaccinations after an earlier bad experience.

In a context where they often miss clinic sessions, women frequently worry greatly that a backlog of vaccinations will have 'stacked up' and that they will have to have several at once. Too many injections at one time is seen as highly problematic. As one mother in peri-urban Gambia put it:

> *Vaccinations are good but not when they are accumulated and given at a go. It makes the child sick. I have seen my co-wife's child get ill because she defaulted and when she took the child, three injections were given on the spot (Mother, Sukuta, April 2003).*

The concern in such cases seems to turn on the idea of 'too much substance' for the blood and body to cope with (rather than any notion of 'immune system overload', as is relevant in the British context that we considered in Chapter 3).

Finally, in certain instances in West Africa people have expressed worries about the effects of vaccination on fertility. This was, for example, the case in the controversy around polio vaccine in northern Nigeria in 2003–2004, when many claimed that the vaccines had been contaminated with anti-fertility agents (Yahya, 2005). It has also been the case in several instances of mass refusal of tetanus toxoid vaccines, especially when delivered in campaigns targeting young girls around puberty. For example in parts of The Gambia in 2001 (Bailey, pers. comm.), and in Cameroon in 1990 (Feldman-Savelsberg et al, 2000), public health workers were accused of delivering 'sterilizing vaccines' in these campaigns. Bodily dimensions to these negative anxieties refer to the importance, across the region, of the quality and balance of fluids in the body to fertility and reproductive potential (e.g. Bledsoe, 1984; Fortier, 2001; Ferme, 2002). Vaccines enter these bodily fluids, and in the case of tetanus toxoid campaigns, at a vulnerable and important time in girls' reproductive careers – a time when cultural values and the initiation rituals and masquerades that express them frequently elaborate the idealization of plumpness and humidity in transitions to fertile womanhood (e.g. Boone, 1986).

Social dimensions of vaccination engag

Vaccine anxieties in the West African context – whether in p
desires for it, or more negative worries about it – are, then, bodily matters. They
are, however, far more than that, as people's reflections on and practices around
vaccination become part of social processes. Relationships between mothers,
within households, within residential compounds and neighbourhoods, and within
communities both shape, and are shaped by, people's practices of attendance (or
not) at the infant welfare clinics and outposts where routine vaccination takes
place, and the experiences they have there.

Different forms of vaccination delivery provide for different sorts of social
experience. In particular, the experience of attending in a group on a designated clinic day or when a mobile vaccination team visits – as is common in
The Gambia, Guinea's mobile clinics, Sierra Leone and Nigeria (albeit often
diminished here by low attendance) – suggests very different social processes
from the individualized appointments and attendance in Guinean towns. In
this section, we begin by exploring these social dimensions in contexts of group
attendance, whether at group clinic days, national immunization days or mobile
visits, focusing particularly on material from The Gambia and from mobile team
visits in Guinea. We then go on to consider gender and generational dimensions
of vaccination practice. Finally we consider people's social experiences of
interaction with 'frontline' staff – nurses and public health workers.

Vaccination attendance as a group experience

As Gambian examples illustrate clearly, attending the infant welfare clinic on its
designated day, or turning up when the mobile vaccination team visit, is often
not just a parental decision. It is also a matter of community orchestration. Thus,
for example, in the village of Marikunda, the night before the mobile team's
scheduled visit, the village health worker rallied the women's organization. This
was one of its several peer-group organizations or *kafou*; a feature of Gambian
sociality that unites people of a particular age-set or interest group to carry out
particular social or economic activities. This particular group, dominated by
women of reproductive age, gathered a crowd that night as it danced, sang and
drummed from compound to compound, accompanied by the village's specialist
musicians, to inform and exhort other mothers to attend the clinic session. The
following morning the group was active again, and once the mobile team had
started work, periodically struck up its songs and dances to encourage women
to wait out the long queue and to accompany the health worker's educational
messages.

Similar forms of community orchestration of vaccination attendance are
common in many West African settings. Thus in The Gambia's new urban
settlements, women often form neighbourhood groups that agree to attend
together on a particular day. In Guinea, whether in urban or rural settings, a
young woman's female entourage of compound relatives and neighbours will
sometimes follow her to vaccination clinics, often in a significant crowd. Local

authorities also help to mobilize women for infant vaccination, both for vaccinators' visits under the mobile strategy and for NIDs. Once informed by the health administration, village and town quarter authorities work through local town criers to inform and encourage parents to attend. Whether the encouragement is from formally or informally organized groups of other women or from local leaders, such orchestration helps to construct a certain sort of community – in the village, or neighbourhood – linked to moral pressure to attend for vaccination. To be a mother in that community, attending is what one does. And in turn this often becomes an accepted and routinized norm, contributing to high levels of community demand (Nichter, 1995; Samuelsen, 2001) for vaccination that may cut across differences of income, education and ethnicity.

Women-centred community networks do not just encourage clinic attendance, but very often also make it something of a social occasion. Thus in the Gambia, as well as in Guinea (Millimouno et al, 2006), Nigeria (Jegede, 2005) and Sierra Leone (Kamara, 2005), designated clinic days or mobile team visits are, for many women, a valued form of social gathering demanding best dress for mother and baby. As an outing that breaks with normal work routines, it is a chance to meet and chat with other mothers from one's own or nearby settlements, to reinforce kin and friendship ties, and to exchange news. By attending, women contribute to and reinforce a valued local community of mothers.

But this does not reflect everyone's experience. In both The Gambia and Guinea, we found a range of worries and forms of competition and exclusion that surround group clinic and mobile vaccination post days. In The Gambia, these worries were particularly important in the urban setting, and played strongly into socially differentiated patterns of vaccination uptake there (Cassell et al, 2006a). Thus for some mothers – perhaps especially those longer term residents with strong social networks – the clinic was indeed a valued group outing. It was more often recent immigrants, the poorer and less well integrated, who felt excluded. A number of features of the social context of a crowded clinic or outreach post play into such differentiated experiences.

First, the infant welfare clinic is a setting for very public display, where mothers and their children are 'on show' to others, and open to their scrutiny. For some, this can be very positive, with the clinic as a place to show pride in one's baby. Thus a young mother in peri-urban Gambia related how:

> *I would find something suitable for my baby, I would also dress beautifully, put on matching shoes, take my bag and go to the clinic. As an adolescent, I loved to draw attention, and I did it (Mother, Sukuta, April 2003).*

This mother described how she fed her baby what she thought was egg powder: 'I wanted my baby to be fat so I could bluff the more.'

However, public display of infant health (or ill-health) is also a matter for status negotiations among women, linked to local understandings that connect bodily processes with morality. Given prevailing bodily understandings of child health, a strong, healthy infant can indicate that one is a good mother who is able to overcome problems, or who has good moral conduct. As we have indicated above, people consider certain child health problems to be linked to the comportment of the parents: whether to attention to bodily hygiene or cleanliness in preparing food, or to inappropriate behaviour that transgresses boundaries between parts of the socio-ecological order. As these can provoke comment and judgement from others, taking a sick child to clinic can be worrisome for mothers. Illness can thus be a reason not to attend the health centre, rather than a reason to go. In particular, having a fat, strong baby can be interpreted as proof of sexual abstinence while breastfeeding, whereas a thin one opens a mother to moral condemnation. Similarly in Guinea, people relate that in most cases where a mother carries a sickly baby, his or her parents will become the object of comment and discussion that judges them incapable of abstaining from sexual relations. Such mothers therefore avoid taking their babies into public, and either eschew vaccination sessions, or wait until everyone else has left with their babies before bringing theirs.

The backgrounds of certain women make them particularly concerned about how others will judge their childrearing. Thus a mother from the praise singing (*griot*) caste in Marikunda, The Gambia, described how:

> *Even within the griot community there is a 'class' type of attitude where some will be superior while others will be interested to see or know how being a griot has improved or worsened one's livelihood. This is not only visible by the number of assets one has but by the way one cares for the children. Therefore if the child is healthy and beautiful she is admired (Mother, Marikunda, March 2003).*

In another case, a Gambian sex worker preferred to attend the infant welfare clinic outside her own neighbourhood, where she was not known. She wanted to distance herself from nurses and other mothers who would know her background, and, she feared, would stigmatize her.

Others find that the health of their baby reflects badly on them. For example a mother in urban Gambia had an infant who refused to be weighed. She described how:

> *Attempts were made to take him but his crying and disturbances worried me and people would comment on it so I stopped. For people to talk on a person regularly is not a good thing; this can affect the child (Mother, Sukuta, March 2003).*

Another mother, in Marikunda, had a very small second baby. She refused to go to the clinic because the baby attracted so much attention when she undressed him, and was only persuaded to resume by a sympathetic health worker. This range of examples suggests that the public display aspects of routine clinic attendance, while positive and attractive for some, are viewed negatively by others who fear unwanted attention on themselves or their baby.

Second, research especially from urban Gambia suggests that infant welfare clinics are also feared as places where children might be harmed by 'bad people' (*moo jawo*). It is to protect them from such hazards that many people – including those who do not normally use them – will put an amulet on their baby especially to go to the clinic. They say that the clinic is a crowded place, rather like a market, and one does not know who might be there, and who might have malevolent intentions towards one's child. One mother in urban Gambia described how she always avoided taking her child to crowded places, and would take her to the clinic only with extreme worry. As she put it: 'When a child undresses, especially if the child is healthy and beautiful, all eyes will be on her, and this I fear when the clinic is crowded ... there are many witches around' (Mother, Sukuta, March 2003).

Many Gambian mothers see weighing as presenting particular hazards. As they explain, certain women have particular amulets which cause their babies to leave behind a trace on the scales. This can cause illness, especially convulsions. If you are not someone with the same amulet yourself, you need to have a general protective one that will counteract this. Occasionally, when a woman who is feared in this way has just weighed her baby, others will not come forward to follow her in the queue, and this can make the nurse impatient. Thus as one older mother described:

> *I observed that at the clinic, each ethnic group has its protection and there are instances where women are scared to put their children after a Fula woman has weighed her child. The Fulas have a special 'horn' for an illness that is transmittable from one child to another. It is even worse when the child passes urine on the scale or when one steps on the mother's footsteps ... an observant mother will never allow her baby to be put on the scale after a Fula woman's baby, she will allow others to go ahead. If the women in the queue also observed that it was a Fula child, none will come forward. The nurse would shout 'next, next' ... they would pretend not to hear (Mother, Sukuta, May 2003).*

As this example illustrates, fears play into ethnic worries, with danger sometimes associated with particular ethnic groups or 'foreigners'. Different ethnic groups are understood to have different forms of protective amulet, so that forms of child protection become ethnic identifiers. They are also markers of who is safe or dangerous to be with in the clinic setting, as one can only be sure of safety among friends or those who have the same amulet as oneself. In this context, solidarity among groups of women at the multi-ethnic urban clinic is as much for security – to keep within a safe group of similar and known people, and to look out for each other – as it is for enjoyment and practical mutual help. In peri-urban Gambia, for instance, mothers from a particular neighbourhood and two outlying villages deliberately grouped to dominate the Tuesday clinic session, and with this solidarity, did not necessarily worry about putting amulets on their babies.

Crowded, group infant welfare clinics and vaccination sessions can therefore be places of worry. This is felt particularly by those who are less well-integrated – such as immigrants in the urban context – or who feel themselves 'different' in some way. But in turn, what happens at the clinic also serves to construct such social differences: to reproduce a notion of community that includes some and leaves others out; to construct a sense of social isolation, or of distinction related to poverty or ethnicity. What are often taken as pre-formed social characteristics shaping vaccination attendance practices should thus be considered, at least in part, as the product of such practices. Such social dimensions of vaccination attendance and access have been little considered in policy debates about immunization in Africa. Yet in our Gambian study, they were clearly part of the explanation for patterns of vaccination uptake. Thus in our survey (Cassell et al, 2006a) a cluster of factors emerged in the urban setting as significantly associated with general non-uptake, including living in a compound of poor appearance; living in a rented compound; not having a mobile phone in the compound; and not being of the Mandinka ethnic group. This cluster of factors is associated both with poverty, and with higher likelihood of being a recent immigrant into the rapidly expanding urban fringe.

Generational and gender relations of vaccination practices

Whether attending a group clinic day or an individual appointment, women make decisions to attend (or not) not as isolated individuals, but within gender and generational relations that extend beyond group orchestration to bring particular forms of advice and pressure to bear. These vary greatly depending on her social and marital circumstances, but there are also changes which occur in the course of a woman's childbearing life.

Gambian material illustrates that women in their first pregnancies, especially if, as is common, they are only teenagers, frequently feel vulnerable and inexperienced. It is common for a woman in her first pregnancy to move to her mother's home for delivery and the first few months of her baby's life. This may mean moving to a village nearby, or across an international border; in the peri-urban fringe, it may mean moving within the town or, for recent immigrants, back to a rural village. There, someone else will help with the 'nursing care' of the baby. It is rare for a first-time mother to do this on her own, unless she is older.

Frequently, then, it is in his or her grandmother's home area that a first child will receive its first vaccinations. In many cases, grandmothers are influential in encouraging clinic visits. Thus one young mother in urban Gambia described how when she had her first child at only 15, she stayed with her mother until the baby was four months old. Her mother 'forced' her to attend clinic, alongside other healthcare advice. Another had her first child while a schoolgirl, out of marriage, and was first taken to the infant welfare clinic by her mother; she introduced her to the nurses and this made subsequent visits easier. Sometimes mothers-in-law play the same role. Mothers and mothers-in-law are also advisors when it comes to traditional medicines; advice that is not easy to refuse given relations of generational authority. Women moving to a new urban settlement are sometimes given a foster mother who plays this role. For example, one young mother found that as part of the expectation that she would associate herself with the people in the area, a foster mother was identified with whom she could deliver and care for her baby.

With accumulating age and subsequent pregnancies, women frequently gain both in personal confidence and in the authority and autonomy ascribed to them by other men and women (see Bledsoe, 2002). Such mothers tend to share advice and learn infant care routines from friends: whether massage, putting on amulets, acquiring other forms of protection, or attending clinic. Several expressed how the clinic itself becomes a learning place where they exchange advice and discuss infant care worries with other mothers, at least those they know well.

Away from their mother's home, Gambian women also negotiate clinic attendance more directly with their husbands. Generally, within the gender relations of parenting, a mother is expected to maintain responsibility for day-to-day infant care and minor ailments, whereas a father would be expected to muster financial and logistical help in the case of a serious illness or injury. Within such divisions, mothers tend to assume unquestioned responsibility for vaccination and routine clinic visits, and few fathers seem to become involved. Even though family planning services (to which most husbands are opposed) are also dispensed at the infant welfare clinic, it appears that few question their wives' attendance on these grounds. On the contrary, most seem to be supportive, and fathers have played a 'backstopping' role, finding transport for a wife who cannot otherwise get to clinic, for instance. Fathers have, at times, used their authority to force attendance against a mother's inclinations. Thus an urban mother described how she was only 13 years old when she first got married, to an influential religious scholar. She feared visiting the infant welfare clinic, but explained how her husband would 'force' her and on occasion even beat her for failing to attend clinic.

In Guinea, the decision to vaccinate might, on occasion, come from a father, but in most cases mothers assume this responsibility. Although in principle it is a father's role to cover any financial costs associated with vaccination, in practice these, like other healthcare costs, are usually met by a child's mother. Only in certain families, predominantly in urban areas where the man has a professional occupation, does he pay. In rural areas, by contrast, a father would help out only if necessary. This reflects differences in prevailing negotiations of intra-household responsibility between rural settings, where women not only make central contributions to household revenue-generating activities, but also earn their own income through fishing, gardening, rice fields, small-scale trade, and so on (see Fairhead and Leach, 1996), and urban households where women's economic opportunities are reduced.

Despite this notional male support for vaccination, it is rare for a child's father or another male relative to take a child to clinic himself, even if the mother is unable to. In both The Gambia and Guinea, the routinized feminization of attendance by pregnant women, mothers and often accompanying female neighbours and kin has led infant welfare clinics to acquire conceptual status as a women's space (see Fairhead et al, forthcoming). This is in a region where gender differentiated social orders are governed by women's and men's power associations that both control knowledge and practices around reproduction, and normalize gendered segregations of space – as in men's and women's initiation places in the forest or special houses (e.g. Leach, 1994; Fairhead and Leach, 1996; Ferme, 2002). An effect, it seems, is that many men feel out of place at health centres, tending to seek their personal curative care in private pharmacies, and often appear reluctant to take their infants for routine weighing and vaccinations if the mother is unavailable. Feminized practices of infant immunization attendance thus reinforce patterns of gendered segregation and solidarity in the region.

Social relations with frontline workers

At infant welfare clinics and outreach posts, mothers encounter health workers – whether nurses, mother–child health aides or public health workers, depending on the context. These encounters are very much social interactions, in which parental and health workers' diverse perspectives interplay in ways shaped by social identity, power and authority. Again, material from The Gambia provides helpful illustration.

Understanding how Gambian nurses consider parents' vaccination attendance practices is essential to comprehending the nature of these social interactions. Nurses generally describe attendance rates as good, and are proud that mothers in The Gambia have, as they put it, 'come to know the importance' of vaccination, and acquired the modern biomedical knowledge that they transmit through their education programmes. Indeed, interviews with nurses in one busy peri-urban health centre illustrated a conviction that mothers had 'active demand' for vaccination, based on modern disease-specific knowledge (something which our earlier discussion illustrated is not generally the case). As one explained, 'our mothers have left behind their traditional practices and come to know the importance of vaccination'. Indeed this nurse claimed that 'their' mothers had abandoned the use of amulets – despite rather obvious evidence of babies wearing them at that very clinic. Nurses express a sense of pride in bringing 'their' mothers into a modern realm of scientific knowledge about child health.

In this context, nurses' discussions also pick out those women who do not comply as an exceptional group; a small category of women who do not fit the generally optimistic image. They usually describe these mothers as 'defaulters'. This strong term with its condemning overtones groups a large variety of particular 'failures', including missing or being late for vaccinations in the schedule, and showing a gap in weighing records of more than about two months. Health workers image defaulters as a particular kind of individual, or at least a negative ideal type, who is ignorant or has misplaced priorities. They include, nurses say, those who travel a lot, and forget to take their children's health cards with them. They include women who prioritize economic activity, such as vegetable gardening and trading, over health and make no time for clinic, and those who neglect clinic visits if their children are well (although when put on the spot, may use travel as an excuse). These reasons for default are at times imaged as a particular ethnic trait (e.g. travel is often linked to Jolas or others from Guinea Bissau, and over-zealous gardening to Mandinka women), or as linked to illiteracy and persistent, traditional views of disease. These categories reflect established modes of discussion among health workers who tend to have passed through forms of education and cultural experience which encourage a sense of superiority in relation to the populations they serve. Denigrating mothers as ignorant or as having misplaced priorities reaffirms their sense of being modern, responsible, scientifically knowledgeable citizens.

Yet their categories do not properly reflect parents' realities. Indeed, they obscure many of the issues that are important to parents and that shape their vaccination practices. As we showed earlier, Gambian mothers' vaccination demand does not depend on literacy and modern biomedical knowledge, but is grounded in ideas around strength and protection that draw together Islamic, naturalistic and biomedical views. And as our ethnographic and survey studies demonstrate, missed or late vaccinations are not systematically associated with a particular 'sort' of person in this way. 'Default' does not necessarily mean a mother is a persistent 'defaulter'; rather, it more often arises due to unexpected circumstances, events or family problems that can affect anyone. These can include extreme family misfortune, or being called away to attend a funeral or visit a sick relative. They can also include temporary pressure of work: for example one mother missed several vaccination sessions with her third baby as she was temporarily responsible for all the family cooking, as her co-wives had travelled. They can include difficulties in finding someone to care for other children, helping to explain why default is significantly more common among women with more children. In urban Gambia, for example, 35 per cent of mothers 'defaulted' with their fifth child, but only 17 per cent with their first child. Circumstances can also embrace the juggling required to sustain diversified livelihoods in economically impoverished settings. Thus women gardeners usually try to reorganize their schedules to enable clinic attendance, by going to the garden in the evening before a clinic day, but are occasionally unable to. A businesswoman also found it hard to make time to attend; her narrative illustrates how shifting gender relations and growing economic autonomy for women can be associated with pressures which make clinic attendance a greater struggle:

> *Women's problems are numerous and now there is the issue of 'empower-ment', whereby women are trying to make ends meet – therefore we women must prioritize. When my child is sick and I have urgent things to do, I either go to the clinic very early and be among the first patients or ask my mother to take the child (Mother, Sukuta, June 2003).*

Occasional failures can also turn on practical difficulties in getting to the clinic. One mother had had three sets of twins, and occasionally could not take them as a helper was not available. Even a short journey may be impossible for mothers who are sick themselves, have a sick child, have no one with whom to leave siblings on a particular day, and when these circumstances coincide with the hot season or heavy rains.

While for a mother, then, 'default' is often a one-off, unavoidable event, for health workers it usually indicates that she is 'a defaulter'. The result can be very problematic interactions at subsequent clinic sessions. Many women complain of ill-treatment and rudeness from health workers when they are late or miss an infant welfare clinic session – something which was also found in other areas of The Gambia by Lovell (1999). Thus an older mother described how:

> *Nurses would embarrass people in front of a crowded clinic. If they fail to take their injections, the nurses would be angry with them. Their clinic cards are sometimes placed at the bottom as a sign of punishment (Mother, Sukuta, June 2003).*

Especially in the urban setting, some mothers reported what they experienced as unsympathetic and disrespectful treatment from the nurses: for example: 'The nurses in [clinic X] are very rude. They have no respect. They embarrass people, even if some of the women are old enough to be their mothers.' Our survey confirmed that such concerns were more common in the urban setting, and that social experiences of clinic there were more varied than in rural areas where mothers usually reported staff to be friendly and respectful.

Emerging strongly from some urban mothers' narratives in The Gambia was a view that prior social connections with clinic staff and strong integration with other women could lead to privileged treatment, while lacking such connections – or not being well-integrated into the neighbourhood or dominant social groups there – could provoke exclusion. The following quotations exemplify such experiences:

> *I know some nurses, as such I don't even stand at queues, they attend to me without delay.*

> *They segregated we [area X, of recent immigrants]. The health centre workers give more attention to women from [area Y, largely long-term residents].*

> *My first day in the clinic was very discouraging. I encountered a long delay due to favouritism. The nurses attended to people according to relations and friendship. I went to the clinic much earlier than most mothers, but most mothers were attended to before me. I consequently got discouraged about the system.*

Similarly, in Guinea where it is commonplace for vaccinators to make informal charges, some mothers claim that they do not pay for vaccinations. As they and their neighbours explain, this is almost always because they have prior connections with the health worker in charge. A vaccinator who is a member of one's kin network, or an in-law, will not usually ask for payment.

Other studies in Africa have identified staff rudeness and attitudes as a problem for vaccination (Streefland et al, 1999; Helman and Yogeswaran, 2004) – often one linked to their low pay and incentives, as well as their training and self-definition as bearers and transmitters of superior western biomedicine. But such social dimensions of interaction also relate to clashes of knowledge and perspective between health workers and parents: over the meaning and value of vaccination, and over reasons for not conforming to the schedule. It also shows how varied experiences are: between settings, and between nurses and clinics, according to mothers' prior social connections or not with nurses. In turn, experiences of vaccination interactions and their social dimensions shape such kinship relations and social distinctions, affirming and reaffirming what it means to be, for instance, an in-law or an immigrant.

Wider political dimensions of vaccination

Perspectives on vaccination are shaped by wider political and political–economic relations whether with the state, with international agencies or wider processes. Without attention to this, the factors that lead everyday technological and social factors to erupt into instances of dissent are lost from view. Yet, as we argued in Chapter 2, without attention to bodily and microtechnological experiences, we cannot properly see why it should be through vaccines in particular that people reflect on wider political structures, and why it is in the way that they do. Moreover, as we outlined in the UK, the very concepts through which people understand bodily health (and vaccines) can become influential in configuring social experience, and indeed wider economic and political experience – and vice versa, with concepts of immunity and flexible adaptation now framing bodily, social and economic reflection alike.

In contrast, in these regions of West Africa, it is notions of proper 'circulatory flow' that frame bodily and also social and political reflection on what it is to be healthy and strong, with social and political problems linked to blockage and inappropriate mixing. A way into understanding this is through the annual celebrations and festivities that accompany the clearing of (unblocking) of paths between neighbouring villages which are found across the region. These maintain healthy social relations between specific neighbouring villages, and have particular relevance in connecting villages to which daughters go in marriage, and from which daughters come; which are also those with historically close political alliances. The annual path-clearing celebrations enable the healthy social interchange that brings the fertility and security needed for prosperity. Ruptures in these paths, and therefore in these interchanges, bring ill fortune. Keeping flows correct and pathways open is a pervasive metaphor. Thus houses have their front and back doors open when possible, to attract visitors. Equally, prosperity is understood to derive from the circulation of traders and their goods and from markets, with blockage leading to hunger and decline. Roads bring prosperity, while decline ensues from blockage, bridge failure and bypasses.

Healthy production and reproduction in the human worlds is conceptually related also to the plant and animal worlds, through the concepts of flow and movement along paths. For hunters, the annual migrations of their prey bring their prosperity. They depend on predicting, manipulating and intercepting the movement of animals, whether in their diurnal feeding and drinking, or in their broader migration.

Problems are associated with paths becoming blocked or 'tied' (*sidi*), engendering hunger. Hunters can find that the bush is tied. Fisherwomen find that the water is tied, blocking the predictable fish movements which are the secret of their success. A blocked path between villages is insulting, and tied menstruation causes infertility, whether the tying is due to incorrect diet, water impurities, or the dirt thrown by sorcerors. Infertile men are similarly 'tied'. Babies' digestion is said to be blocked by breastmilk impurities. Blood becomes tied, solid and 'asleep' when cool, 'like red palm oil'. And like red palm oil, it becomes liquid as it warms and 'wakes up' on feeling the sun's rays in the morning. People do not go to work in the fields until mid-morning when their blood begins to flow and strength returns to them. Medical cures commonly seek to unblock and untie to restore flow.

An analytic that strength and prosperity derive from proper circulatory flow thus transcends body, body social and body politic, in a broader framing. Strength (bodily, social and political) derives from maintaining such flows. The political significance and strength of leaders can be gauged by the coming and going of people, and the significance of a market by those that frequent it. A wealthy man is one who can attract and maintain many followers, have many clients, and have many wives and children along with the social networks and flows they build. A wealthy woman is one who has many children, and who maintains relations with wider family. To be strong and powerful is to be at the centre of healthy flows. Strong, successful settlements and areas are also at the centre of flows: they might be close to trade routes, house important periodic markets, and have a continual circulation of economic goods and products. They also attract an inflow of immigrants, and are successful at retaining links with emigrants, and the material influx they bring.

Such notions of strength linked to circulatory flow underlie the great political value of having a health centre or post in one's village. Which village or neighbouring administrative locale will be allocated an area's health centre has been a matter of extreme competition and tension in each of our study locations. To house the health centre is to be the political centre. It means that people flow into and through the settlement. It also means that the health post becomes part of that community's authority and social relations. In a similar way to the sense in which vaccination as a bodily project strengthens the body, housing a vaccination centre is a route to strengthening the local body politic. In both real and metaphorical terms, it is a route to having a strong population, to realizing a desire or anxiety for local political strength. It is an injection that makes the community strong. It is also an indicator of how connected a community or local polity is to wider patron–client relations and networks that extend up to national and even international levels. This underlies the disappointment that villagers and settlement authorities often feel when mobile vaccination teams fail to turn up. More than a simple failure of vaccine supply chains or transport, in local understandings this can represent a failure or blockage of flows and connectedness that also suggests political failure.

Furthermore, in both our Gambian and Guinean study sites, tensions between settlements and localities over the location of health posts were tensions between different local political jurisdictions. Settlements that command authority within modern administrative structures – as a district or sub-prefecture headquarters – were in competition with settlements with their importance grounded in 'traditional' political structures and historical claims to authority, for instance as the original 'founding settlement' of a territory. Whichever of these came to prevail became, more broadly, an indicator of whether the state recognized or overlooked a local political structure and its centre, and thus of the relative significance of different forms of political authority.

In the context of West African politics and political culture, communities tend to experience the state as operating through patronage. This can be an experience of benevolence: of a state that, through its agents, brings a supportive flow of goods and services in recognition of mutual interests. On the other hand, it can also be an experience of extraction, as communities and their members are preyed upon to boost the political and material strength of a state and its agencies whose interests are seen to lie elsewhere. Through the metaphor of strength/power, vaccination can be implicated in both kinds of relationship.

Thus vaccination delivery can, at times, be experienced as part of the benevolent flows of goods and support that build strength – indeed the very essence of these. Vaccination has long been delivered primarily through the state, promoting strong bodies that in turn become part of, and contribute to, a populous, strong body politic at national level. Indeed such national connections often became part of and were reinforced through the rhetorics of African statehood in the 1960s. Whether the chosen path was socialist or capitalist, these commonly promoted vaccination and public health within a frame that emphasized modernization and development, for the common good of a nation's people. Thus in contradistinction to a recent colonial past, White (2005) suggests that:

> In what is normally considered the optimistic first years of African independence ... inoculation campaigns should, in theory at least, have been free of the taint of colonial health endeavours and should have represented African nations' abilities to better the lives of their citizens (White 2005, pp11–12).

In this context, people have often experienced 'failures' of the state in the post-independence period through failures of health delivery. Whether linked to conflict and civil war, or to neoliberal reforms emphasizing a rolling-back of the state and cost-recovery for basic services, benevolent flows of good and services from state agencies to communities have often been blocked. Other analysts have written of the effects of neoliberal reform on people's acceptance of vaccination. For instance Birungi (1998) suggests for Uganda that vaccination acceptance was predicated on state provision of health services, which supported a climate of collective goodwill and responsibility. As this was undermined by neoliberal moves towards health service cost recovery and community 'self-help' that accelerated during the 1980s, so these trustful contracts became more fragile and often broke down. However, the failures of delivery that have frequently accompanied cost-recovery policies signal something more and different than simply a 'breakdown of trust'. Within concepts of strength and fluidity, they signal a more fundamental rupture in connecting people with nation. Either the nation, or body politic, has lost strength, or been undermined by rivals; or its interests have turned to privileging and building the strength of other clients elsewhere.

Such broader relations can be localized in the practices of hosting state agents in vaccination. Village authorities are often anxious to ensure that mobile vaccination teams at least stay and eat in the community, even if they cannot be persuaded to stay overnight. Hosting 'strangers' in this way is an established regional stock-in-trade for drawing them into a family or village arena of influence and indebtedness; for establishing some degree of control and allegiance, and ensuring that future actions towards the settlement are benevolent and supportive. A state that is not sending out its agents, or whose agents make only fleeting visits and will not enter into these mutual obligations, is a disconnected state. This is, potentially, a state to worry about, since its benevolence and interests may turn to other, possibly rival clients elsewhere.

Vaccination can certainly come to be understood as part of an extractive politics, or to the benefit of others. Extracting from and weakening local polities for the material benefit of the colonial or post-colonial state has been a vivid part of political experience for many in the region. So, too, are experiences of state leadership that rely on ethnic and geographical power bases for support, thus tending – in the distribution of benefits – to favour specific areas. The social experience of vaccination benefits flowing more to a favoured political constituency is a logical extension of state politics.

At times, vaccination programmes are understood to actively weaken a polity and be a positive danger, as is the case when they are understood to contain sterilizing agents or HIV. Yet to understand why, it is important to recognize this wider field of political representation concerning the nature of benevolence and prosperity, of which sterilization is the inverse, linking bodily weakening with weakening of a body politic, as a population, area or polity is sapped of fertility or strength. In the case of the rejection of oral polio vaccines (OPV) in northern Nigeria in 2003–2004, for example, the chairman of the Supreme Council for Sharia in Nigeria (SCSN), Dr Datti Ahmed, claimed that the OPV campaign was a genocidal move aimed at weakening the populations of the Islamic northern states:

> *We believe that modern-day Hitlers have deliberately adulterated the oral polio vaccines with anti-fertility drugs and contaminated it with certain viruses which are known to cause HIV and AIDS.*[5]

As Yahya (2005, 2007) shows, the interpretations of northern state governors, Islamic leaders and of local authorities and populations alike connected this move with wider political struggles. These included international tensions around Islam and American imperialism post 9/11, given many Nigerians' concern about US foreign policy towards Africa and the Islamic world. Thus as a Nigeria-based Ghanaian doctor who supported the boycott put it:

> *We all know that WHO is just an extension of the US government, we also know that the US feel they can control the rest of the world. At least the Sharia states are telling the Americans that they can't just do what they like (Doctor, Kaduna, July 2005).*

Interpretations also interplayed with long-standing tensions in Nigerian politics between the north and the south, and between federal and state government. Objecting to a vaccine delivered through a top-down campaign that literally came in vehicles from the south, and by a technocracy linking the central Ministry of Health with international organizations, was part of a broader disquiet about patronage politics that weakened and subjugated northern and state concerns to southern and central ones. In boycotting the OPV, northern state governors substantively, as well as symbolically, challenged these political processes.

We have suggested above that within local political framings, ensuring benevolent, strengthening support from the state is partly to be achieved through establishing social connectedness and regular flow with its agents. Top-down vaccination campaigns contrast with this, and consequently risk being understood and experienced very differently. In these, as in the global polio eradication initiative in Nigeria, global finance and orchestration is often highly visible, in the foreign vehicles and personnel employed. Even if local, state personnel are involved, it is in forms outside their routine identity. Vaccination campaigns often bypass established political geographies: rather than being connected with located places and polities, they come from outside and move from door to door. Their temporary character – in one-off NIDs or events – also means that they do not create or maintain connections; they do not become part of strength-building relations. Instead, it is easy for campaigns to be experienced as invasive and alien, and this calls into question their agenda. If not obviously strengthening a local or national polity, then they are easily interpreted as strengthening a polity elsewhere or a global polity – whose interests may be far from complementary, and indeed better served by weakening one's area. The likelihood of such reflections, which seem to have been in play in the Nigerian polio case, may be greatest where campaigns appear most at odds with routine, state delivery systems (see Streefland, 2001). In northern Nigeria this was starkly so, given the prevailing breakdown and only minimal operation of government primary healthcare systems. With the collapse of routine vaccination infrastructure, such benevolence as there was is no more. In contrast, in Guinea – where routine state vaccination delivery does operate, albeit in constrained ways – people seem to see NIDs as an extension of more routine state relations, often involving the same personnel and employing a door-to-door strategy that has, at times, been part of routine delivery.

These West African conceptualizations, rooted in understandings of strength-building and depletion that link bodily processes with wider national and international politics, thus provide a further layer to White's (2005) argument that international disease eradication programmes in Africa have often been experienced as a kind of 'un-national sovereignty'. Thus from the 1960s onwards, global institutions came increasingly to influence and shape the direction of national policies, in ways that increased the fragility of new African statehood. As White recounts, this was nowhere more obvious than in health and vaccination. Thus in the 1960s, the WHO, the US Centres for Disease Control and USAID planned and implemented the smallpox eradication campaign that was to have such a significant effect in reducing the global incidence of the disease. Yet in

White's terms, this involved practices that subordinated African statehood and rode roughshod over national and local sentiments. It thus revealed 'the triumph of global humanitarian concerns at the expense of local sovereignty and local humanitarian concerns' (2005, p12). The involvement of global institutions in African health issues has only increased in intervening decades, through the WHO Expanded Programme on Immunization, and a series of further disease eradication campaigns including the Global Polio Eradication initiative in the 1990s–2000s, and now to initiatives led by global philanthropic organizations and public–private partnerships. Considering the connections between body and body politic, and the concepts of strength and fluidity that enable these, reveals why such broader political shifts provide a context in which vaccine anxieties can flourish, and the significance of worries about strength depletion in these.

Interactions between policy and parental framings

For parents in many West African settings, then, we have described how vaccine anxieties – whether in the positive sense of a desire and striving for child health and socio-political success, or in the negative sense of worry about vaccination effects – often turn on understandings that link bodily with social and political experiences through the notions of strength and healthy fluid flow. This framing is not shared by health workers and those in public health policy, who tend to interpret public engagement with vaccines through a dominant vocabulary that highlights supply-side factors, and relates non-acceptance either to ignorance or to rumour. In this final section, we indicate some ways in which these gulfs in framing are themselves produced and reproduced through encounters between parents and public health institutions, first as taking place in the context of routine vaccine delivery in clinic settings, and then in interpretations of resistance to large-scale campaigns.

Health worker interactions, default and 'compounded default'

As we illustrated in the Gambian context, health workers tend to describe mothers whose practices fail to fit the prescribed vaccination schedule as 'defaulters', assuming them either to be ignorant of the modern scientific benefits of vaccination or to have wrongly placed priorities. As we also illustrated, mothers' reasons for sometimes not attending for vaccination, or for coming late, are usually rooted in more contingent issues; issues related either to their social relations and livelihood struggles, or to specific factors in a child's personal health trajectory – such as being thin, so that a mother risks moral approbation from other mothers. Worries about the social setting of the clinic and the risks of 'bad people' or problems from other ethnic groups can also deter attendance, or lead mothers to hang back in the queue. As we also saw, parents are not ignorant of vaccination but bring to their reflections a range of forms of knowledge, albeit framed not in strictly biomedical terms. As these contrasting perspectives interact in clinic settings, so each can be reinforced.

Thus health workers, interpreting mothers' practices as indicating that they are 'defaulters', often subject them to embarrassing, degrading or hasslesome treatment. For instance they might shout at or insult them in front of other mothers, send them to the back of the queue, or ignore them. Mothers so treated become even more reluctant to attend and might deliberately come late the next time to avoid the crowds and queues, or stay away altogether. Thus as one Gambian mother explained:

> *Some who feared being embarrassed and have defaulted, stayed away and would instead send their children to clinic only when very ill. Others will take their children to the outpatients (Mother, Sukuta, June 2003).*

Worries that missed clinic sessions will lead to an accumulated backlog of injections can also deter attendance. Fear of being forced to have catch-up injections, given anxieties that 'too much substance' in the blood can cause sickness, sometimes means that women keep their babies away for further months, compounding non-attendance. The story of a woman in Sukuta illustrates how these dilemmas can arise and give rise to worry that contributes to late vaccination:

> *I delivered on the 4th of April 2001 and had a naming ceremony on the eighth day, which was on a Tuesday, our clinic day. The following Tuesday coincided with a Muslim feast 'Ketimo' so I could not go to the clinic. The following Tuesday was a public holiday and the fourth Tuesday the nurse responsible for registering newborns was not at work. I became very worried because for four weeks I could not register my baby and she was also not weighed but my greatest worry was surrounded my daughter receiving many injections at one go. I feared that this would make her sick. As clinic days go by without being registered, I became worried. I have seen babies receiving three to four injections at one go, two on the arms and one or two on the thigh(s). When I was finally registered, I reluctantly accepted the injections prescribed for me, as refusal would mean either being put aside by the nurses or receiving several shots during my next visit (Mother, Sukuta, May 2003).*

Health workers, failing to appreciate the logics of parents' worries, tend to interpret such lateness and non-attendance as further evidence that the mother is a defaulter. In this way, their views are confirmed, so further widening the gulf between parental and health worker perspectives.

Health worker interactions and supply dilemmas

A related set of dynamics sometimes unfolds in settings of constrained vaccine supply and delivery, as cases from Guinea illustrate. Here, as we have seen, the financial problems faced by health centres mean that health workers often find it necessary to charge, informally, for vaccination services that are officially free to parents. Parents are generally willing to pay, here as in Sierra Leone (Kamara, 2005); an indication of their strong anxiety for vaccination. However, willingness aside, some parents – especially those from the poorest families, or who have experienced a recent family crisis – cannot pay. Sometimes they simply do not bring their children for vaccination, as these mothers in Kissidougou, for example, explained:

> *I did not have the means to follow vaccination for my child – for each vaccine one needs to hand over a sum of money.*

> *It is for lack of money that my child does not follow vaccination. Rice is very expensive and money is not forthcoming. It is not refusal.*

According to some mothers, many who are in this position prefer to say that they have lost their baby's health card to avoid embarrassment when health agents ask them to pay and they are unable to. Health workers sometimes humiliate such mothers in front of others, accusing them of not prioritizing their baby's health over other expenditures. So as one Dinguiraye mother explained:

> *Others prefer to stay at home, lacking financial means, in order to avoid humiliation by the health agents.*

At the same time, given the economic problems facing vaccination services, it is often the case that mothers arrive at a health centre for a vaccination appointment only to find that no vaccines are available. Health staff are highly aware that this can put them off future attendance:

> *Often in Kissidougou we lack vaccines for polio, DTP, BCG. The crisis of vaccines is making itself felt even at national level and progressively, because of this rupture in provisioning, mothers lose confidence and no longer refer their children (Health worker, Albadaria, June 2004).*

It can be particularly frustrating for mothers who must walk long distances to reach the health centre, only to find that there are no vaccines, as the case of this mother from Beindou in Kissidougou exemplifies:

> *The reasons for my child's insufficient number of vaccinations are the lack of vaccines in Beindou health centre. This has made me no longer go. The distance is more than 15km and as a woman, I do not dare to go alone (Mother, Beindou, June 2004).*

Other parents, who live in remote areas and rely on the visits of mobile vaccination teams, have become frustrated at their erratic visits; a frustration that, as the last section illustrated, can stem from a broader sense of political failure and lack of connectedness, as well as bodily worries about lack of vaccinations per se. Thus women in one village in rural Kissidougou lamented that the mobile team had not been to their village for nearly six months. At first they had waited and cooked for the team on the day they were expected; now they do not bother, and just get on with their work. Frustrated with the failure of the government health system to provide the services they need, many people are turning more and more towards the ever-growing range of private providers available, at least for curative services. This in turn further undermines health centre income and its capacity to vaccinate.

The Guinean situation exemplifies the vaccination supply problem that international debates emphasize for Africa. However, such supply-side problems play out in very particular ways, depending on broader political–economic factors and the ways health workers respond to these in their interfaces with parents. In this case, broader economic crisis, health service pluralization and privatization, health centres' funding crises and health agents' informal charging have all interacted to shape problematic interactions between parents and vaccination providers that, in a dialogical way, serve to discourage some from vaccination.

Interactions around campaign refusal

In instances where mass refusal of vaccination campaigns occur, dialogical processes are also at work, in which vaccinators and the policy world, and parents and local authorities, interpret each other's actions in ways that can create and sustain a gulf between their perspectives. Yahya's study of polio vaccines in Nigeria in 2003–2004 exemplifies this.

International and central government agencies, for the most part, interpreted the boycott of the OPV campaign by three northern states as based on rumour; a rumour of conspiracy to render people infertile. Rumour, as we saw in Chapter 2, has provided a very common conceptual frame through which policy makers have interpreted vaccine anxieties in the developing world; a frame which frequently serves to delegitimize the content of any concerns expressed by writing them off as ill-founded. In contrast, for parents and local authorities, refusing the campaign had a logic rooted in bodily understandings of polio as a spiritual affliction not amenable to vaccination; concerns about vaccines, fluids and fertility, and wider political anxieties about an alien campaign amid a weakening of the Islamic north, manifested, for instance, in the virtual collapse of the routine health services that were part of benevolent government patron–client relations there. Yet these linked bodily and political understandings, united through the concepts of strength and fluidity, went unappreciated by international agencies. Interpreting refusal in terms of rumour, there was little need to investigate further. Rather, the WHO and others focused on addressing refusal by re-implementing the campaign with greater determination and resources, and through educational campaigns emphasizing the importance of polio vaccination in biomedical terms. These strategies, however, contributed further to parental views that the vaccination campaign was a highly financed, external initiative separate from the routine health system, and that it was irrelevant to polio as they understood it.

Thus even after the formal end to the boycott in mid 2004, when the last of the three states, Kano, finally agreed to resume the campaign after vaccines were sourced from a company in a Muslim country (Indonesia), fear and instances of OPV refusal continued within many northern communities. As a rural woman put it:

> *There is a mistake in what the white man understands polio to be. We know what it is and we have our own way of handling it... I will not allow any one to put anything in my baby's mouth. We are very aware of what they are doing ... we know that it causes infertility in women (Mother, Bauchi, July 2005).*

In this, she expressed the persistence of a gulf in interpretation of what the polio campaign was about; a gulf only widened by policy makers' dismissal of parental anxieties as ill-founded rumour.

Conclusions

This chapter has ranged widely across West African settings, tracking parents' understandings and experiences of vaccination across rural and urban places from The Gambia and Guinea to Nigeria and Sierra Leone. This has involved considering various forms of organization in vaccination delivery – from campaign to routine, and within the latter, from group clinic and mobile visit days to individualized appointments, amid varied supply constraints. Nevertheless, some common themes have emerged. Central are concepts of strength and of fluids, their flows and connectedness; concepts which often serve to integrate understandings of bodily, social and wider political issues. Vaccination is commonly understood in these terms: as a technological and technocratic intervention that affects strength, whether of a child's body, or a body politic. Much of the time and in many settings these conceptualizations shape strong anxiety for vaccination. Yet they also coordinate negative anxieties about the ways that vaccines can weaken a body or polity, whether directly – as a substance that interferes with the fluid relations of health and fertility – or relatively, by strengthening others elsewhere.

Concepts of strength and connectedness also underlie the very different ways in which routine vaccination services and campaigns are often experienced. Analysts have noted the tendency for vaccination worries and mass refusal to focus on campaign style delivery (e.g. Greenough, 1995; Streefland, 2001). Here we have offered further explanations for this that go beyond the view that people simply reject their top-down and sometimes coercive style. Playing on people's anxieties, too, are the polarizing effects of interpretations that write their worries off as rumour, and the disconnectedness of campaigns from routine services, in settings where the latter exemplify, par excellence, the strength-building connectedness and flows of benefits from a benevolent state. This suggests that strengthening routine delivery systems and integrating disease eradication campaigns more fully into them may be an essential step in addressing vaccine anxieties. West African politicians may be well-positioned to appreciate this, and its reasoning. Thus it is telling that in a strategic response to the OPV crisis, Nigeria's president, Olusegun Obasanjo, emphasized in talks with senior WHO and UNICEF officials in October 2005 that childhood immunization would, from 2006, become routine and integrated into the country's health delivery system, with direct management and ownership of immunization services by state and local governments, as against the current focus on polio campaigns and national immunization days.[6]

Yet as the case of The Gambia shows, even when an effective, high coverage, routine immunization system is operating, further polarizing problems can occur. Gulfs between policy and parental framings – of why vaccines are desirable, and what processes shape uptake – persist, and can be widened through interactions between parents and health workers in ways that can reduce attendance for some. This suggests the need for a more thoroughgoing integration – into health systems, and into the training of health workers – of attentiveness to the conceptual worlds of parents, and sensitivity to the social struggles that many face in negotiating clinic attendance with particular children's health trajectories, and social and moral relations.

Notes

1 We have conducted ethnographic research in Malinke- and Kissi-speaking parts of the prefecture of Kissidougou intermittently since 1992 (see Fairhead and Leach, 1996, 2003). This was our first research covering Dinguiraye. Divisions and prefectures are both approximately equivalent to the WHO's concept of a 'health district': the main administrative unit responsible for organizing health service delivery at the local level.
2 In Guinea, apart from ourselves, the research team consisted of Dr Alpha Ahmadou Diallo (Ministère de la Santé Publique) and Dominique Millimouno (Centre Universitaire de Recherche sur le Développement, CURA), and their assistants. In The Gambia, the team consisted of ourselves and Mary Small, a Gambian nurse, then of the Gambia Committee on Traditional Practices (GAMCOTRAP) and her assistants.
3 This is a pseudonym.
4 Mothers' textual responses from the survey, where cited in this chapter, are not specifically referenced, in contrast with narrative interviews in The Gambia and Guinea which we reference by place and month of interview.
5 'Vaccine boycott spreads polio', www.news24.com/News24/Africa/Features/0,6119,2-11-37_1481952,00.html, accessed 11 February 2004.
6 'Federal Government integrates immunization into health delivery system', Nigeria First News: www.allafrica.com, accessed 5 October 2005.

6

Anxieties over Science: Engaging Vaccine Trials in The Gambia

Introduction

This chapter shifts attention from routine vaccination and its delivery in West Africa, to the conduct of vaccine trials and how those drawn into their ambit understand and engage with them. The trial of a new vaccine, in this case in The Gambia, would appear to provide an ideal lens for viewing how people engage with vaccine science. However as the chapter unfolds, the limited extent to which people interpret the practices they encounter as 'science' and as a 'trial' becomes part of the story; a story which calls into question the self-evident nature of 'public engagement with science'.

Again our focus in this chapter is on anxieties – positive or negative. Here the anxieties are about children participating in something that the medical research community regarded as a vaccine trial. To understand both desires to participate and fears about doing so, we again address bodily, social and wider political dimensions to parental experience. In particular, we discern how these dimensions are integrated through an understanding of health in relation to blood calculus and exchange; an 'economy of blood' that extends from the body into international political economy, and which makes sense within the concepts that we discussed in the previous chapter that relate circulatory systems to health and strength. As we show, such perspectives contrast starkly with those of the scientists and administrators organizing what they see as a scientific trial. Once again, we consider how these contrasting perspectives – in this case, of those organizing the trial and those invited to join it – have been shaped and consolidated in dialogical relation to each other.

In The Gambia, there is a long history of vaccine trials and related medical research, linked to the UK's Medical Research Council (MRC) laboratories which were founded in 1949 when The Gambia was still a British colony. This still remains the UK's principal public investment in medical research in Africa. The coastal campus and three main field stations further inland house advanced laboratories and orchestrate clinical trials that operate over much of the country.

Their research focuses on malaria, tuberculosis, pneumonia, HIV/AIDS and other viral diseases, nutrition and non-communicable diseases, and is particularly strong in vaccine evaluation. The MRC in The Gambia is now the country's third largest employer. Of employees, a third are Gambian fieldworkers who 'enable us to work effectively throughout the whole country and help establish our credibility with the Gambian people' (MRC, 2002, p6). The MRC also offers clinical services which provide it with public visibility (MRC, 2002, p6).

As we shall see, there is a widespread view that the MRC offers good and often free medication to 'those registered with it', but this is balanced with a concern that the MRC steals good, African blood that, people speculate, they send to Europe or America whether for transfusions or to make medicines. Those organizing trials tend to interpret blood stealing as an unfortunate and ill-founded rumour, in much the same way as we found in relation to worries about vaccination programmes.

Indeed, in social science analysis, blood stealing has often been grouped with other phenomena such as body-part theft, or the spread of sterilizing agents, as rumours and idioms through which African people responded to medical research and other forms of health-related intervention, whether historically or recently (for a review, see Geissler and Pool, 2006). Such a grouping is made possible only by considering all these phenomena under the singular umbrella of 'rumour'. But again, we argue that the concept of rumour conceals more than it explains. It overlooks the specific meanings of blood, and the wider social and political worlds in which people come to construe it as being 'stolen'. Attention to the importance of blood reasoning, and how it enables health to be connected to wider economic orders reveals a more embedded and enduring logic to 'vampiritic' anxieties – a logic just as powerful as the logics underlying vaccine anxieties, and indeed sharing similar conceptual framings.

This case focuses on the huge Pneumococcal Vaccine Trial (PVT) conducted jointly between the MRC and the Gambian Government between 2001 and 2005. This was a 'phase III' trial of a vaccine against pneumonia and invasive pneumococcal disease, designed to ascertain its impact on mortality and illness in African contexts, having already been subjected to trials concerning safety and efficacy (phases I and II). A positive result in an African context would be important to support the introduction of this vaccine into routine immunization schedules throughout Africa, despite its relatively high cost. The PVT was a randomized, double-blind, placebo-controlled trial, which, between 2001 and 2003, eventually recruited 17,437 infants between 6 weeks and 51 weeks old from areas of The Gambia's Central and Upper River Divisions (Cutts et al, 2005), but which had been planned to be three times as large, and cover half the country.

The trial involved a huge surveillance exercise, including stencilling numbers on each compound, geo-referencing each one, and taking a photo of the compound head. The trial recruited existing village health workers and employed further assistants in villages to track births, encourage clinic attendance, and report deaths. MRC fieldworkers recruited babies at government infant welfare clinics, where, if accepted, the trial vaccinations (or placebo) were mixed with routine infant immunizations. Informed consent required a mother's signature, after discussing a take-home information sheet with others. The support to government vaccination infrastructure, trial conduct and monitoring involved a huge logistical presence, visible in the trial's Land Rovers and motorbikes that crisscrossed the otherwise hardly used tracks. The MRC monitored children for 30 months after their vaccination, tracking illness and mortality, and visiting each child at home every three months.

Notably, the trial utilized state-of-the-art communication involving radio, public meetings and 'traditional' media, as well as fieldworker-administered explanations and information sheets to assist informed consent, in line with internationally recognized best practices in the ethics of medical research in developing countries (see Nuffield, 2002). The trial did *not* involve taking blood samples, although this had been necessary in a range of preparatory and associated studies, and in diagnosing certain ill children during this trial. Notably too, and in contrast with many other MRC studies, this trial did not officially offer free health care to study subjects and their families. Senior staff suggested that the MRC tried to help anyone with a serious illness, irrespective of whether they were in the trial. In practice, however, the majority of fieldworkers and participants did consider free treatment as an entitlement linked to trial participation (Fairhead et al, 2006).

Our research concerning parental engagement with the trial employed both ethnographic and survey methods. It took place after the recruitment and trial vaccination of children had finished (although monitoring continued), so our data on these aspects of trial practices and experiences are based on people's recent recollections. We focused our ethnographic work on the village of Marikunda, which had been covered by earlier MRC research as well as by the PVT. As ever, our focus was on bodily, social and wider political dimensions of parents' perspectives on the trial, but in the context of their broader perspectives on child health and its protection. We carried out participant observation and informal discussions in settings where parents take infants and where people discuss the issues of the day. We held group discussions in the five areas of the village, observed clinic interactions, interviewed frontline health professionals including MRC fieldworkers, and followed up with 50 longer narrative interviews with mothers identified through participant observation. We then considered the generalized significance of the key themes that emerged from this focused fieldwork among a wider population in Upper River Division, through an interviewer-administered questionnaire survey of a random sample of 800 mothers of children aged 12–24 months. The survey explored mothers' perspectives on engagement with MRC studies within their broader understandings and experiences of child health and its protection (Cassell et al, 2006b; Fairhead et al, 2006). The survey included many narrative responses which, in this chapter, supplement our ethnographic evidence from Marikunda.

Blood-stealing anxieties

Our survey showed that of the mothers invited to participate in the PVT, 85 per cent accepted. In probing what people thought the study was about, the survey found that 45 per cent of mothers invited to join either did 'not know', were 'not told' or had 'forgotten'. A proportion of 30 per cent said it was for improved child health, and 18 per cent said that it concerned free checking and treatment for their children. Only 6 per cent mentioned pneumonia or the phrase 'pneumococcal vaccine trial'.

Work in the village of Marikunda had revealed that people speak not about joining a particular trial, but about 'joining MRC' or 'having a child registered with MRC'.[1] When we asked about the benefits of 'having a child registered with MRC', 55 per cent of those invited to join mentioned good treatment, and a further 26 per cent specified that this was also free. A further 14 per cent also mentioned free food and transport. When asked if they had heard any negative ideas about MRC, 28 per cent said they had. Notably, many mothers participated despite this, and virtually all those reporting hearing negative things about MRC also saw benefits. The negative ideas, in all but one case turned on the notion that MRC 'takes' or 'steals' blood (the exception being a single case where worry was expressed about an 'experimental vaccine'). The local language term they used for stealing, *sunya* in Mandinka, is the general term for 'steal' in many other contexts.

These blood-stealing anxieties were expressed forcefully in some of the narrative accounts that mothers gave as part of the survey. Many statements such as the following were made:

> *MRC takes blood from healthy people and sells it.*

> *When one joins the MRC study, they will take much blood from your child and if you are not lucky the child may die.*

> *I heard from people that MRC would treat your child until he/she grows older. Then they take his/her blood and give it to others.*

> *I heard MRC steals and sells people's blood.*

> *MRC takes blood from those children that they claim to be helping and sell it to others.*

> *I heard that MRC people take blood from their patients in large quantities continuously.*

In a number of cases, people seemed unsure whether to believe these ideas, suggesting that they are part of a field of uncertainty:

> *I used to hear MRC takes the children's blood; I don't know if they sell it or not. I don't believe it. I have no fear of MRC.*

> *I heard when your blood is good MRC will steal it. I don't know, maybe they sell it. I cannot believe it. I will not however join MRC. I fear they will steal my child's blood.*

People elaborated on these themes during our ethnographic work in Marikunda. Several of the earlier studies that MRC had carried out in the village had involved venous blood taking, even though the PVT did not. One man, for example, explained how he had registered his child with MRC but later dropped out, as he was unnerved by conversations in the men's resting shelter. Here, other men told him that MRC would '*weedeh* [empty, from the French *vider*] the child's blood'. When his child next became ill, he instructed his wife to take him to the government clinic instead of MRC.

Bodily understandings

To understand these blood-stealing anxieties, it is important to focus on their bodily dimensions, and specifically to see how people understand blood and its significance. We consider here how people understand the relationship between health and blood, how blood is conceptualized, and, importantly, how it has recently come to be transacted.

Many aspects of life in Marikunda, in The Gambia more broadly and in the wider West African region are conceived of as a 'struggle for blood'. As we discussed in the previous chapter, maintaining the flow, quantity and quality of blood and other bodily fluids is understood as vital to health and strength. The struggle for blood is evident, for instance, in women's reproductive lives. As Bledsoe (2002) describes elsewhere in Mandinka Gambia women relate that they have only a restricted number of pregnancy chances, and strategize to ensure that each will lead to a healthy, surviving child. A major problem is to recuperate after each childbirth, to prepare for the next. This is conceived of as rebuilding strength, and is often spoken of as recuperating blood.

Indeed as people in Marikunda emphasized to us, women's lives more generally are fraught by blood loss: in the making of a child, in the events around childbirth, and in their arduous agricultural and domestic labour that hinders blood recuperation. Avoiding practices that might lead to blood loss, and seeking means to replenish and strengthen one's blood, are thus major preoccupations – for women especially, but for men and children too. Thus people often evaluate foods and medication for their impact on blood. Meat, certain leaf vegetables, red palm oil and now vitamin pills are sought after to build or replenish blood and thus strength.

People's concerns with blood recuperation are focused in attitudes towards and practices around blood donation. There is a general reluctance to give blood, even to close family or friends. As Cham (2000) describes, one of the reasons why men so rarely accompany women to hospital when they are in need of treatment is their fear that they would be obliged to give blood. These fears reflect understandings of blood and gender, which suggest that women are often needy recipients. Thus in the words of a poorer man, 'Usually only men give blood. It is more dangerous for a woman because of a woman's heavy workload. If a woman's blood lessens it is worse, as she still has to continue with her work' (Marikunda, May 2003). Women who accompany the sick, by contrast, are usually found by hospital staff to be unfit to give blood; practices which one can assume interplay with local understandings of blood and gender.

Thus blood logic is not only important to understanding strength, but through this configures perspectives on gender difference and indeed on wider social difference. As we shall see, people differentiate Africans from Europeans partly through the idea that Africans have 'stronger blood' – and they consider that Europeans seek it for this reason.

People associate blood depletion not simply with depleted strength and repro-ductive resilience, but also with susceptibility to other dangerous conditions. It is not the quantity of blood in the body alone that is important here, but also the balance between blood and other body 'water'. An excess of water over blood[2] is thought to predispose one to a serious condition called *fonyo* associated with swelling, and for which it is futile, and indeed dangerous, to receive injections (see also Bierlich, 2000).

Much ethnography relating to East Africa (Weiss, 1998; White, 2000; Geissler, 2005) suggests that blood is an important concept in defining kin relations. Audrey Richards writes of the importance of blood to the physiological under-standing of matriliny among the Bemba (Richards, 1939). Weiss (1998) describes how among the Haya, pacts solidified by the mutual drinking of blood created relatedness among clan members, such that subsequently they could marry only outside the clan. Geissler, for example, writes that 'Among people in Uhero, blood – of humans and of cattle – is identified with people's relations and the ties between the living and the dead (Geissler, 2005).

In contrast, throughout much of Islamic West Africa, including The Gambia, relatedness is not conceptually linked to blood, but to the different and con-trasting circulatory system that is sometimes referred to as 'white blood'. As we discussed in the last chapter, the white blood system links semen, breastmilk and foetal growth. Through these, it also shapes kinship (e.g. Cros, 1990; Fortier, 2001). Many people in Marikunda spoke in this way, describing how the spinal fluid is the origin of a man's semen, and how this helps constitute and build a foetus through continued sex during pregnancy. This also encourages the 'rise' of breastmilk and gives it, and through it the baby, a man's character and kinship identity. Thus, otherwise unrelated children who have shared maternal milk (through wet-nursing) should not marry. In contrast, red blood is associated with personal strength, and with the liver, the organ of self and of emotion. It is the stuff of life – the vital force of living things – but not the stuff of relatedness or identity. As the stuff of personal strength, blood is in turn linked to plumpness, considered a physical sign of a person's health, power and material prosperity (see also Ferme, 2002).

Transfusions establish blood as a potential commodity. Marikunda is about 10km from the local hospital at Basse, and 60km from the regional hospital at Bansang which both use transfusions. Yet blood is rarely readily available for transfusion. Cham (2000) has studied the economy of blood provisioning at Bansang. He found that when blood is needed, relatives are told to 'find blood' for 'their patient' in one of three ways. First, they can give blood themselves if the blood group matches. Second, they can give their own blood to the blood bank,

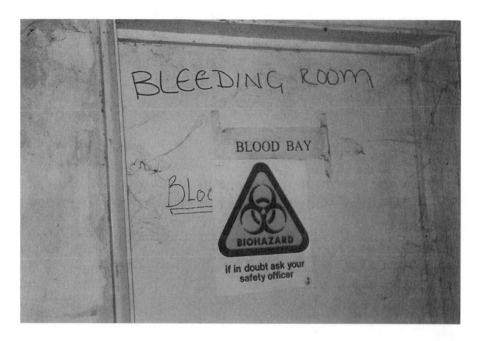

Figure 6.1 *The blood testing room in a district hospital, Upper River Division, The Gambia*

and draw out blood of the right group, if it is available. Last (but most usually), they can buy blood for cash. In this, the patient's family is asked to pay up front to laboratory staff who act as intermediaries to obtain blood from 'professional donors'. Cham found that patients and their escorts often complain that they pay for more blood units than they use, and accuse lab personnel of reselling the blood. This trade in blood is somewhat clandestine: Cham reports a patient saying that lab staff would sometimes call someone sitting inside the lab who pretends to be a commercial donor, in order to trick patients and make money from them. In the 14 cases of transfusion that he followed, blood cost about 150 dalasis (about £5) per pint, and the average amount spent on a transfusion was 363 dalasis. This is slightly more than a month's salary for a menial worker. Blood has thus acquired a high cash value. It has become part of an economy, as a commodity that can – and is – bought and sold.

The availability of transfusions is one of several medical practices and other factors which appear to have interplayed with existing local framings to render blood all the more central to local health calculus. Blood sampling has also become central to biomedical diagnostic practice in government clinics, as well as in the MRC's work in the region. In primary education, the importance of nutrition for strong blood is accentuated. Thus, while we do not have the historical evidence to track an evolving significance of 'blood calculus', there is strong reason to believe that it has become more important in recent decades. This is also suggested by the emergence of what people talk about as new conditions relating to blood.

An example might be 'high blood', an ailment that resonates with popular and African clinical use of the term 'hypertension', but in the words of a village healer, concerns the lightening and rising-up of 'bad blood' within the body, 'just as a bad egg floats', leading to dizziness.

Ideas linking strength and health to blood now inter-animate with a field of suspicion and imagination around the MRC's interest in blood and shape anxieties around participating in MRC activities. This is important for an understanding of the social world which the trial plays into, and of the wider political world in which it is also interpreted.

Social dimensions of vaccine trial engagements

Our studies in Marikunda and our survey indicate that many people considered joining the PVT in terms of a balance of danger and benefit. The dangers principally concerned blood taking. The benefits concerned the better or free treatment that people associated with the MRC. Survey responses indicated that many people associated both these possibilities with MRC activities. They balanced their worries against the benefits of joining MRC, as a kind of quid pro quo:

> *I heard MRC steals blood. I believe it. I saw them take blood from patients. I feared for my child to join but I had to hence she gets treatment there.*

> *I have heard that MRC takes blood from their registered children but didn't pay heed to this, I just wanted to register my child with them for better treatment.*

How people assessed this balance, and how this balancing translated into actual decisions to participate or not in the vaccine trial, were not simply questions for an individual parent. Rather, they implicated and were shaped by both gender relations and by relations of status and power in people's compounds and in the wider village. It was such social processes that led to Marikunda becoming what, in the eyes of the PVT organizers, was seen as a successfully 'accepting' village, in which all eligible infants except one became enrolled in the trial.

Perspectives on the balance of benefits and dangers in registering an infant with MRC often varied significantly between women and men, so that PVT registration was at times an issue of tension between husbands and wives. Husbands frequently expressed concerns around MRC's motivations and blood taking, sharing these anxieties with other men in the men's meeting-place (*bantaba*). Their reflections included sharing stories of prior involvement with MRC studies, and the blood-taking incidents that they had experienced. In contrast, while women often shared these worries, they seemed more likely to relegate them to the background in relation to their prior concern with and main responsibility for day-to-day infant care. People reported quarrels between husbands and wives taking place over the issue of registering an infant with the PVT, with mothers in most cases pushing for it, and fathers being against. Indeed in the single case in the village where PVT registration was declined, this seems to have been the husband's decision in the face of serious opposition from his wife.

Mothers, while acknowledging dangers, generally emphasized registering an infant with the trial as a positive step amid the multitude of strategies and practices they use to keep their infants well. Whatever they had earlier learned of the trial, they came to experience it through both the presence of MRC fieldworkers alongside government nurses at the monthly trekking clinic, and the practices associated with the consent procedure. A signature of agreement would then usher in further practices of registration and surveillance. These included the taking of a photograph of the mother and baby for their registration card, and the placing of a special number and stickers on the child's health card. The stickers were seen by mothers to denote 'being with MRC' in general terms. Indeed, like village men, women expressed their engagement not as 'with a trial', but in a far more general way as being 'with MRC' as one among many health-providing institutions. They described 'joining MRC' in a way more akin to registering a child with the government health service or creating a social relationship with a prominent marabout, than to consenting to participate in a trial.

Registering with MRC, in local perception, gives access to much the same sort of biomedical services as government clinics, but MRC is perceived as being more regular and having more reliable drug supplies and diagnostic techniques. It offers medicines free of charge. The benefits of good quality, free medical care extend from their children, to themselves and sometimes other family members. Thus while the PVT's formal trial protocol and procedures did not grant special treatment privileges to study subjects, there was a pervasive view among villagers in Marikunda that joining MRC did bring such privileges. For example, one woman, when asked what the PVT meant to her, said she could not recall what was said to her during the information/consent session but 'one thing I know is that it offers good treatment leading to good health, and my stepmother's children [registered with the trial] are doing well' (Mother, Marikunda, April 2003). Another woman described how:

> *I have registered with MRC and seen the benefits. One good thing about it is that, there is no money involved. The parents would also benefit from the treatment given. Drugs are so expensive and are not available in government hospitals (Mother, Marikunda, April 2003).*

Experience at the monthly outreach clinic for infant welfare in Marikunda reinforced the differences between being 'with' and 'not with' MRC, and the implications of these for infant care. The usual team of government nurses would be preceded by an MRC Land Rover containing a group of MRC fieldworkers and occasionally a doctor.[3] The four queues that used to form in different parts of the clinic building – for initial registration, weighing, vaccinations and antenatal checks – were now joined by a fifth, MRC line, under a tree on the other side of the courtyard. This separate MRC line, there primarily to screen and monitor children, was generally perceived by mothers as 'for treatment', and those registered with the PVT could queue there if they were concerned about their infant's health. Here, they would have a consultation with a team consisting of a nurse, a fieldworker and occasionally a doctor. This appeared to women as a far greater level of attention than they might receive from one of the government nurses. The MRC table had beside it a large trunk which appeared to women to be filled with drugs (even though it also contained documentation). In contrast, women suggested that the government team rarely carried a wide selection of drugs and would usually refer cases requiring treatment to the hospital in Basse, requiring a difficult half-day's walk or an expensive, and usually unavailable, taxi or donkey cart. MRC protocol stated that any seriously ill child, whether a study participant or not, would be transported to hospital. Nevertheless, some villagers perceived this as a benefit reserved for study children. In general perception then, in Marikunda at least, entitlement to join the MRC line represented not just 'free' treatment, but on many occasions, any treatment.

On one clinic day that we observed, for example, a woman anxious about the rash on her 2-month-old baby lamented the fact that he had just missed joining the PVT, for which registration closed a month before his birth. She tried queuing up at the MRC table, but was turned away as she was not a trial participant. Several other women had similar experiences, with children who fell either side of the trial age bracket. Seeing registered children and their siblings receiving medicines reinforced their sense of being denied access to something which had become 'normal' to many of their kin, friends and neighbours.

In some respects, MRC fills in for what would normally be a father's role in an infant's health care: that is, stepping in with financial and logistical assistance when serious health problems arise. From this perspective, it is not surprising that some men make a different calculus of benefit and danger, and welcome MRC health provision as 'letting them off the hook'. This is particularly the case for men who have travelled or out-migrated, whether to Banjul or abroad. Thus one woman registered her third child for the PVT on the recommendation of the child's father, who was working in Banjul. It seems that he saw MRC as a kind of insurance, in his absence: 'my husband asked me to go to MRC as they have good medicines. The father stays away and if the child had an attack it would be difficult, but with MRC one prevents as well as cures' (Mother, Marikunda, June 2003).

The tenor and outcomes of such husband–wife negotiations were also shaped by the practices associated with the informed consent process. People relate that it was women who were handed the PVT information sheet and consent form at their first clinic attendance with a new baby. Only an exceptional few could read the Arabic translation on the reverse, let alone the English explanation. Most brought them home to their husbands, who again often had difficulty comprehending the sheets. Nevertheless, it was generally they who made the decision about whether or not their infant would join. Talking about this issue in a group discussion, women in Marikunda denied any power over such decisions; 'it is up to our husbands to decide'. Similarly in our wider survey, only 44 per cent of mothers said that they had been involved in the decision (either alone or jointly with others). The rest said their husband, compound head or other senior men

Figure 6.2 *Medical researchers on a village visit during the pneumococcal vaccine trial in The Gambia, checking the health of enrolled children*

her words, the 'informed consent' process is overshadowed by
within the household and compound. Nevertheless, it is also the
decisions usually coincided with women's interests, so they had
resist them. Where quarrels did arise – and there are many reports
of hea.   :s – it is in those households where a man's resistance based on
earlier blood-taking experience clashed with a woman's interests in registering,
largely to guarantee treatment for her infant.

Decisions about trial engagement in Marikunda were not just left to individual
households, but also involved village authorities. First, the MRC fieldworkers
liaised with and supported the village health worker in communicating the trial
aims to prospective participants. In Marikunda, he is a local man who has played
this role for 18 years, and is regarded by both villagers, government and MRC
staff as exceptionally active and enthusiastic. He encouraged eligible mothers
to register with the trial, whether one-on-one or during his monthly 'rallying'
calls to women to take their babies to the mobile clinic. He also worked through
several people who were influential in the village – including two powerful local
traders – to push the message that MRC was proposing 'nothing bad' and that
it would be 'good to join'. Even more significantly, the village chief (*Alkalo*) and
his council of elders agreed, in conjunction with the village health worker, that
Marikunda parents 'should accept'. At a village meeting, he exhorted the entire
village to register their infants. Ultimately, as many parents expressed, it was this
village-level decision and the pressure exerted through the chief and elders that
led them to join. This put an end to dithering for many – although not necessarily
to their anxiety about whether this had been the right decision. It was certainly
a key moment in the social process that eventually led Marikunda to have near-
universal acceptance.

The power and solidarity of village authorities varies enormously from settlement to settlement. Chiefs and elders would not wield the authority to bring about
such an orchestrated community response everywhere. Indeed some villages
are riven by political factions that divide over questions of MRC engagement,
as over other matters. However, these variations only serve to emphasize the
interrelationship between trial engagement and socio-politics at the village level,
as well as within households. Bringing about an orchestrated mass 'acceptance'
can serve as a demonstration and affirmation of the power of local political
structures. In a similar way, so can bringing about a successful mass 'refusal' – of
which there were several examples during the MRC's recruitment process for
the PVT.

Anxiety about blood stealing in a political–economic context

People's worries about the MRC taking blood are not simply about its possible
bodily effects, depleting the health and strength of a blood-sampled subject.
Rather, people's anxieties – and the circumstances in which they understand the

MRC's blood taking as stealing – relate also to their understandings of a wider political economy.

People are unsure exactly what MRC does with the blood it takes. Their speculations on this include the notion that the small vials they collect (as blood samples) are amalgamated into quantities sufficient to make treatments and medicines:

> *I heard that MRC people take blood from their patients, put that together and treat others with it.*

People also speculate that blood is exported for its qualities, becoming part of a transnational economy. For example, and as originally recorded in our notes:

> *One man joined a trial several years ago. He thought that he had been chosen because his blood was amongst 'the best in the village'. He recalls how they tried to take a lot of blood, but after the first intravenous syringe-ful he felt a pain in his chest and told them to 'stop or I will fight you'. He recalls no reason being given for the blood-taking, only that a promise of gifts of medicine failed to materialise: 'I received nothing, and felt very offended.' While he initially thought the blood was to help treat Gambians, as time went by he reflected that it was probably to treat Europeans, as 'African blood is stronger' than theirs.*

Similarly, a man who became unhappy with the frequency and quantity of blood taken from his son during treatment at MRC facilities in the 1990s maintained that:

> *MRC are attracted by my son's blood, because our blood is of higher quality than that of the white people (Father, Marikunda, April 2003).*

People's perceptions of MRC recruitment procedures in studies past and present played into their reflections that high-quality blood was being sought. For instance as men in Marikunda related:

> *They would also pick and choose those children to join and those not to join. If the intention is to protect children why do they accept some and reject others? (Marikunda, April 2003).*

> *They are interested in healthy fat babies. Sometimes they go in for thin and beautiful babies. I remembered about six months ago two healthy, fat, handsome male children from different families joined the programme. Unfortunately they died. Their deaths followed each other, so MRC was responsible (Marikunda, April 2003).[4]*

In our survey too, a mother said, for example: 'I heard they look for healthy children and take their blood.'

Many parents' narratives contain within them a sense of transaction. Sometimes these transactions are perceived as reasonable, but in other instances they are perceived as robbery. Thus some indicate a sense of fair transaction, for instance when blood giving is reciprocated with free medication or indeed with what people have understood as blood replenishing medicines (in most cases vitamins) given by MRC. For example:

> *People are gradually accepting MRC now, because they offer good treatment. Whenever blood is taken, they ensure that enough medicines are given to replace the loss. They will never do what is bad (Father, Marikunda, May 2003).*

However the exchange relationship can become unfair in many ways. One man had the ill fortune see his child die in his arms and attributed the death to earlier MRC blood-taking intervention, here described as we originally noted it:

> *Initially, the child joined the MRC programme. They were supplying things to encourage people to join. They brought soap and other things during the naming ceremony. Later, the child fell ill and was taken to MRC by his wife. He heard that they took blood, and put it in a container. After returning home the child did not improve, and he was taken back where some blood was again taken. The child died four days later. Since then, MRC have asked him to sign his younger children up to other trials, but he refuses. Now known as a 'refuser', when MRC pass him by in a Land Rover they don't stop for him. This has made him furious. He has told his wife never to seek a lift but to walk even when offered. He has 'turned his back on MRC'.*

Some people have become suspicious of blood taking because they do not receive any results, in contrast with the blood taken for diagnosis in hospitals. For example:

> *They do not say what they do with the samples. They do not provide results about the blood taken to the person concerned [as the clinics do when one has a blood test]. As this is not done, the rumour that is spreading about selling blood must be true, as we do not know what was done with the blood (Male villager, Marikunda, April 2003).*

Without feedback, the taking of blood is likened to 'robbery'.

The tremendous resources of MRC and especially their fleet of vehicles themselves engender suspicion of wider motives. For instance:

> *It is amazing to see a vehicle being fuelled to come all the way from Basse just to identify or transport one small infant. What is the rationale behind their action? This made us afraid of their programme (Male villager, Marikunda, May 2003).*

This concern with the material wealth of MRC trials puts the value of any blood that they might take into a different register: a sense that the little taken has a far greater value measured by the entire value of a trial and its logistical support. In turn, such speculation interplays with wider worry about 'white people' and their wealth more generally. As a spokesperson from a nearby village known for its reticence to join MRC studies described:

> *It shocked the villagers to see and hear white people coming to this part of the country saying they are offering services to promote health. Compared to Europe where conditions are favourable, Africa is quite the opposite. Why do they have to leave their comfort to stay in a hot humid environment? Why do they have to leave their mosquito-free country to come to a place infested with mosquitoes and be taking prophylaxis regularly, is it worth it? I have travelled to many parts of Europe and then settled down in Japan for 10 years. I am a living witness of what the white people do to the blacks. They are terrible. The whites would never do anything free of charge (Male villager, Gambisara, May 2003).*

And another:

> *The whites would never do anything for free; they are after their self-interest. They make themselves the priority and overwork you. Sometimes they pretend to be nice or good but behind this they have a different motive (Male villager, Gambisara, May 2003).*

For some, such reflections on international political economy interplayed with reflection on national politics. People's discussions often reflected on the extent to which the MRC was 'with' the government (which it was in the case of the PVT, as a joint government-MRC trial), as well as the extent to which the government itself could be relied upon to promote their interests. Unsurprisingly, opinions on this point varied, depending not least on whether people supported the party in power or not. For instance several men in Marikunda who were linked with the party in power expressed a view that the Gambian government would protect them from MRC:

> *When MRC first came, some people were scared, saying that MRC will take people's blood. But others said the MRC and the government had discussed this a lot, and that the government does not sell its people. They will not sell their children's blood. After assessing the situation, I became brave enough to accept. The Gambian government will never allow someone to trick its citizenry (Male villager, Marikunda, May 2003).*

Evident in people's reflections, then, is the sense that blood transactions implicate a national and international political economy. Blood taking becomes part of a set of relationships between economically poor people and the visibly wealthy institution of MRC, and by extension, between Africa and Europe. Anxieties about blood taking and interpretations that this is stealing reflect both the sense of extreme inequality in these relationships, and the exploitation that often appears to accompany transactions.

Perspectives on trial participation: interactions between framings

The world of the researcher is framed in terms of 'the trial'. Most staff recruitment, line management, financing, administration, work practices, ethical conduct, accountability, and so on are organized around particular trials and their protocols. For researchers, connectivity with the world outside is regulated by the globalized institutions and practices of biomedical ethics, also focused on 'the trial'. Connectivity turns on internationally recognized 'best practices' in communicating trial aims and procedures to the community (by radio, traditional media and public meetings), and to potential research subjects (through information sheets and the regulated way frontline research staff explain the trial), who can on this basis give their 'informed consent'. The assumption is that subjects' interpretations of what researchers are up to can be strongly determined by such trial-by-trial communication.

Yet rather than understand the MRC on a trial-by-trial basis, the prevailing views of those living with the trial focus on MRC as an institution, and its historical reputation sedimented through many engagements, not particular trials. They focus on the MRC as a health provider more than as a research institution. For the majority of Gambian people, then, what is at stake when reflecting whether or not to 'join MRC' is not a particular trial, or even anything much to do with 'science' or 'research', but a historically embedded and far broader relationship with an institution – the MRC – and its global location and meanings. These meanings, as we have shown, include both potential danger (of blood stealing) and benefit (of good, free treatment). Both of these are highly significant amid people's conceptions of the interrelationship between blood and strength, and the dilemmas of keeping infants well. Balancing these is often a negotiated path with worries along the way, involving struggles around gender, generation and authority amid social and power relations. It is the outcome of such negotiations that led to particular households and sections of communities deciding to register their infants.

Such framings contrasted with the perspectives of the scientists and managers involved with the PVT. Given that for them, what is at stake is a particular trial, they developed particular views on why people did not participate, and what it would take to encourage them to; views that often lay badly at odds with the villagers' perspectives we have outlined in this chapter. Moreover, these contrasting framings were sometimes drawn into interaction in the context of the trial in ways that served to reinforce them.

Fieldworkers and their supervisors presented two related sets of views. First was the notion of the trial as a scientific enterprise that populations could and should come to understand. Such understanding, or scientific enlightenment, was linked with – seen as the key to – people participating. This link was exemplified in the following statement from one of the PVT's field supervisors:

> *We gauge people's understanding from the acceptance rate. If it is high, we assume that people have got our message. If they refuse, we assume misunderstanding, and sensitise them (Trial supervisor, Basse, April 2003).*

In this way acceptance or refusal becomes a proxy for people's comprehension of the trial, ignoring the possibility that people might be accepting for quite other reasons. Thus in Marikunda, as all but one eligible infant was registered for the trial, MRC fieldworkers and senior staff alike had come to consider the village to be 'accepting', its parents presumed to have 'understood' and to have taken on board MRC assurances, following communication and consent practices. There was, therefore, some surprise when an attempt to recruit participants for a follow-up immunogenicity study (that required blood sampling) encountered significant numbers who refused to participate. What MRC had understood as 'acceptance' evidently did not reflect a transformed mentality, but a calculus in 'joining MRC' that had gone one way, and was now going the other. MRC's claim that parental concerns with blood stealing were ill-founded rumour which would pass as people acquired scientific modernity begins to ring hollow.

Second, managers and fieldworkers tend to describe trial 'acceptors' and 'refusers' as distinct categories – whether applied to individuals or to whole communities – in ways that overlook the uncertainty, balancing and negotiation involved with people's decisions. They explain refusal in various ways, attributing it to certain social categories. As interviews with fieldworkers at the MRC field station in Basse revealed, many ascribe refusal to ethnicity, singling out the Serahuli people in this respect. They also ascribe refusal to 'tradition', leaving ambiguous whether this means a greater respect for Islamic authority, health practices less shaped by biomedicine, or disengagement with state administrative structures. In some contradiction, others ascribe refusal to people having 'travelled' – considering villages with larger levels of refusal to have more diasporic connections to the capital, Banjul, and beyond, bringing external distortions to benign local sentiments. In other cases, they attribute refusal to communities that are new to MRC trials, and who have not yet come to know and trust the MRC. These categories of trial acceptor and refuser, and explanations for them, are rooted in the institutional needs of public health and research institutions, and in established modes of discussion among health workers, as developed through the long history of these institutions. The categories have put into play a particular reasoning around the nature or character of rural society, and differences within it, centred on the degree to which people accept (or reject) scientific modernity. In this, the trial's imperatives are shaping knowledge not just about health, but about the social world.

Given these views, both trial managers and fieldworkers place great emphasis on communicating the objectives of the trial, establishing participation, and addressing 'refusal', which they see as a problem. Yet the interactions generated in this sometimes served to drive perspectives further apart. Thus when faced with villages where refusal was widescale, trial officials tended to respond primarily by investing in more intensive publicity efforts. Re-explaining the trial's aims and purpose, using locally appropriate communications methods, was seen as the key way to reduce the proportion of refusers. Given villagers' rather different framings of the issue, however, such publicity was eclipsed for parents by their broader reflections on MRC – reflections often articulated through blood-stealing anxieties. That trial communication did not generally achieve its aims is suggested by our survey findings, in which 94 per cent of those invited to join could not say what the study was about – although as we have also seen, people participated despite this lack of trial-specific knowledge. For trial managers, however, it was easy to assume that a high or increased acceptance rate after enhanced consultation and communication proved the effectiveness of its techniques, reinforcing their view of the link between trial-specific understanding and acceptance. Equally, it was easy to assume that continued refusal despite sensitization indicated continued ignorance, suggesting the need to apply sensitization with even greater vigour. Both outcomes thus reinforced their dominant perspectives on refusal.

As fieldworkers made clear in discussions with us, for them, not having refusals, or gaining acceptances in 'problematic' villages, became a point of pride. Yet positioned as they were at the front line in villages, fieldworkers often had a different view of village–MRC interactions than did the more distant trial managers. This was rooted more in the transactional logics that were important to villagers and which fieldworkers themselves became a part of (see Geissler et al, 2005, for a discussion of such transactions in another Gambian MRC study site). In this context, fieldworkers understand all too well that villagers are primarily motivated to participate in the trial by their desire for privileged free treatment. In interviews, several explained how they sought to increase participation by emphasizing this when they explained the trial, and by using discretion in administering free treatment so as to maintain good relations in the village. For example one fieldworker said:

> We explain that in the PVT there are 40,000 children so there are not the resources for everyone. We cannot treat the whole family, only immediate family, the mother and siblings, but if the father goes with the PVT card he will be assisted.

Another said: 'What they want is the free treatment. This is clarified during the time of recruitment.' Such examples of fieldworker discretion are disputed by the trial's senior managers. They emphasize that the PVT protocol did not provide for such free treatment, and that instead the MRC tried to help anyone with serious illness, irrespective of whether they were in the trial. They also deny that fieldworkers could be exercising such agency and discretion, stressing that they all follow standard, mandated trial procedures. Through such denial, trial managers uphold and reinforce a view of the trial and acceptance/refusal as based on formal, trial-specific procedures and logics, and villagers' understanding and acceptance of them. In this, they distance themselves further from the more transactional logics in which both villagers' and fieldworkers' everyday experiences are embedded.

Finally, there are instances where interactions have been expressly designed to improve mutual understanding between scientists and villagers, and to quell worries about blood stealing. Yet in dialogical ways, these attempts can misfire, widening gulfs further. Thus MRC has attempted to explain better what it does by organizing visits to its laboratories to 'demystify science'. Such visits have been organized in the context of a number of recent MRC studies. In the case of the PVT, a group of women who participated in one of the preparatory studies was taken to the MRC field station in Basse with such aims in mind. Yet as one described:

> *I witnessed an incident where a blood sample was taken from a baby, put in a small bottle and mixed with the boro [serum] in the laboratory. After it was mixed, the women who were present misinterpreted it to be whole blood withdrawn from the baby. This was circulated in the village and people were scared (Mother, Marikunda, April 2003).*

Far from demystifying science, then, this visit – within villagers' reasoning about the transnational economy of blood – served to confirm its reality, showing them what MRC does with what it steals.

Conclusions

In the Gambia, blood has distinct, particular meanings which are central to the ideas of blood stealing that now circulate. Here, we have tried to show how blood calculus has become the dominant way in which they reflect on trial participation. The 'struggle for blood', the significance of its accumulation in the body, its capacity to be extracted, transformed or transfused, and its relative independence from relational physiology, all make it a remarkably easy product to consider as transactable. Moreover, ideas about transactions in blood relate understandings of the body rather seamlessly to understandings of the economy. Blood reasoning enables those in Marikunda to link their evaluation of bodily process, health and health chances to economic success/hardship and lifestyle. Through blood accumulation, one can make savings (or lose out) in one's very body. In many respects, the path to good health in contemporary West Africa is construed as a build-up of blood, linked to notions of strength. People could thus be understood as living in an 'age of blood', the latter describing a substantive relation that connects the body and the economy. Blood logic interrelates bodily processes and wider political–economic processes through understandings of accumulation and depletion that both take place within and transcend the body.

The perception of a European desire for African blood can be seen as a projection of such blood logic onto Europeans whom, it is thought, benefit financially and medically from the medications presumed to be based on it. Appreciation of this substantive, ontological relation between blood and economy is, we argue, vital to understanding current anxieties about blood stealing. Such anxieties are neither groundless rumours that circulate amid scientifically unenlightened publics, nor part of a realm of the occult, resurfacing as superstitious Africans come to grips with modernity. Rather, views that the MRC is involved in stealing blood are grounded in local practices fostering health in which blood calculus is involved, as well as their intersection with technological and trial practices, as interpreted through locally embedded meanings of blood. Ideas around blood stealing, when an anticipated transaction unfolds as unreasonable or unjust, also provide a potent way of expressing concerns with the wider political–economic relations in which medical research is embedded, and sometimes – through trial refusal and mobilization – directly challenging them. We suggest that blood stealing only has this power as a lens to reflect and refract wider political–economic experience because of its grounding in localized understandings and experience of technological and trial practices. Blood-stealing anxieties provide a logical way for people to connect their bodily experiences – the economy of blood in their bodies, and its links with health – with their experiences of international political economy, and the inequalities and extractions it involves.

The mystery of how some acquire huge wealth while others remain poor has long been a topic of lively reflection and speculation in societies across Africa (Geissler and Pool, 2006, p979). Indeed it is such 'mysteries' that some anthropologists have – as we argue, often misleadingly – linked to a resurgence of belief in 'occult economies' in Africa (e.g. Comaroff and Comaroff, 1999). As people engage with globally supported medical research, it is not surprising that speculation turns logically to the transnational economic disparities in which it is so evidently embedded. Geissler and Pool have reviewed a wide range of instances in which local populations have accused medical researchers as well as promoters of health interventions, such as vaccination, of engaging in nefarious practices – whether stealing blood, engaging in satanic acts, or distributing anti-fertility substances. They argue that such accusations should be seen as valid local commentary on medical research ethics – and, one might add, the wider political economy in which they are embedded (see Angell, 2000; Farmer, 2005), the political economy of top-down global public health programmes, or the political economy of the state or international relations more broadly. The vampiritic anxieties that we have explored in this chapter have, in this respect, much in common with vaccine anxieties – and indeed are often interconnected with them.

Indeed in the Gambian case, for those who see a rise in expressed anxieties about blood stealing as part of a resurgent set of rumours as Africans confront modernity, we can also offer a rather less mystified and more material reading. Any rise in concern about blood stealing could reflect perceptions of a rising value of blood to others (as medical research proliferates, blood-based pharmaceuticals develop and blood transfusion technologies spread) amid the country's pervasive and deepening poverty. Impoverishment accentuates the material inequality between the world of medical researchers and the world of potential study subjects: between those perceived to want blood and those who have it in their bodily reserves. Poverty also makes it more difficult to replenish blood; in the Gambia a pint of blood has only recently come to represent half a month's salary. In this context, it cannot be expected that blood-stealing anxieties will just fade away as people become more 'scientifically enlightened'.

Notes

1   This notion of 'joining MRC' also prevailed in relation to another MRC research project that we studied – an infant cohort study exploring immune responses located in Sukuta, Western Division (see Fairhead et al, 2004; Leach and Fairhead, 2005).
2   Whether this means more diluted, or in relation to water elsewhere in the body, is difficult to discern.
3   It is important to note that Marikunda and other villages within the catchment of the main Basse clinic may have differed in this respect from other areas of the PVT which did not experience such high attendance by MRC staff.
4   The PVT had strict procedures requiring the investigation of reports of serious side effects, and found no cases where mortality was linked with the trial vaccine.

7

Conclusions

There are many versions of the story of childhood vaccination – past, present and future. For many it is a simple and optimistic saga of disease eradication, in which science and technology gradually conquer nature and ignorance in equal measure for humanity's good. Others narrate a story of coercion, control and conspiracy towards deception and even genocidal ends. Yet for many it is a field of heightened anxiety: a balance of the opportunities and dangers that this unfolding and most global of technologies offers to that most intimate, personal and closely observed world which is the nurturing of new life.

This book has tracked today's contradictory engagements with vaccination and vaccine science in very different social contexts. It has considered how a ubiquitous and rather singular technology, and its globalized technocracy plays into diverse social worlds in parts of the UK and West Africa. We have been keen to identify how broader conceptual, social and wider political orders are significant to people's unfolding experiences of technology, and have developed an analytical framework to discern links between these and how they unfold in dialogical relation to vaccination services and sciences.

Our approach has been to focus on parental anxieties about vaccination. While in some cases anxiety carries negative connotations – such as uneasiness, concern and their causes – it also has a more positive sense of an earnest desire *for* something: to strive for improved immunity, strength or resilience, however conceived. To understand these anxieties, we have found it necessary to consider not only parents' reflections and practices concerning health and vaccination, but also the social worlds of which these reflections are a part, and the wider political and economic issues that become drawn into such reflection. As we consider here, a strong theme in this work has been to expose repeatedly how these bodily, social and wider political domains are conceptually connected and co-produced, coming together in broader framings. Yet to understand these framings, we have also needed to see how they emerge and are reinforced in engagement with the rather different framings that emerge from the health and policy institutions concerned with vaccination.

We now review bodily, social and political–economic dimensions to parental framings, drawing out comparisons and commonalities across the UK and West African cases that earlier chapters have considered separately. As we show, some of these commonalities serve to qualify and question stereotypes that have depicted Europe and Africa as 'two worlds' in relation to science and technology. As we go on to show, this discussion also questions the use of concepts of risk, trust and rumour that have been cornerstones to existing policy and social science discourse on vaccination anxieties. In many ways, this vocabulary is part of the problem. Instead, attention to the contextual and dialogical way that gulfs emerge between parental and policy worlds suggests ways towards bridging these gulfs, and making life easier for all concerned.

Body, sociality, politics – emerging vaccination experiences in the UK and West Africa

In the body

Whether in the UK or West Africa, parents have a range of ways of thinking about vaccines and their effects. Some broadly correspond with modern western biomedicine, but others draw on different therapeutic frames, whether Islamic, herbalist or homeopathic. Even where therapeutic frames are distinct, they often share framing concepts (such as the immune system, or particular notions of circulation and strength in the West African context).

In both settings, parental evaluation of a particular child's health history interplays with reasoning that has a wider cultural salience. The notion of a child having a personalized pathway through the numerous uncertainties that can influence his or her health, and of the importance of building strength and robustness is key in West Africa as much as in the UK. And in both settings, it is often in relation to a child's particular pathway and strength that parents evaluate the appropriateness of vaccination.

Yet, whereas in the UK, the path to strength, robustness and good health is seen as a build-up of immunity, in West Africa good health is conceived of as a build-up of blood, and its proper circulation. Both immune system reasoning and blood reasoning are broad conceptual fields that orientate, and can integrate, diverse dimensions of health and effects on it. Each has emerged and come to dominate through the interplay of medical science and popular, cultural conceptions. Just as concepts of immunity have seeped between immunology and popular media and reflection in Europe and the US, so in West Africa, attention to blood circulation, quantity and quality as an index of health – a long-standing mode of cultural reasoning in the region – has been heightened by medical interest in blood testing and transfusion.

In sociality

In both British and African settings, the world of vaccination creates new social relations and forms of sociality. MMR talk, neighbourhood groups at African clinics, and mobilization around vaccine concerns are part of the processes through which social relations are made, and through which people come to find similarity and difference between themselves and others. Discussions and practices around vaccination are part and parcel of gender and generational relations, and communities, networks and emergent social solidarities which sometimes extend transnationally. We have seen how vaccination is quintessentially social, something that is often overlooked in approaches that see it simply as a technical issue about which people 'make decisions'. Vaccination exemplifies how science and technology are implicated in the construction of kinship and social worlds, involving particular forms of exclusion and differentiation, and forms of tolerance and relationality.

Yet how the social dimensions of vaccination unfold is configured in specific ways linked not just to social history and context, but also to reasoning concerning the body. Some differences have emerged in the nature of this between the British and West African settings. Thus in the UK, the values of personal responsibility and choice connect with ideas around personalized immunity and individuated pathways of child health. These enable a moral world highly tolerant of personalized decisions, even as people discuss and compare these among themselves within households and social networks. In contrast, our West African examples reveal how the conceptual world of blood and bodily fluids links child health to social and moral orders: to appropriate behaviour and worry about the consequences of other's behaviour, whether vindictive or accidental. This produces a world in which child health and vaccination are bound up with maintaining social and moral propriety, and thus with the associated forms of authority (age and gender hierarchies, village authorities, compound heads, women's groups, and so on).

This is not, however, the stereotypical contrast sometimes drawn between Europe's post-industrial 'risk society' and a 'traditional', community-focused developing world. Such configurations do not negate personalized reflection and negotiation in West Africa, just as they do not negate reflection on the morality of vaccination in the UK. It is just that these reflections have different forms and emphases. Issues of confidence and power to go against expectations, and responsibility towards both one's own child and towards one's community, prove to be important in both Britain and West Africa. Social relations and notions of community and morality are being actively forged around vaccination in both settings.

By understanding how parents are coming to consider their child's health in relation to community good, we can see that – contrary to common arguments in health policy circles – anxieties are not simply personal or selfish, but are rooted in particular framings of how a particular child's health relates to the community. Thus in the UK, parents who avoided MMR evoked notions of a community good both in concerns that MMR may be safe and good for the community 'but not for my child' [because of personalized immunity issues], and in concerns that vaccination is damaging children and thus society. In West Africa, parents who avoided oral polio vaccine or declined to participate in vaccine trials were concerned that these were bad not only for their own children, but also for their societies. This exemplifies how different kinds of collectivities and solidarities are emerging, shaped through shared experiences or positionalities in relation to technologies and technocracies.

In both the UK and West African settings, frontline health workers – whether British GPs, nurses and alternative therapists, or West African clinic staff, research fieldworkers, healers and NGO workers – are critical brokers between the large-scale nature of national and international vaccination programmes, and the personal and social worlds of parents. Rather than acting as the one-way conduits for information and pro-vaccination advice that policy discourses often assume, however, encounters are often far more negotiated. Whether in dialogue or through practices, parents do not bow to or accept professionals' expertise unquestioningly, but rather relate it to their own experiential knowledge and expertise.

A common theme across the British and West African cases is that interactions with health workers are social. They are shaped by prior relations of power and authority. They are also shaped by social and personal connections which affect the quality of interaction: whether in seeking advice from health workers who are friends and relatives in the UK; or in the ways that relatedness affects interactions with clinic nurses in Africa. Parents' experiences of these interactions of course vary greatly depending on who they are, and their own social backgrounds – while parents' interactions with health workers take place within a much broader field of social interactions around vaccination decisions and advice. How parents feel in relation to these social and authority relations affects how far they express vaccine anxieties, and how these translate into practices – in ways that counter prevailing stereotypes. Thus, in the UK, it is less that the middle classes are newly anxious (and that parents from more deprived backgrounds are not), than that their educational and social experiences give them confidence to express their questions and, in some cases, not to vaccinate. In The Gambia, refusal to participate in vaccine trials is less rooted in ethnic identity or poor education, than in material circumstances that render its benefits unnecessary.

Parental encounters with the work of health staff serve to make the global and national intimate. Parents come to experience vaccination programmes through such highly local encounters, and the particular settings – the doctor's office, the infant welfare clinic courtyard – in which they take place. The personality of the professional, and the material trappings of the encounter, all shape what vaccination comes to mean. Yet at the same time, frontline workers are representatives of national and in some cases international programmes and imperatives. This sometimes makes them feel conflicted; it also influences encounters with parents who often see beyond the person to the wider political and economic issues at stake.

In political and economic orders

The cases reveal just how far vaccine anxieties relate to wider concerns: with the political economy of science, with the state and with the global political, economic or religious order. While such links are clear in many other works and popular commentary, we have sought to understand how and why vaccines – and particular vaccines – become the focus of wider reflection. It is easier to assert that anxieties are 'meta-commentaries' on, or idioms for expressing concerns with, global capitalism, geo-politics and inequalities than it is to show and to understand why anxieties become manifest in the ways that they do.

The chapters reveal how both immune system reasoning and blood reasoning link bodily processes with those in wider society and economy, but configure this in rather different ways. Thus in our West African examples, blood-thinking interrelates bodily processes and wider political–economic processes, through understandings of strength building, accumulation and depletion that both take place within and transcend the body – connecting the body and wider polity and economy. Immune system thinking, as Martin (1994) has pointed out for the US, and as we have discerned for the UK, similarly relates bodily processes to wider social and economic transformations that emphasize 'flexible specialization' in business and lifestyle, as well as a personal responsibility and flexibility to cope with threats.

These linkages should not be seen as simply metaphorical, connoting both a likeness in health and political–economic reasoning but at the very same time, separateness. Rather, in their thinking about child health and vaccination, parents are sometimes tracking more substantive relations between body, society and political economy. In The Gambia, for example, blood calculus traces substantive connections between bodily and economic wellbeing, and between bodily transactions of blood in trial sampling and blood donation, and a trans-national political economy of medical research and European–African relations in which it is seen to have value. In the UK, notions of personalized immunity are linked to real desires for choice and flexibility in vaccination regimes that have been frustrated by what some parents see as an inflexible and dogmatic state, aligned with the commercial interests of pharmaceutical companies. Personalized immunity is also linked substantively with people's economic conditions – it can be compromised by poor food, living environments, pollution – and the broader political–economic relations that shape these.

These interpretative frames also enable experience in one domain to shape experience in another. Thus for many Brighton parents, the triple MMR vaccine was considered 'too much in one go'. While this relates to ideas about 'overloading' the immune system, it also echoes personal experiences of 'too many things going on'; of everyday experience of complexity, and of government, corporate and technical systems working in ways that bring unpredictable results. This is not simply an anxiety that vaccines might upset a delicately balanced body in which external threats are disruptive to natural bodily orders (Fitzpatrick, 2004). It is not a case of 'pollution' reasoning; a generic response to things being 'out of place' (Douglas, 1966). Rather, it reveals parental appreciation of uncertainty complexity and the emergence of unknowable outcomes in the body politic as much as in the body, as vaccination enters bodies that are also understood in complex and individualized ways.

In West African blood reasoning, concerns are framed within ideas of properly channelled flow, and problems arise from inadequate blood, its blockage and inappropriate mixing. Again, it is possible to discern echoes connecting bodily anxiety and wider social and political anxieties: the anxieties that arise from blockage of flow – of life support systems which when working 'flow' properly, and of unblocked roads, regular markets, migration patterns, reciprocities, seasonal cycles and animal migrations, and of state support. Perspectives on all these are predominantly configured through the flow of a working system versus one that is disrupted and blocked, with the flow bringing strength and prosperity.

In short, anxieties around vaccination and vaccine-related science are grounded in particular notions of the body and body politic that reinforce each other. These give rise to particular ways of interpreting the practices of vaccination or medical technology and technocracy. Vaccination is thus at one and the same time micro-technological and macro-political experience. What we have sought to show is how these two dimensions come together within particular configurations. Without the wider political dimensions, many aspects of people's concerns are lost. Without the bodily, microtechnological dimensions, analysis remains 'thin'; we cannot see why, for instance, it should be through oral polio vaccines that people in northern Nigeria expressed worries about US imperialism.

Viewed in this way, a health system is not just a set of infrastructures for delivering a set of technical services and associated expert knowledges. Rather, it is embedded within a set of moral and social orders and a set of bodily and wider political reflections. It is this wider interpretative and experiential complex that shapes parental thinking and practice.

Dialogical encounters

While until now we have focused on the bodily, social and wider political dimensions of parents' perspectives on vaccination, a missing yet central issue is the way these are co-produced in dialogical engagement with vaccination technocracies.

The ways that those working for vaccination technocracies – whether as policy makers, medical researchers, health service managers, or frontline professionals – interpret parental anxieties and hesitancies in vaccination are configured by their particular institutional worlds. This extends, for instance, from emphases on mass childhood immunization as a top-down population-level intervention, to the labelling of vaccination 'compliers' and 'defaulters' according to categories of education, class or ethnicity. As each of the chapters has revealed, such interpretations often gives rise to emphases that contrast rather starkly with parental framings. They support interventions that parents interpret within their own logics, acting accordingly. Policy makers and professionals, in turn, very often interpret parental action within their own, technocratic framings. This dialogical process, we have suggested, is a central force shaping the production of views on each 'side'. It is through ongoing engagements that such views are continually reiterated and re-instantiated. It is this process that produces what can sometimes come to appear as two contrasting cultural and discursive worlds, of parents and policy makers. To understand either, it is necessary to understand the other and their interaction.

This process is visible, for instance, in the ways that health workers in some West African settings label mothers who are late for vaccination appointments as 'defaulters', with such mothers seeing the nurses as incomprehending of their real desires for vaccination and the social circumstances that prevent them getting there. It is visible in the MRC in The Gambia considering parents who participate in vaccine trials to have 'understood' the importance of trials, whereas parents are actually balancing desires for free treatment and fears of blood stealing. It is visible in the MMR information put out by the UK DH, that is premised on notions of risk at a population level, in contrast with the personalized reflections on uncertainty that dominate parental thinking. And it is visible in the engagements between the UK government and parental groups over claims of MMR damage, where each has used (differently framed) science and accusations of bias in science to dismiss the other's position. While such cases can appear simply as instances of contrasting framings, the chapters have shown how dynamics can unfold that reinforce these positions. More significantly, in such dynamics, there is often a shift from differences simply of perspective on vaccination, to broader ascriptions of enduring personality and identity: 'the defaulter', 'the newly irrational middle class', 'the Serrahuli', 'the arrogant doctor', and so on.

This is not to deny that there are many situations and circumstances that blur and call into question the kinds of categorical (or essentialist) distinction that emerge. For instance while encounters at the interface between health professionals and parents can be a vehicle for divergence, many doctors and health professionals, as people and parents themselves, can articulate private views and equivocate. Medical research fieldworkers often make creative compromises in discussions with those they recruit to trials, brokering the imperatives of their work with the social imperatives of everyday village life. Yet as the chapters have shown, the imperatives, practices and analytical positions of the health institutions concerned often delegitimize the more personalized engagements that would otherwise undermine more categorical perspectives.

At a larger scale, we can now see how stereotypical contrasts between Africa and Europe in relation to vaccination have emerged: at their starkest, contrasting a compliant African poor whose only problem is access or irrational tradition, with a newly irrational and media-misled British middle class. While these stereotypes are rooted in particular dynamics in each setting that we have described in the chapters, they also emerge in relation to each other. Thus in broader, globalized reflection, contrasts are drawn between Europe and Africa, for instance, in assertions of African compliance given the prevalence of diseases such as measles, contrasted with European post-modern complacency where measles 'has been forgotten', or in concerns that European anti-vaccinationism is 'polluting' Africa. While such globalized reasoning draws life from the categories that have emerged in each setting, it also feeds back to reinforce such views. The result is often an appearance of very distinct African and European worlds and experiences.

These views are those emergent from health institutional positions and a powerful globalized policy and media world. Our chapters have shown how far they are contradicted by the variety of parents' perspectives and experiences, showing up similarities that transcend and deny these stereotypical Europe–Africa contrasts. Although the settings and details may be different, the depth of parental concern and experiential expertise around particular pathways of child health, and a concern about how state and global institutions affect rights to pursue this, are more broadly shared. In both settings, too, parents expressing anxieties about vaccination are also commenting on, engaging with and sometimes challenging the politics and political-economy of public health programmes, of science, and of states and global institutions more broadly.

Other stereotypes about Europe and Africa emerge, however, from parental settings, having their own logics reinforced through dialogical engagements with health institutions. These include, for example, the views of the extractive, selfish 'whites' that circulate in some Gambian villages, and of a transnational political economy in which Europeans desire good African blood. They include views within parental movements questioning vaccination of the power of 'big pharma' and its capacity to override local and national interests worldwide. While these hard-felt views clearly have roots in other areas of experience beyond vaccination, the everyday worlds of vaccination that we have been describing in this book continually re-instantiate them.

Our analytical approach has attempted to provide an integrative, not merely comparative, way of understanding British and West African experiences of this global technology and technocracy. Anxiety connotes active engagement with an uncertain world, recognizing a grappling creativity. This contrasts with a view of vaccination as habit – or perhaps more theoretically, a reading of habitus in Bourdieu's sense (1990) that highlights the routinized and unreflected-on nature of practice. A view that vaccination has been (or needs to be) established as a normalized routine, and that this has been disrupted by agents of rumour and individualized risk awareness, can follow from this reading. Yet our ethnography does not support this, questioning assumptions of normalized routine and a disruption of past order. We have focused on anxiety as desire and worry, finding that even where people appear to be subscribing to routines, these emerge from an active, agentive desire albeit subject to the bodily, social and political framings that we have outlined. Again, it could be argued that the idea of routine or habit is an idea rooted in the perspectives of the technocracy.

The way health institutions understand public action (and thus how they endeavour to shape it) that we have been exploring can be understood in Foucault's terms as discourses of biopower – forms of governmentality over processes of life (Gordon, 1991). This study reveals three particular aspects to governmentality arguments. First, governmentality is fragmented. Thus for instance UK health institutions lock into two very differently framed discourses – one rooted in notions of routinization and self-subjection to (public health) authority and the other hailing critical reflection and active public choice. These are discourses not controlled by the health world, but the health world helps shape them. Second, these can be distinct from parental discourses, and often starkly so. Discourses of governmentality associated with institutions of health engage with conceptual framings of wider publics that also configure bodily, social, political and economic experience. Yet, third, what we have shown is that the 'poles' of policy and parental thinking are not just perceptually opposed, but are co-produced through encounters with each other; through a dialogical process of governmentality and response, politics and counter-politics. Thus a theory of anxiety does not presume a separability of parental and policy worlds (or discourses), but focuses on the active production of such distinctions. The case of vaccination, read through such an approach, sheds light more broadly on the production of distinction – of distinct lifeworlds – in the relations of governmentality. The cases from Africa and Europe show the many forms this takes, in this case shaped around distinctions between policy versus parent. But, as we have shown, such distinctions are not pre-ordained, but emerge from encounters.

Revisiting ignorance, risk, trust and rumour

We now revisit some of the core terms of policy debate about public engagement with technologies with which we began in Chapter 2. What might we now say about ignorance, risk, trust and rumour?

The cases show how far parental evaluations of child health and vaccination emerge from parents' experiential expertise – the knowledge that comes from daily observation and interaction with particular children on whom parents and everyday carers are clearly, in many respects, experts. In the context of parents' knowledge and expertise – gained and maintained in interaction with a diversity of other experts – those who do not accept vaccination should be seen neither as ignorant, nor, necessarily, as 'resisting' in a negative sense. Rather, such parents are often following positive, informed strategies geared to the health of their child.

Moreover, commonalities in this respect between the European and African settings cast major doubt on stereotypes that have cast Africa as 'traditional' compared with Europe's 'modernity', on the basis of supposed knowledge of and attitudes to biomedicine. Some have argued, in more dynamic terms, that societies in Africa are emerging from a traditional, superstitious past to become biomedicalized, post-traditional and rational/modern. At the same time and in contrast, some see Britain and Europe as becoming de-medicalized (Williams and Calnan, 1996), post-modern and more irrational. Thus Fitzpatrick (2004) sees the apparent rise in popularity of complementary and alternative therapies in Britain as evidence of a 'rise of irrationality in society'. But our evidence suggests an ongoing pluralism in thinking about child health, drawing on diverse therapies and notions of healing, in both settings. Within this, biomedical and non-biomedical discourses and practices have always interplayed, although in different ways in different times and places. And the resulting conceptual fields have provided logical – rational – ways for parents to think about and evaluate their children's health and the possible roles of vaccination in it. Nevertheless, parental rationalities in both settings often fail to correspond with the very particular forms of rationality and of medical discourse that underlie vaccination and public health programmes. It is in relation to these very particular logics that public rationalities are so often evaluated, and either found wanting – or optimistically seen to be evolving along the right path, with just a bit of biomedical education needed to get them there.

The case material also reveals that debates couched in terms of risk often have little traction on parental perspectives and experience. What is important to parents is rarely risk in its strict sense of calculable probabilities, but broader uncertainties and ambiguities. In many of the controversies we have considered, the issues concerned were framed in highly contrasting ways; these were not controversies that research could reduce to calculable risk probabilities, or at least not in a way that would have been convincing to both sides. Moreover, risk debates narrow and occlude from view the multiple meanings that vaccination carries for parents, across a spectrum from considerations of the microtechnological practices around vaccination in relation to prevailing notions of immunity, blood and health; through reflections on parental lifestyle, responsibility, confidence and control; to considerations and concerns about delivery regimes and the motivations and political economy of the institutions involved. Even parents that 'talk risk' reveal such broader dimensions of meaning in their narratives, in their discussions with other parents, and in their practices.

Similarly, concepts of trust have only limited purchase, obscuring many other meanings of greater relevance to parents. Thus, for instance, in describing their relationships with doctors and health professionals, Brighton parents rarely evoked a notion of trust. More significant were ideas of whether a relationship was supportive, and whether a parent felt confident to express their views and raise questions – issues that were shaped by a variety of social and personal circumstances. Where people do use the term 'trust', it is often of a socially remote institution, rather than one with which they have personal relationships. Thus people did use the term 'trust' in relation to the government and pharmaceutical companies over the MMR issue, but they did so as shorthand to refer to a range of political experiences, of negative experiences where they felt misled by government sources over other issues such as BSE, and perceived relationships between vaccine companies, science and policy. It is such understandings that need to be analysed if public engagement with vaccination, and the reasons for vaccine anxieties, are to be understood and addressed.

In West African settings, it seems even more starkly clear that to evoke a term such as trust would be an impoverished way of addressing the issues of knowledge, power and social relations that are at play in vaccination practices and controversies. When poorer, socially marginalized Gambian mothers stay away from peri-urban clinics because they fear that nurses and other mothers will embarrass them and harm their children, is this best described as 'distrust' (of the nurse? Of the clinic as an institution?)? Or are the logics of these fears – in the understood connections between immoral sexual behaviour and thin, weak babies; in the potential for sorcery in crowded places; and in social experiences of exclusion in the context of ethnicity and migrant relations – worthy of attention? When, in northern Nigeria, villagers and their leaders boycotted the oral polio vaccine, was this simply a question of 'distrust' (of the vaccine, of the federal government, of the WHO, of the US, or all of these)? Or are the meanings of people's relationships with technologies and institutions, shaped through local understandings of polio, past experiences of international pharmaceutical trials, and recent religious, national and international political history, worthy of analysis? Our analyses of vaccination practices, anxieties and controversies in earlier chapters gave priority to an ethnographic focus on the content and meaning of people's knowledge and relationships and, in such an analysis, the notion of trust rarely proved helpful. When we used it, on reflection, it is rather as our informants did: as a convenient shorthand to express a more complex, embedded set of meanings that it was perhaps not the moment to articulate in full.

In this light, it becomes apparent that policy arguments about 'breakdown of trust' or an emerging culture of suspicion are part of particular and simplifying policy framings. They hark back to an imagined good and orderly world of solidarity – whether the world of the UK's national health service in the post-war years, or an Africa isolated from global rumours – which has given way to an anxious individualized, globalized, modern world. In short, analyses in terms of trust and its breakdown are themselves part of a dialogical process that creates and reproduces misleading stereotypes.

If, as we argue, it is important to take the content of people's vaccine anxieties seriously, then the terminology of 'rumour' – at least as commonly used in relation to health and vaccination – is also unhelpful. In much policy and popular discourse, rumour has become a shorthand for an idea that can be dismissed; that needs to be replaced with proper 'facts'.

However, to understand why many Gambians consider that MRC steals blood, for instance, it was important to understand the locally embedded meanings of blood, and the centrality of blood calculus to health practices. For many villagers, anticipated transactions with MRC unfolded as unreasonable or unjust, and were thus experienced as stealing. Blood stealing is certainly not an unrooted rumour circulating out of nowhere, credulous somehow to minds befuddled by contradictory modernity.

What policy discourses often describe as rumour has, in our cases, been revealed instead as struggles around knowledge and science, often strongly linked to parents' observations and experiential expertise. Vaccine and vampire anxieties are often part of wider concerns with the political economy of science, with the state and with the global political, economic or religious order. But rather than reflect alien or activist-spread ideas, such interpretations are made apparent and logical to people through their everyday experiences and conceptualizations of children's health, and their experiential encounters with vaccination delivery, scientific and health-providing institutions in the ways that we have described. It is the intersection of these micropolitics of technological experience with macropolitics that today involve a supercharged field of contemporary genocides, AIDS, war on terror and religious politics, that give vaccine anxieties such power, becoming part and parcel of critical engagements with state and global technocracy more broadly. Discarding and delegitimizing these anxieties by labelling them as rumour is problematic indeed.

One might, however, recapture the sense of rumour as an unproven statement; a status that should open up inquiry and reflection, and enable people to debate current events without necessarily 'believing' the rumour. Rumours in this sense become particularly relevant in contexts of uncertainty, providing a mode through which people can reflect on the issues at stake in a wide-ranging and non-committal way.

Implications

We have found strong contrasts in perspectives on vaccination, and have tried to describe the conditions which have given rise to them, and how they shape parental anxieties. These contrasting perspectives are not linked directly to singular outcomes – not all parents think alike. But they do configure dilemmas from which decisions emerge, as anxieties play into much more haphazard personal circumstances and everyday processes. Thus they influence vaccination uptake rates and outcomes, with very big implications for child health and survival.

We have found these contrasting perspectives to emerge in dialogical relations with each other, in ways that create and sustain gulfs between the technocracy and parents who are seeking child health: a gulf that, no matter what one's perspective, cannot be helpful in making the most of the technological opportunities that vaccines offer. Approaches to vaccination policy making and delivery that are dismissive of the conceptual worlds of parents, and which are insensitive to the social struggles that they face in negotiating clinic attendance with health trajectories and social and moral relations, are unlikely to be successful in creating and sustaining the high coverage rates that health services desire, social immunity needs, and which might ultimately improve the health of us all.

The analysis in this book would suggest two linked strategies to address these problems: finding ways to recognize, reinforce and build on the positive dimensions of vaccine anxieties, and linked to this, finding ways to turn the dialogical relations between parents and policy makers into ones that draw them together rather than drive them apart. For instance, in the UK social transformations added to the media and information explosion have enabled a massive increase in attention to health, food, lifestyle, and also child care. The emergence of particularistic ways of understanding child health which is associated with this has much that is very positive about it, and which is indeed nurtured by other areas of health support. To focus only on loss of trust, cultures of suspicion, heightened risk awareness and the problems of individuated calculus is to see only its negative implications for vaccination. Not only is it to miss positive elements which could be built upon, in parental attentiveness and active health seeking, but in doing so, it is to misunderstand where parents are coming from and to risk alienating them.

In Nigeria, to take another example, it is equally problematic to dismiss anxieties with the polio vaccine only as negative, linked to unfortunate rumour and religious dissent. Again, parental anxiety about polio vaccines was linked to a striving for children's health in a more positive way. Nigerian parents want functioning, effective routine health and vaccination services that address the wider range of illnesses that they prioritize. They want to be confident that those vaccinating their children have local interests at heart, and in this context are worried about the alien, top-down global polio eradication initiative.

The emergence of parental networks and mobilization around vaccination, equally, should not be written off in negative terms simply as problematic 'anti-vaccination' movements. Again, there are often more positive dimensions, striving for child health, sometimes appreciating some aspects of vaccines, but expressing concerns and uncertainties about others. Such mobilizations are an inevitable corollary of the fact that there are diverse experiences and ambiguities that, at certain moments, clash with public health perspectives to such an extent that controversy results. Mobilizations need to be taken seriously as valid forms of public participation in the politics of knowledge around vaccination, as indeed around the directions and impacts of science and technology more broadly.

The use of alternative, non-biomedical therapies and practices in child health seeking, too, need not be simply dismissed in negative terms. Alternative therapies – whether 'traditional' or emergent – are not necessarily counter to vaccination, but are often used in ways that parents see as congruent with and complementary to vaccination. These complementarities need to be appreciated, bringing opportunities, too, to appreciate their purveyors – whether healer or homeopath – and involve them in more inclusive approaches to child health.

It is thus important for those associated with vaccine development and delivery to be in a position to understand these positive dimensions. This must involve attention to core framings – such as the blood reasoning and immunity reasoning so important in the settings of this book – which render comprehensible the details of vaccine anxieties. This is crucial not just to avoid misunderstanding, but also to build more unifying interactions.

This carries a range of practical implications for vaccination policy making and programming: for the research that informs it, for its institutional arrangements, and for forms of public involvement. These are closely linked.

Thus, in the UK, a strand of debate in the medical profession now recognizes that in contemporary society the top-down approach to immunization policy currently pursued by the DH is likely to work less and less well, and advocates greater public involvement in decisions about vaccination policy and programmes. The editor of the *British Journal of General Practice* has suggested that it is time for a new approach that listens to the public, rather than relying excessively on 'experts' (Jewell, 2001). Others suggest that it is time to move from expectations of compliance to concordance in vaccination, paralleling a similar move advocated with regard to medicine taking (Vernon, 2003). Public policy about immunization illustrates and reflects a tension in wider health policy between an increased reliance on scientific evidence, and a wish for a patient-centred approach, between needs as defined by experts, and desires as expressed by the public. To bring about such shifts and move towards resolving these tensions requires ongoing research and reflection into how publics think. But it also involves more. It requires an opening-up of definitions of science and evidence, to encompass a wider plurality of views. It requires a redefinition and a pluralization of expertise: as Stilgoe et al (2006) argue, 'Rather than getting trapped in an unproductive "expert vs public" debate, the challenge is to embrace the different forms of expertise on offer, to view these as a resource rather than a burden' (Stilgoe et al, 2006, p40). And it may also require shifts in the institutions and organizations of vaccine policy, and their associated power relations, if those in the policy world are to act on what they learn of parents' desires through, for instance, enabling more flexible, individuated approaches to vaccination schedules.

Furthermore, the heightened importance of immunity that is apparent in the UK case, and the personalized ways that people understand their own and their infants' immune system, embedded within much more than just understandings of health, means that generic medical research at population levels will encounter difficulties. A challenge to the science of vaccinology will be to draw out and respond to more differentiated vaccine needs, effects and vulnerabilities.

In the West African context, and in the wake of controversies such as that over polio in Nigeria, it is increasingly recognized that ensuring the effectiveness and sustainability of vaccination delivery and uptake requires ongoing support to basic health service delivery on the part of national and local government staff, donor agencies and NGOs (e.g. Health Partners International (HPI), 2006). Policy approaches to improving vaccine delivery need to be informed by an understanding of how different delivery styles are perceived and interpreted by parents in particular social and political settings. In particular, campaigns can stand out starkly amid weak state services, and – in different circumstances – contribute to heightened anxieties and be valued as a substitute for routine services in ways that undermine schedule completion. Better integration of campaign and routine activities, and greater public dialogue about their interrelationship, will be critical if both current and new vaccine technologies are to be developed and delivered effectively in the future. Given trends towards growing pluralization and privatization in the health sector, policy dialogue about its implications for vaccination, and debate over strategies for achieving more effective relationships (perhaps through forms of local public–private–community partnerships around vaccination) are also needed. At the same time, a better understanding of parental framings could inform more appropriate policy approaches to education and communication. Instead of simply delivering top-down disease specific messages, these could usefully develop more dialogue-based approaches which work with and build on the concepts through which people already think about vaccination.

These vaccine-focused suggestions, in both the UK and African settings, chime with broader arguments for democratization in science and technology. If technologies are to meet diverse public needs, such arguments run, then there also needs to be public debate and more democratic decision making about the directions in which they are developed and promoted, and the values and purposes they serve (see Jasanoff, 2005; Leach et al, 2005). This can be assisted by deliberative approaches to policy making and technology governance, in which public, scientific and policy perspectives are brought together and negotiated (Fischer, 2003; Hajer and Wagenaar, 2003) – whether the result is the hoped-for reaching of consensus, or the identification of irreconcilable views and trade-offs, requiring further political debate and action. It can also be assisted by approaches to technology and programme appraisal that broaden out the range of inputs to include the framings of the public, and that open up the outputs to specify the different possible options that might suit different groups of people or settings (Stirling, 2005). Both demand attention to the power relations between participants, to ensure that all framings, including those of the public, acquire influence in the process. A more democratic approach to science and technology also demands reflexivity in the institutions involved with technocracy; for them to reflect on their own assumptions, framings and positions, and the ways these might be excluding others (Wynne, 2005).

These are challenges indeed for any technological domain, and none more so than vaccination, where a singular approach to mass childhood immunization, backed by particular sorts of science, has long been deeply interlocked with institutional imperatives, professional hierarchies and power relations. Yet these very characteristics of vaccination technology and technocracy, given the problems we have highlighted in this book, underpin the vital need for a more deliberative, democratic approach.

The challenge for vaccination is not just to improve microdeliberation, however. Vaccination is part of a now highly globalized technocracy, backed by globalized science and promoted through global institutions. Current hopes for and investments in mass childhood immunization and new vaccines are set to expand the scope and reach of this globalized technocracy further. This could become part of further polarization between vaccination technocracy and the children and parents it is supposed to serve, unless ways can be found to mediate these global and local worlds more effectively. Understanding localized contexts and framings, and the particular vaccine anxieties and desires they give rise to, is central in this, and essential if the polarizing problems this book has identified between technocracies and parental worlds are not to recur, writ large, across local and global scales.

To date these problems have often been masked by the very effectiveness of vaccination technology. It is perhaps easy for those in the technocracy to see these problems as marginal and temporary – as small aberrations in a broader context of success and progress in disease eradication through science. Indeed, and sometimes despite worries about vaccines, most parents, in most places, are having their children vaccinated when they can. This may continue to be true for big-hitting vaccines; those that address widespread diseases of which there is widespread fear. Yet vaccine technologies are increasingly being applied to ailments for which there is less self-evidence. In this context, we might foresee more instances where vaccine anxieties as reflection become manifested in vaccine refusal.

If vaccine technologies and technocracies continue to attract international investment, manifested in further expansion of global technocracy, we can also expect heightened media attention and popular reflection. In a world of global political tensions and uncertainties, public reflection on the political dimensions of vaccines is also likely to intensify. How global vaccination technocracy and its framings comes to intersect with more located framings of the bodily, social and political dimensions of vaccination will be crucial in what ensues. Understanding vaccine anxieties, and using this understanding to build positive, inclusive strategies will thus become ever more vital if the potentials of vaccination – immense as they are – are genuinely to be harnessed towards improved child health in our globalized world.

References

Aaby, P. (1995) 'Assumptions and contradictions in measles and measles immunization research: Is measles good for something?', *Social Science and Medicine*, vol 41, no 5, pp673–686

Aaby, P., Jensen, H., Mulholland, K., Barreto, M. L. and Folb, P. I. (2001) 'Routine vaccination and child survival in Guinea-Bissau', *British Medical Journal*, vol 322, p360

Agrawal, A. (1995) 'Dismantling the divide between indigenous and scientific knowledge', *Development and Change*, vol 26, pp413–439

Agrawal, A. (2005) *Environmentality: Technologies of Government and the Making of Subjects*, Duke University Press, Durham, NC

Allen, A. (2007) *Vaccine: The Controversial Story of Medicine's Greatest Lifesaver*, WW Norton, New York, NY

Anderson, P. (1999) 'Another media scare about MMR vaccine hits Britain', *British Medical Journal*, 12 June, vol 318, no 7198, p1578

Anderson, W. (2002) 'Introduction: Postcolonial technoscience', *Social Studies of Science*, vol 32, no 5–6, pp643–658

André, F. (2003) 'Vaccinology: Past achievements, present roadblocks and future promises', *Vaccine*, vol 21, pp593–595

Angell, M. (2000) 'The ethics of clinical research in the third world', *New England Journal of Medicine*, vol 337, no 12, pp847–849

Bache, I. and Flinders, M. (eds) (2004) *Multi-level Governance*, Oxford University Press, Oxford

Baker, J. P. (2003) 'The pertussis vaccine controversy in Great Britain, 1974–1986', *Vaccine*, no 21, pp4003–4010

Barnes, B., Bloor D. and Henry, J. (1996) *Scientific Knowledge: A Sociological Analysis*, Athlone, London

Barry, A., Osborne, T. and Rose, N. (eds) (1996) *Foucault and Practical Reason: Liberalism, Neo-liberalism and Rationalities of Government*, University of Chicago Press, Chicago, IL

Bauman, Z. (1999) *In Search of Politics*, Stanford University Press, Stanford, CA

Beck, A. (1960) 'Issues in the anti-vaccination movement in England', *Medical History*, no 4, pp310–321

Beck, U. (1992) *Risk Society: Towards a New Modernity*, Sage, London

Beck, U. and Beck-Gernsheim, E. (2002) *Individualization: Institutionalized Individualism and its Social and Political Consequences*, Sage, London

Beck, U., Giddens, A. and Lash, S. (1994) *Reflexive Modernization: Politics, Tradition and Aesthetics in the Modern Social Order*, Polity Press, Cambridge

Beck-Gernsheim, E. (2000) *Reinventing the Family: In Search of New Lifestyles*, Polity, Cambridge

Bedford, H. and Elliman, D. (1998) *Childhood Immunisations for Carers and Parents*, Health Education Authority, London

Bedford, H. and Elliman, D. (1999) 'Vaccines and their real or perceived adverse effects', *British Medical Journal*, vol 318, pp1487–1488

Begg, N., Ramsay, M., White, J. and Bozoky, Z. (1998) 'Media dents confidence in MMR vaccine', *British Medical Journal*, vol 316, p561

Bennett, P. G. and Calman, K. C. (eds) (1999) *Risk Communication and Public Health*, Oxford University Press, Oxford

Berkes, F. (ed) (1989) *Common Property Resources: Ecology and Community-Based Sustainable Development*, Belhaven Press, London

Bicego, G. T. and Boerma, J. T. (1993) 'Maternal education and child survival: A comparative study of survey data from 17 countries', *Social Science and Medicine*, vol 36, no 9, pp1207–1227

Bierlich, B. (2000) 'Injections and the fear of death: An essay on the limits of biomedicine among the Dagomba of northern Ghana', *Social Science and Medicine*, no 50, pp703–713

Bijker, W., Hughes, T. and Pinch, T. (eds) (1987) *The Social Construction of Technological Systems*, MIT Press, Cambridge, MA

Birmingham Post (2002) 'Parents trust in MMR jab halts measles epidemic', 27 December. Available at www.uvig.org/archive_summaries.asp?_PubDate=#id108

Birungi, H. (1998) 'Injections and self-help: Risk and trust in Ugandan health care', *Social Science and Medicine*, vol 47, no 10

Bledsoe, C. (1984) 'The political use of Sande ideology and symbolism', *American Ethnologist*, vol 11, pp455–470

Bledsoe, C. (2002) *Contingent Lives: Fertility, Time and Aging in West Africa*, University of Chicago Press, Chicago, IL

Bloom, G. and Standing, H. (2001) 'Pluralism and marketisation in the health sector: Meeting health needs in contexts of social change in low and middle-income countries', *IDS Working Paper*, no 136

Blume, S. (2006) 'Anti-vaccination movements and their interpretations', *Social Science and Medicine*, no 62, pp628–642

BMA (2002) Annual meeting. Tuesday business, 2 July. Motion 354. Available at www.bma.org.uk/ap.nsf/Content/arm+2002+order+of+business%5Carm+2002+tuesday?OpenDocument&Highlight=2,target,payment

Boone, S. (1986) *Radiance from the Waters: Ideals of Feminine Beauty in Mende Art*, Yale University Press, Newhaven, CT

Bourdieu, P. (1990) *The Logic of Practice*, Polity, Cambridge, UK

Bradstreet, J. (2004) 'Biological evidence of significant vaccine related side-effects resulting in neurodevelopmental disorders', Presentation to the Vaccine Safety Committee of the Institute of Medicine, The National Academies of Science, 9 February

Brown, A., Foster, M., Norton, A. and Naschold, F. (2001) 'The status of sector wide approaches', *Working Paper 142*, Overseas Development Institute, London

Brown, P. (1992) 'Popular epidemiology and toxic waste contamination: Lay and professional ways of knowing', *Journal of Health and Social Behaviour*, no 33, pp267–281

Brugha, R., Starling, M. and Walt, G. (2002) *New Products into Old Systems: GAVI from a Country Perspective*, Save the Children Fund and London School of Hygiene and Tropical Medicine, London

Burchell, G., Gordon, C. and Miller, P. (eds) (1991) *The Foucault Effect: Studies in Governmentality*, pp1–52, University of Chicago Press, Chicago, IL

Cabinet Office Strategy Unit (2002) *Risk: Improving Government's Capability to Handle Risk*, Cabinet Office, London

Calman, K. (2002) 'Communication of risk: Choice, consent, and trust', *The Lancet*, vol 360, no 9327, pp166–168

Camara, M. (nd) 'Programme élargi de vaccination integré aux soins de santé primaries et médicaments essentiaux', Ministère de la Santé Publique, Conakry, République de la Guinée

Casiday, R., Cresswell, T., Wilson, D. and Panter-Brick, C. (2006) 'A survey of UK parental attitudes to the MMR vaccine and trust in medical authority', *Vaccine*, no 24, pp177–184

Cassell, J.A., Leach, M., Fairhead, J. R., Small, M. and Mercer, C. H. (2006a) 'The social shaping of childhood vaccination practice in rural and urban Gambia: A quantitative survey of mothers based on ethnography', *Health Policy and Planning*, vol 21, no 5, pp373–391

Cassell, J. A., Leach, M., Poltorak, M. S., Mercer, C. H., Iversen, A. and Fairhead, J. (2006b) 'Is the cultural context of MMR rejection a key to an effective public health discourse?', *Public Health*, no 120, pp783–794

Castel, R. (1991) 'From dangerousness to risk', in G. Burchell, C. Gordon and P. Miller (eds) *The Foucault Effect: Studies in Governmentality*, pp281–298, University of Chicago Press, Chicago, IL

Castells, M. (1997) *The Power of Identity: the Information Age, vol 2*, Blackwell, Oxford

Cave, S. and Mitchell, D. (2001) *What your Doctor May Not Tell You About Children's Vaccinations*, Warner Books, New York, NY

CEPT (2004) The Chief Executive Policy Team, Research and Consultation Unit, Brighton and Hove City Council, Brighton, available at: www.citystats.org/cityStats/

Cham, M. (2000) 'Maternal mortality in the Gambia: Contributing factors and what can be done to reduce them', MPhil Thesis, Faculty of Medicine, University of Oslo

Chataway, J. and Smith, J. (2006) 'The International AIDS Vaccine Initiative (IAVI): Is it getting new science and technology to the world's neglected majority?', *World Development*, vol 34, no 1, 16–30

Cleland, J. G. and Van Ginneken, J. K. (1988) 'Maternal education and child survival in developing countries: The search for pathways of influence', *Social Science and Medicine*, vol 27, no 12, pp1357–1368

Colgrove, J. (2006) *State of Immunity: The Politics of Vaccination in Twentieth-century America*, University of California Press, Berkeley, CA

Collins, H. (2004) 'Experts, expertise and participation in decision-making', in Healey, P. (ed) *Scientific Connoisseurs and Other Intermediaries – Mavens, Pundits and Critics*, Report on ESRC Science in Society Programme Workshop, Economic and Social Research Council, Swindon, p14

Collins, H. M. and Evans, R. (2002) 'The third wave of science studies: Studies of expertise and experience', *Social Studies of Science*, vol 32, no 2, pp235–296

Comaroff, J. and Comaroff, J. L. (1999) 'Occult economies and the violence of abstraction: Notes from the South African postcolony', *American Ethnologist*, vol 26, no 2, pp279–303

Cookson, C. (2002) 'Benefit and risk of vaccination as seen by the general public and the media', *Vaccine*, vol 20, pp85–88

Coulter, H. (1990) *Vaccination, Social Violence, and Criminality: The Medical Assault on the American Brain*, North Atlantic Books, Berkeley, CA

Coulter, H. L. and Fisher, B.L. (1991) *A Shot in the Dark: Why the P in the DPT Vaccination May be Hazardous to your Child's Health*, Avery, New York, NY

Croll, E. and Parkin, D. (eds) (1992) *Bush, Base, Forest, Farm*, Routledge, London

Cros, M. (1990) *Anthropologie du Sang en Afrique : Essai d'Hématologie Symbolique chez les Lobi du Burkina Faso et de Côte d'Ivoire*, Harmattan, Paris

CSM (1999) *Report of the Working Party on MMR Vaccine*, Committee on Safety of Medicines, London

Cutts, F. T., Glik, D. C., Gordon, A., Parker, K., Diallo, S., Haba, F. and Stone, R. (1990) 'Application of multiple methods to the study of the immunization programme in an urban area of Guinea', *WHO Bulletin*, vol 68, no 6, pp769–776

Cutts, F. T., Zaman, S. M. A., Enwere, G., Levine, O. S., Okoko, J. B., Oluwana, C., Vaughan, A., Obaro, S. K., Leach, A., McAdam, K. P., Biney, E., Saaka, M., Onwuchekwa, U., Yallop, F., Pierce, N. F., Greenwood, B. M. and Adegbola, R. A. (2005) 'Efficacy of a nine-valent pneumococcal conjugate vaccine against pneumonia and invasive pneumococcal disease in The Gambia: Randomised, double-blind, placebo-controlled trial', *The Lancet*, vol 365, March 26, pp1139–1146

DETR (2000) *Measuring Multiple Deprivation at the Small Area Level, The Indices of Deprivation 2000*, Department of the Environment, Transport and the Regions, London, available at: http://neighbourhood.statistics.gov.uk

DeWilde, S., Carey, I., Richards, N., Hilton, S. and Cook, D. (2001) 'Do children who become autistic consult more often after MMR vaccination?', *British Journal of General Practice*, no 51, pp226–227

Douglas, M. (1966) *Purity and Danger: An Analysis of Concepts of Pollution and Taboo*, Routledge, London

Douglas, M. (1992) *Risk and Blame: Essays in Cultural Theory*, Routledge, London

Dunn, A. (2005) *Synthesis Report – Addendum to Existing Qualitative and Quantitative Immunisation Survey*, PATHS Programme, Nigeria

Durbach, N. (2000) 'They might as well brand us: Working-class resistance to compulsory vaccination in Victorian England', *Social History of Medicine*, vol 13, no 1, pp45–63

Durbach, N. (2005) *Bodily Matters: The Anti-vaccination Movement in England, 1853–1907*, Duke University Press, Durham and London

Ekbom, A., Wakefield, A. J., Zack, M. and Adami, H. O. (1994) 'Perinatal measles infection and subsequent Crohn's disease', *Lancet*, no 344, pp508–510

Elliman, D., Bedford, H. and Miller, E. (2001) 'MMR vaccine: Worries are not justified', *Archives of Disease in Childhood*, no 85, pp271–274

Eng, E., Naimoli, J., Naimoli, G., Parker, K. A. and Lowenthal, N. (1991) 'The acceptability of childhood immunization to Togolese mothers: A sociobehavioral perspective', *Health Education Quarterly*, vol 18, no 1, pp97–110

Epstein, S. (1996) *Impure Science: Aids, Activism and the Politics of Knowledge*, University of California Press, Berkeley, CA

European Commission (2001) 'Ethical, legal and social aspects of vaccine research and vaccination policies', report of a European Commission research project, Psychoanalytic Institute for Social Research, Italy

Evans, M., Stoddart, H., Condon, L., Freeman, E., Grizzell, M. and Mullen, R. (2001) 'Parent's perspectives on the MMR immunisation: A focus group study', *British Journal of General Practice*, no 51, pp904–910

Fairhead, J. (1992) 'Indigenous technical knowledge and natural resources management in Sub-Saharan Africa: A critical review', Paper prepared for SSRC project on African Agriculture, US

Fairhead, J. and Leach, M. with D. Millimouno and M. Kamano (1996) *Misreading the African Landscape*, Cambridge University Press, Cambridge

Fairhead, J. and Leach, M. (2003) *Science, Society and Power: Environmental Knowledge and Policy in West Africa and the Caribbean*, Cambridge University Press, Cambridge

Fairhead, J., Leach, M. and Small, M. (2004) 'Childhood vaccination and society in The Gambia: Public engagement with science and delivery', *IDS Working Paper*, no 218, Institute of Development Studies, Brighton

Fairhead, J., Leach, M. and Small, M. (2006) 'Public engagement with science? Local understandings of a vaccine trial in The Gambia', *Journal of Biosocial Science*, no 38, pp103–116

Fairhead, J., Leach, M., Millimouno, D. and Diallo A. A. (forthcoming) 'New therapeutic landscapes in Africa: Parental categories and practices in seeking infant health care in the Republic of Guinea', *Social Science and Medicine*, Special Issue on Future Health Systems

Farmer, P. (1999) *Infections and Inequalities: The Modern Plagues*, University of California Press, Berkeley, CA

Farmer, P. (2005) *Pathologies of Power: Health, Human Rights and the New War on the Poor*, University of California Press, Berkeley, CA

FBA (2005) 'The state of routine immunisation services in Nigeria and reasons for current problems', FBA Health Systems Analysts, report for DFID

Feldman-Savelsberg, P., Ndonko, F. T. and Schmidt-Ehry, B. (2000) 'Sterilizing vaccines or the politics of the womb: Retrospective study of rumour in Cameroon', *Medical Anthropology Quarterly*, no14, pp159–179

Ferme, M. (2002) *The Underneath of Things*, University of Chicago Press, Chicago, MA

Fidler, D. (1998) 'Microbialpolitik: Infectious diseases and international relations', *American University International Literature Review*, no 14, pp1–53

Fischer, F. (2000) *Citizens, Experts and the Environment: The Politics of Local Knowledge*, Duke University Press, Durham and London

Fischer, F. (2003) *Reframing Public Policy: Discursive Politics and Deliberative Practices*, Oxford University Press, Oxford

Fitzpatrick, M. (2002) 'MMR: The making of junk science', www.spikedonline.com/Articles/00000002D39E.htm, accessed July 2003

Fitzpatrick, M. (2004) *MMR and Autism: What Parents Need to Know*, Routledge, London

Fletcher, J. (1995) 'Fair warning: Jackie Fletcher describes the work of JABS', *Health Visitor*, February, vol 68, no 2, p82

Fombonne, E. (2001) 'Is there an epidemic of autism?', *Pediatrics*, no 107, pp411–413

Ford, G. (2001) *The Contented Little Baby: The Simple Secrets of Calm, Confident Parenting*, Penguin, London

Fortier, C. (2001) 'Le lait, le sperme, le dos. Et le sang?', *Cahiers d'Etudes Africaines*, no 161(XLI-I), pp97–138

Foucault, M. (1976) *The History of Sexuality: An Introduction*, Penguin, Harmondsworth

Foucault, M. (1978) 'Governmentality', Lecture, College de France, reproduced in G. Burchell, C. Gordon and P. Miller (eds) *The Foucault Effect: Studies in Governmentality*, pp87–104, University of Chicago Press, Chicago, IL

Furedi, F. (2001) *Paranoid Parenting*, Allen Lane, London

Gabe, J., Kelleher, D. and Williams, G. (eds) (1994) *Challenging Medicine*, Routledge, London

Gage, A. J., Sommerfelt, A. E. and Piani, A. L. (1997) 'Household structure and childhood immunization in Niger and Nigeria', *Demography*, vol 34, no 2, pp295–309

Gauri, V. and Khaleghian, P. (2002) *Immunization in Developing Countries: Its Political and Organizational Determinants*, World Bank, Washington, DC

Geissler, P. W. (2005) 'Kachinja are coming: Encounters around a medical research project in a Kenyan village', *Africa*, vol 75, no 2, pp173–202

Geissler, P. W. and Pool, R. (2006) 'Editorial: Popular concerns about medical research projects in sub-Saharan Africa – a critical voice in debates about medical research ethics', *Tropical Medicine and International Health*, vol 11, no 7, pp975–982

Geissler, P. W., Kelly, A., Imoukhuede, B. and Pool, R. (2005) 'Substantial transactions and an ethics of kinship in recent collaborative malaria trials in The Gambia', paper presented at the conference on 'Locating the field: The ethnography of medical research in Africa', Kilifi, Kenya, 4–9 December

Giddens, A. (1991) *Modernity and Self-identity: Self and Society in the Late Modern Age*, Polity Press, Cambridge

Gordon, C. (1991) 'Governmental rationality: An introduction', in G. Burchell, C. Gordon and P. Miller (eds) *The Foucault Effect: Studies in Governmentality*, University of Chicago Press, Chicago, IL, pp1–52

Gottlieb, A. (2001) *Under the Kapok Tree: Identity and Difference in Beng Thought*, Indiana University Press, Bloomington, IN

Gottlieb, A. and De Loache, J. (2000), *A World of Babies*, Cambridge University Press, Cambridge

Greenough, P. (1995) 'Global immunisation and culture: Compliance and resistance in large-scale public health campaigns', *Social Science and Medicine*, vol 41, no 5, pp605–607

Gunn, T. (1992) *Mass Immunization – A Point in Question*, Cutting Edge Publications, UK

Hajer, M. and Wagenaar, H. (2003) 'Introduction', in M. Hajer and H. Wagenaar (eds) *Deliberative Policy Analysis*, Cambridge University Press, Cambridge

Hall, S. (1997) *Representation: Cultural Representations and Signifying Practices*, Open University, Milton Keynes

Ham, C. and Alberti, K. G. M. M. (2002) 'The medical profession, the public and the Government', *British Medical Journal*, vol 324, no 7341, pp833–842

Hancock, B. (2000) 'The culprit behind asthma and allergies: Vaccination', *New Vegetarian and Natural Health*, Winter edition. Available at www.vaccination. inoz.com/asthma2.html, accessed 17 April 2004

Hanlon, P., Byass, P., Yamuah, M., Hayes, R., Bennett, S. and M'Boge, B. H. (1988) 'Factors influencing vaccination compliance in peri-urban Gambian children', *Journal of Tropical Medicine and Hygiene*, vol 91, no 1, pp29–33

Haraway, D. (1991) *Symians, Cyborgs and Women: The Reinvention of Nature*, Free Association Books, London

Hardy, A. (2006) 'Liberty, equality and immunisation c.1800–1970', Paper presented at the Wellcome Trust conference on the history of vaccination, London, 29–30 June

Hargreaves, I., Lewis, J. and Spears, T. (2002) *Towards a Better Map: Science, the Public and the Media*, ESRC, Swindon

Health Promotion England (2001) *MMR: The Facts*, National Health Service, London

Heaton, A. and Keith, R. (2002) *A Long Way to go: A Critique of GAVI's Initial Impact*, Save the Children Fund UK, London

Heggenhougen, H. K. and Clements, C. J. (1990) 'An anthropological perspective on the acceptability of immunization services', *Scandinavian Journal of Infectious Diseases Supplement*, no 76, pp20–31

Helman, C. G. and Yogeswaran, P. (2004) 'Perceptions of childhood immunisations in rural Transkei: A qualitative study', *South African Medical Journal*, vol 94, no 10, pp835–838

Hobson-West, P. (2003) 'Understanding vaccination resistance: Moving beyond risk', *Health, Risk and Society*, vol 5, no 3, pp273–283

Hobson-West, P. (2007) '"Trusting blindly can be the biggest risk of all": Organised resistance to childhood vaccination in the UK', *Sociology of Health and Illness*, vol 29, no 2, pp198–215

Horton, R. (2004) *MMR: Science and Fiction*, Granta Books, London

House of Lords (2000) 'Science and Society', 3rd report of Select Committee on Science and Technology, HMSO, London

HPA (2004) 'COVER programme: October to September 2003', *CDR Weekly* vol 14, no 13. Available at www.hpa.org.uk/cdr/archives/archive04/news04_1.htm#13 accessed March 2004

HPI (2006) *Reviving Routine Immunization in Northern Nigeria*, proposal to DFID, Health Partners International, Save the Children UK and Grid Consulting Ltd, Health Partners International, Lewes, UK

Hupcey, J. E., Penrod, J., Morse, J. M. and Mitchem, C. (2001) 'An exploration and advancement of the concept of trust', *Journal of Advanced Nursing*, vol 36, no 2, pp282–293

IHSD (2004) *Private Sector Participation In Health, Institute for Health Sector Development. Immunisation Survey*, PATHS Programme, Nigeria

Imperato, P. and Traore, D. (1969) 'Traditional beliefs about measles and its treatment among the Bambaro of Mali', *Tropical Geography and Medicine*, vol 21, no 62

Irwin, A. (1995) *Citizen Science: A Study of People, Expertise and Sustainable Development*, Routledge, London

Irwin, A. and Wynne, B. (eds) (1996) *Misunderstanding Science? The Public Reconstruction of Science and Technology*, Cambridge University Press, Cambridge

Jamison, A. (2001) 'Science and Social Movements', *International Encyclopaedia of the Social and Behavioural Sciences*, Elsevier

Jasanoff, S. (2003) 'Breaking the waves in science studies', *Social Studies of Science*, vol 33, no 3, pp389–400

Jasanoff, S. (ed) (2004) *States of Knowledge: The Co-Production of Science and Social Order*, Routledge, London

Jasanoff, S. (2005) *Designs on Nature*, Princeton University Press, Princeton, NJ

Jasanoff, S. and Wynne, B. (1997) 'Science and decision-making', in S. Rayner and E. Malone (eds) *Human Choice and Climate Change*, Battelle Press, Columbus, OH

Jefferson, T., Price, D., Demicheli, V. and Bianco, E. (2003) 'Unintended events following immunization with MMR: A systematic review', *Vaccine*, no 21, pp 3954–3960

Jegede, A.S. (2005) 'The cultural and political dynamics of technology delivery: The case of infant immunisation in south western Nigeria', West African Social Science and Immunisation Network (WASSIN) paper 3, www.ids.ac.uk/ids/KNOTS/Projects/vacc3.html#Outputs

Jewell, D. (2001) 'MMR and the age of unreason', *British Journal of General Practice*, Editorial, vol 51, pp875–876

Kamara, C.W. (2005) 'The cultural and political dynamics of technology delivery: The case of infant immunisation in west Africa. Comparative fieldwork and report on Sierra Leone'. West African Social Science and Immunisation Network (WASSIN) paper 5, www.ids.ac.uk/ids/KNOTS/Projects/vacc3.html#Outputs

Kaul, I. and Faust, M. (2001) 'Global public goods and health: Taking the agenda forward', *WHO, Bulletin*, vol 79, no 9, pp869–874

Keeley, J. and Scoones, I. (2003) *Understanding Environmental Policy Processes: Cases from Africa*, Earthscan, London

Knorr-Cetina, K. (1981) *The Manufacture of Knowledge*, Pergamon Press, Oxford

Knorr-Cetina, K. (1999) *Epistemic Cultures: How the Sciences Make Knowledge*, Harvard University Press, Cambridge and London

Last, M. (1980) 'The importance of knowing about not knowing', *Social Science and Medicine*, no 15, pp387–392

Latour, B. (1987) *Science in Action*, Harvard University Press, Cambridge, MA and London

Latour, B. (1993) *We Have Never Been Modern*, Harvard University Press, Cambridge

Latour, B. and Woolgar, S. (1979) *Laboratory Life: The Social Construction of Scientific Facts*, Sage, Los Angeles, CA

Leach, M. (1994) *Rainforest Relations: Gender and Resource Use Among the Mende of Gola, Sierra Leone*, Edinburgh University Press for the International African Institute, Edinburgh

Leach, M. (2005) 'MMR mobilisation: Science and citizens in a British vaccine controversy', *IDS Working Paper*, no 247, Institute of Development Studies, Brighton

Leach, M. and Fairhead, J. (2002) 'Manners of contestation: "citizen science" and "indigenous knowledge" in West Africa and the Caribbean', *International Social Science Journal*, no 173

Leach, M. and Fairhead, J. (2005) 'Being with MRC: Infant care and the social meanings of cohort membership in Gambia's plural therapeutic landscapes', paper presented at the conference on 'Locating the Field: The ethnography of medical research in Africa', Kilifi, Kenya, 5–9 December

Leach, M., Scoones, I. and Wynne, B. (eds) (2005) *Science and Citizens: Globalization and the Challenge of Engagement*, Zed Press, London

Leach, P. (2003) *Your Baby and Child*, Dorling Kindersley, London

Lindbladh, E. and Lyttkens, C. H. (2003) 'Polarization in the reaction to health-risk information: A question of social position?' *Risk Analysis*, no 23, pp 841–855

London Evening Standard (2003) 'Doctor blames ministers for loss of faith in MMR', 15 January

Long, N. (2001) *Development Sociology: Actor Perspectives*, Routledge, London

Long, N. and Long, A. (eds) (1994) *Battlefields of Knowledge*, Routledge, London

Lovell, N. (1999) 'Anthropological study and report on the workings of the Expanded Programme on Immunisation in The Gambia', report prepared for the European Commission DGVIII by UNECIA, EU, Brussels

Luhmann, N. (1979) *Trust and Power*, Wiley, Chichester, UK

Lupton, D. (1994) *Medicine as Culture: Disease, Illness and the Body in Western Societies*, Sage, London

Madge, C. and O'Connor, H. (2006) 'Parenting gone wired: Empowerment of new mothers on the internet?', *Social and Cultural Geography*, vol 7, no 2, pp199–220

Mambro, F. (2002) 'A fascinating article about Kok Ksor', www.montagnard-foundation.org/comm-101102.html , accessed 17 May 2007

Marcus, G. (1995) 'Ethnography in/of the world system: The emergence of multi-sited ethnography', *Annual Review of Anthropology*, no 24, pp95–117

Martin, E. (1994) *Flexible Bodies: Tracking Immunity in American Culture from the Days of Polio to the Age of AIDS*, Beacon Press, Boston, MA

Mattingly, C. and Garro, L. C. (eds) (2002) *Narrative and the Cultural Construction of Illness and Healing*, University of California Press, Berkeley, CA

McAdam, D., Tarrow, S. and Tilly, C. (2001) *Dynamics of Contention*, Cambridge University Press, Cambridge

Melucci, A. (1989) *Nomads of the Present: Social Movements and Individual Needs in Contemporary Society*, Hutchinson, London

Melucci, A. (1996) *Challenging Codes: Collective Action in the Information Age*, Cambridge University Press, Cambridge

Miller, E. (2002) 'MMR vaccine: Review of benefits and risks', *Journal of Infection*, no 44, pp1–6

Millimouno, D., Diallo, A. A., Leach, M. and Fairhead, J. (2006) 'The social dynamics of infant immunisation in Africa: Perspectives from the Republic of Guinea', *IDS Working Paper*, no 262, Institute of Development Studies, Brighton

Mills, H. M. (2002) 'MMR: The story so far', *Private Eye Special Report*, May

Misztal, B. (1996) *Trust in Modern Societies: The Search for the Bases of Social Order*, Polity Press, Cambridge

Mol, A. M. (2003) *The Body Multiple: Ontology in Medical Practice*, Duke University, Durham, NC

Moore, H. and Sanders, T. (eds) (2002) *Magical Interpretations, Material Realities: Modernity, Witchcraft and the Occult in Postcolonial Africa*, Routledge, London

Moulin, A.-M. (1989) 'Immunology old and new: The beginning and the end', in P. Mazumdar (ed) *Immunology 1930–1980: Essays on the History of Immunology*, Wall and Thompson, Toronto

Moulin, A.-M. (2007) 'Immunization: science, politics and the media', presentation at Anglo-French seminar on Immunization, 27 March, London

MRC (2001) *Review of Autism Research – Epidemiology and Causes*, Medical Research Council, London

MRC (2002) *Annual Report of the UK Medical Research Council Laboratories, The Gambia*, MRC, London

Muraskin,W. (2004) 'The global alliance for vaccines and immunisation (GAVI): Is it a new model for effective public–private cooperation in international health?', *Joint Learning InitiativeWorking Paper*, no1–2, Global Health Trust

Muraskin, W. (2005) *Crusade to Immunize the World's Children*, Global Bio Business Books, Los Angeles, CA

Musambachime, M. C. (1988) 'The impact of rumor: The case of the Banyama (vampire men) scare in northern Rhodesia, 1930–1964', *International Journal of African Historical Studies*, vol 21, no 2, pp201–215

Napier, A. D. (2003) *The Age of Immunology: Conceiving a Future in an Alienating World*, University of Chicago Press, Chicago, IL

Nasir, L. (2000) 'Reconnoitering the antivaccination websites: News from the front', *Journal of Family Practice*, vol 49, no 8, pp731–733

Netley, F. (2002) *Holy Oak: A History of Whitehawk and Manor Farm 1934–1974*, Phoenix News, Wellsbourne Centre, Brighton

NHS (2002a) *MMR: Information for Health Professionals*, Department of Health Publications, London

NHS (2002b) *MMR: Information for Parents*, Department of Health Publications, London

NHS (2004) 'MMR: The facts', Immunisation Information website, Immunisation Information, Department of Health, www.mmrthefacts.nhs.uk

Nichter, M. (1995) 'Vaccinations in the Third World: A consideration of community demand', *Social Science and Medicine*, vol 41, no 5, pp617–632

Norris, M. (1998) 'Modernism and Vietnam: Francis Ford Coppola's *Apocalypse Now*', *Modern Fiction Studies*, vol 44, no 3, pp 730–766

Nuffield (2002) *The Ethics of Research Related to Healthcare in Developing Countries*, Nuffield Council on Bioethics, London

Obaro, S. K. and Palmer, A. (2003) 'Vaccines for children: Policies, politics and poverty', *Vaccine*, no 21, pp1423–1431

Offit, P. A., Quarles, J., Gerber, M. A., Hackett, C. J., Marcuse, E. K., Kollman, T. R., Gellin, B. G. and Landry, S. (2002) 'Addressing parents' concerns: Do multiple vaccines overwhelm or weaken the infant's immune system?', *Pediatrics*, vol 109, no 1, pp124–129

O'Neill, O. (2002) *A Question of Trust: The BBC Reith lectures 2002*, Cambridge University Press, Cambridge

Onuoha, G. B. (1981) 'Factors responsible for under-utilization of available health services by the rural people in Nigeria', *East African Medical Journal*, vol 58, no11, pp859–866

Ortner, S. (1995) 'Resistance and the problem of ethnographic refusal', *Comparative Studies in Society and History*, no 35

Ostrom, E. (1990) *Governing the Commons: The Evolution of Institutions for Collective Action*, Cambridge University Press, Cambridge

Pareek, M. and Pattinson, H. (2000) 'The two-dose measles, mumps and rubella (MMR) immunisation schedule: Factors affecting maternal intention to vaccinate', *British Journal of General Practice*, no 50, pp969–971

Petts, J (2005) 'Health, responsibility and choice: Contrasting negotiations of air pollution and immunisation information', *Environment and Planning A*, vol 37, pp791–804

Petts, J. and Niemeyer, S. (2004) 'Health risk communication and amplification: Learning from the MMR vaccination controversy', *Health, Risk and Society*, vol 6, no1, pp8–23

Pickering, A. (ed) (1992) *Science as Practice and Culture*, University of Chicago Press, Chicago, IL

Poland, G. A. and Jacobson, R. M. (2001) 'Understanding those who do not understand: A brief review of the anti-vaccination movement', *Vaccine*, vol 19 pp244–245

Poltorak, M., Leach, M., Fairhead, J. and Cassell, J. (2005) 'MMR talk and vaccination choices: An ethnographic study in Brighton', *Social Science and Medicine*, vol 61, no 3, pp709–719

Porter, D. (1999) *Health, Civilization and the State: A History of Public Health from Ancient to Modern Times*, Routledge, London

Porter, D. and Porter, R. (1988) 'The politics of prevention: Anti-vaccinationism and public health in nineteenth century England', *Medical History*, no 32, pp 231–252

Ramsay, M., Yarwood, J., Lewis, D., Campbell, H. and White J. (2002) 'Parental confidence in measles, mumps and rubella vaccine: Evidence from vaccine coverage and attitudinal surveys', *British Journal of General Practice*, no 52, pp912–916

Rhodes, R. A. W. (1997) *Understanding Governance*, Open University Press, Buckingham.

Richards, A. I. (1939) *Land, Labour and Diet in Northern Rhodesia: An Economic Study of the Bemba Tribe*, Oxford University Press, London

Richards, P. (1985) *Indigenous Agricultural Revolution*, Longman, London

Richardson, K. (2005) *Internet Discourse and Health Debates*, Palgrave, London

Rogers, A. and Pilgrim, D. (1995) 'The risk of resistance: Perspectives on the mass Childhood Immunisation Programme', in J. Gabe (ed) *Medicine, Health and Risk: Sociological Approaches*, Blackwell, Oxford

Rose, N. (1999) *Governing the Soul*, Free Associations Books, London

Samuelsen, H. (2001) 'Infusions of health: The popularity of vaccinations among Bissa in Burkina Faso', *Anthropology and Medicine*, vol 8, pp.164–175

Scheibner, V. (1993) *Vaccination: 100 Years of Orthodox Research Shows that Vaccines Represent a Medical Assault on the Immune System*, Minerva Books, London

Schmidt, K., Ernst, E. and Andrews, D. N. (2002) 'Aspects of MMR: Survey shows that some homoeopaths and chiropractors advise against MMR', *British Medical Journal*, vol 325, p597

Science Media Centre (2002) 'MMR learning lessons', a report on the meeting hosted by the Science Media Centre, 2 May

Scoones, I. and Thompson, J. (1994) 'Knowledge, power and agriculture: Towards a theoretical understanding', in I. Scoones and J. Thompson (eds) *Beyond Farmer First*, IT Publications, London, pp16–31

Shiels, O., Smyth, P., Martin, C. and O'Leary, J. J. (2002) 'Development of an allelic discrimination type assay to differentiate between strain origins of measles virus detected in intestinal tissue of children with ileocolonic lymphonodular hyperplasia and concomitant developmental disorder', *Journal of Pathology*, Pathological Society of Great Britain and Ireland, London

Simms C., Rowson, M. and Peattie, S. (2001) *The Bitterest Pill of All:The Collapse of Africa's Health Systems*, Medact/Save the Children, London

Singh, V. K., Lin, S. X., Newell, E. and Nelson, C. (2002) 'Abnormal measles-mumps-rubella antibodies and CNS autoimmunity in children with autism', *Journal of Biomedical*, vol 9, no 4, pp359–364

Smailbegovic, M. S., Laing, G. J. and Bedford, H.(2003) 'Why do parents decide against immunization? The effect of health beliefs and health professionals', *Child Care Health and Development*, no 29, pp303–311

Smith, R. D. and Woodward, D. (2003) 'Global public goods for health: Use and limitations', in R. Smith et al (eds), *Global Public Goods for Health*, Oxford University Press, Oxford

Spier, R. E. (2002) 'Perception of risk of vaccine adverse events: A historical perspective', *Vaccine*, vol 20, pp578–584

Spock, B. (1976) *Baby and Child Care*, Pocket Books, New York, NY

Statview (1999) *Evaluation de la Couverture Vaccinale de PEV et des Journées Nationales de Vaccination 1998 dans la commune de Matoto: Rapport Final*, Statview, Conakry, République de la Guinée

Stilgoe, J., Irwin, A. and Jones, K. (2006) *The Received Wisdom: Opening Up Expert Advice*, Demos, London

Stirling, A. (2003) 'Risk, uncertainty and precaution: Some instrumental implications from the social sciences', in F. Berkhout, M. Leach and I. Scoones (eds), *Negotiating Change*, Edward Elgar, Cheltenham

Stirling, A. (2005) 'Opening up or closing down? Analysis, participation and power in the social appraisal of technology', in M. Leach, I. Scoones and B. Wynne (eds), *Science and Citizens*, Zed Press, London, pp218–231

Stirling, A. and Mayer, S. (1999) *Rethinking Risk:A Pilot Multi-criteria Mapping of a Genetically Modified Crop in Agricultural Systems in the UK*, SPRU, University of Sussex, Brighton

Streefland, P. (2001) 'Public doubts about vaccination safety and resistance against vaccination', *Health Policy*, no 55, pp159–172

Streefland, P., Chowdhury, A. M. R. and Ramos-Jimenez, P. (1999) 'Patterns of vaccination acceptance', *Social Science and Medicine*, no 49, pp1705–1716

Tarrant, C., Stokes, T. and Baker, R. (2003) 'Factors associated with patients' trust in their general practitioner: A cross-sectional survey', *British Journal of General Practice*, no 53, pp798–800

Tarrow, S. (1998) *Power in Movement: Social Movements, Collective Action and Politics*, Cambridge University Press, Cambridge

Taylor, B., Miller, E., Farrington, C. P., Petropoulos, M., Favot-Mayaud, I., Li, J. and Waight, P. A. (1999) 'Autism and measles, mumps and rubella vaccine: No epidemiological evidence for a causal association', *Lancet*, no 353, pp2026–2029

Taylor, C. C. (1992) *Milk, Honey and Money: Changing Concepts in Rwandan Healing*, Smithsonian Institution Press, London and Washington, DC

Thrower, D. (2002) 'MMR and acquired autism (autistic enterocolitis): A briefing note'. www.autism-arch.org/thrower/thrower-1july2002.doc

Uhlmann, V., Martin, C. M., Shiels, O., Pilkington, L., Silva, I., Killalea, A., Murch, S. B., Walker-Smith, J., Thomson, M., Wakefield, A. J. and O'Leary, J. J. (2002) 'Potential viral pathogenic mechanism for new variant inflammatory bowel disease', *Journal of Clinical Patholology: Molecular Pathology*, vol 55, no 2, pp84–90

UNICEF (2003) *Combatting Antivaccination Rumours: Lessons Learned from Case Studies in East Africa*, Eastern and Southern Africa Regional Office, UNICEF, Nairobi

Van Zwanenburg, P. and Millstone, E. (2003) 'BSE: A paradigm of policy failure', *The Political Quarterly*, vol 74, no 1, pp27–37

Vaughan, M. (1991) *Curing Their Ills: Colonial Power and African Illness*, Stanford University Press, Stanford, CA

Vernon, G. (2003) 'Immunisation policy: From compliance to concordance?' *British Journal of General Practice*, vol 53, no 490, pp399–404

Wakefield, A. J. (2002) 'Enterocolitis, autism and measles virus', *Molecular Psychiatry*, vol 7, supplement 2, S44

Wakefield, A. J. (2003) 'The emerging picture of persistent measles vaccine virus in autism', www.visceral.org.uk/science.php

Wakefield, A. J., Pittilo, R. M., Sim, R., Cosby, S. L., Stephenson, J. R., Dhillon, A. P. and Pounder, R. E. (1993) 'Evidence of persistent measles virus infection in Crohn's disease', *Journal of Medical Virology*, no 39, pp345–353

Wakefield, A. J., Murch, S. H., Anthony, A., Linnell, J., Casson, D. M., Malik, M., Berelowitz, M., Dhillon, A. P., Thomson, M. A., Harvey, P., Valentine, A., Davies, S. E. and Walker-Smith, J. A. (1998) 'Ileal-lymphoid-nodularhyperplasia, non-specific colitis and pervasive developmental disorder in children', *Lancet,* no 351, pp637–641

Wakefield, A. J., Puleston, J., Montgomery, S. M., Anthony, A., O'Leary, J. J. and Murch, S. H. (2002) 'Review article: The concept of entero-colonic encephalopathy, autism and opioid receptor ligands', *Alimentary Pharmacology and Therapeutics*, no16, pp663–674

Walls, J., Pidgeon, N., Weyman, A. and Horlick-Jones, T. (2004) 'Critical trust: Understanding lay perceptions of health and safety risk regulation', *Health, Risk & Society*, vol 6, no 2, pp133–150

Weiss, B. (1998) 'Electric vampires: Haya rumours of the commodified body', in M. Lambeck, and A. Strathern (eds) *Bodies and Person: Comparative Perspectives from Africa and Melanesia*, pp172–194, Cambridge University Press, Cambridge

White, L. (2000) *Speaking with Vampires: Rumour and History in Colonial Africa*, University of California Press, Berkeley, CA

White, L. (2005) 'The needle and the state: Immunization and inoculation in Africa. Or, the practice of un-national sovereignty', paper presented at the conference on 'Locating the Field: The ethnography of biomedical research in Africa', Kilifi, Kenya, December 4–9

WHO/UNICEF (1996) *State of the World's Vaccines and Immunisation*, WHO, Geneva

Whyte, A. (2002) 'Nurses needled by mistrust over MMR', *Nursing Times*, vol 98, no 11, pp10–11

Whyte, A. and Liversidge, K. (2001) 'Should nurses encourage parents ...?', *Nursing Times*, vol 97, no 6, p17

Williams, S. J. and Calnan, M. (1996) 'The "limits" of medicalization? Modern medicine and the lay populace in "late" modernity', *Social Science and Medicine*, no 42, pp1609–1620

Wolfe, R. M. and Sharp, L. K. (2002) 'Anti-vaccinationists past and present', *British Medical Journal*, vol 525, pp403–432

Worcester, R. M. (2002) 'Public opinion and opinion polling', in A. Weale (ed) *Risk, Democratic Citizenship and Public Policy*, Oxford University Press, Oxford, pp13–37

Wynne, B. (1992) 'Misunderstood misunderstandings: Social identities and public uptake of science', *Public Understanding of Science*, no 1, pp281–304

Wynne, B. (2005) 'Risk as globalizing "democratic" discourse: Framing subjects and citizens', in M. Leach, I. Scoones and B. Wynne (eds) *Science and Citizens: Globalization and the Challenge of Engagement*, Zed Press, London, pp66–82

Yahya, M. (2005) 'Polio vaccines – difficult to swallow? The story of a controversy in Northern Nigeria', *IDS Working Paper*, no 261, Institute of Development Studies, Brighton

Yahya, M. (2007) 'Polio vaccines – no thank you! Barriers to polio eradication in Northern Nigeria', *African Affairs*, vol 106, no 423, p185

Yarwood, J. (2007) 'Immunisation communication in the UK: Lessons learned', presentation at the Anglo-French meeting on 'Immunisation: Science, politics and the media', Novartis Foundation, London, 27 March

Zola, I. K. (1975) 'In the name of health and illness: On some socio-political consequence of medical influence', *Social Science and Medicine*, vol 9, no 83

Index